THE
O. J.
SIMPSON
TRIALS

THE
O. J.
SIMPSON
TRIALS

Rhetoric, Media, and the Law

EDITED BY

JANICE SCHUETZ AND LIN S. LILLEY

Southern Illinois University Press
Carbondale and Edwardsville

Copyright © 1999 by the Board of Trustees,
Southern Illinois University
All rights reserved
Printed in the United States of America

02 01 00 99   4 3 2 1

Library of Congress Cataloging-in-Publication Data

The O.J. Simpson trials : rhetoric, media, and the law / edited by Janice Schuetz
  and Lin S. Lilley.
    p. cm.
  Includes bibliographical references and index.
    1. Simpson, O. J., 1947–   —Trials, litigation, etc. 2. Trials (Murder)—
California—Los Angeles. I. Schuetz, Janice E. II. Lilley, Lin S., 1948– .
  KF224.S485O15 1999
  345.73'02523'0979494—dc21   99-20621
  ISBN 0-8093-2281-1 (cloth : alk. paper)   CIP

The paper used in this publication meets the minimum requirements of American National Standard for Information Sciences—Permanence of Paper for
Printed Library Materials, ANSI Z39.48-1984. ∞

Contents

Preface

THE O. J. SIMPSON CRIMINAL AND CIVIL TRIALS brought forth a mountain of discourse about the trials and the participants. Some participants sought to explain their individual roles and attempted to blunt criticism. Some discourse came from attorneys conducting postmortems and second guessing the trial strategy. Most of the commentary came from the media. None of the commentary focused on the trial transcripts or on how the Simpson saga formulated by the media affected the public's perceptions not only of the trials but also of the American system of justice.

The goal of the following chapters is to move the commentary on the trial from the media and the mass market to the academic venue. To accomplish this goal, the authors' analytical book investigates the transcripts of the two O. J. Simpson trials; reviews the jurors' posttrial statements and the participating attorneys' explications, as well as the extensive postmortems and media commentaries; and focuses on relevant legal concepts and practices. All of these factors give insight into the content, form, and style of the rhetoric. The goal of this work is to increase public understanding about the connections between rhetoric and law.

Chapter 1 identifies the qualities of telelitigation by focusing on the personalities of the trial participants, the conflict and dramatic elements of the case, the feelings of the public about the trial issues and participants, and the social issues arising out of the case. Additionally, this chapter shows how the telelitigated trials of O. J. Simpson created new media genres of television programs, books, and Internet sites.

Chapter 2 defines the characteristics of a media spectacle, focusing on the traits of the Simpson trials. The chapter shows that this spectacle was unscripted, appeared in multiple media outlets, embodied elements essential to entertainment due to the celebrity status of the participants, generated high levels of interest and involvement from the public, featured high levels of the accessibility of the media, and created a competitive impulse among the media outlets. All of these factors combine to produce a new model focusing on the media spectacle, an important construct for interpreting the Simpson trials.

Chapter 3 compares the opening statements in the criminal and civil trials. This chapter focuses on the influence of telelitigation reflected in the structure, content, and language of the presentations. The chapter also argues the importance of opening statements, shows the procedural differences between opening statements in the civil and criminal trials, and analyzes the statements in detail.

Chapter 4 focuses on the issue of racism as it emerged in the criminal trial with the testimony of and about Mark Fuhrman and continues with the apology Fuhrman gives for his testimony in his book, *Murder in Brentwood*. The chapter analyzes the uses of denial, apologies, justifications, and excuses as they appeared in the testimony, off the record, and in the posttrial media explanation of Fuhrman.

Chapter 5 considers the content of personal justification. The author examines Simpson's deposition and trial testimony and the testimony about him in the civil trial. The theoretical focus of the chapter is on the rhetorical process of credibility attribution and on rhetorical strategies of accusation and defense. The emphasis in the chapter is on the direct and cross-examination of Simpson in the civil trial and how his testimony related to the evidence presented by plaintiffs.

Chapter 6 compares and contrasts the closing arguments in the criminal and civil trials by examining legal procedures and issues, communication strategies, legal refutation strategies, and style of presentation. This chapter stresses how the elements of telelitigation altered the situational, substantive, and stylistic qualities of the closing arguments and how the organizing principles differed between the closing arguments of the civil and criminal trials. The chapter emphasizes the performative and dramatic elements of closing arguments as media events.

Chapter 7 evaluates the processes of juror decision making as they occurred in the criminal and civil cases. The chapter focuses on the discussions of jurors that were presented in media accounts. The chapter investigates how jurors responded to the evidence at trial; how they reconstructed the narratives of the prosecution, plaintiffs, and defense; and how they deliberated. The chapter compares the deliberation processes of the two Simpson juries to the existing research on communication and jury deliberation.

Chapter 8 summarizes the key factors that influenced the trials, including the celebrity status of the defendant, the role of money, and the impact of race. All of these factors alter the type of rationality in these trials. As a result, the trials no longer demonstrate traditional and deductive models of reasoning based on legal rules and procedures, but instead these cases reveal the commonsense rationality of the courtroom as it is influenced by the media, by the social realities of wealth and race, and by the experiences of jurors and public spectators.

Chapter 9 identifies factors that legitimated the evaluation of these trials as "trials of the century." The chapter first summarizes the findings of the various chapters and then develops a specific analysis of the effects of these cases on the media, on society, and on the legal process.

THE
O. J.
SIMPSON
TRIALS

1

Introduction: Telelitigation and Its Challenges to Trial Discourse

Janice Schuetz

THE 1990S BROUGHT WHAT JONATHAN ALTER (1997, February 17) called "The Great Age of Trials." Alter noted that "bad news about crime tends to drive out good or important news about anything else. Today's jealous mistress of law is seducing the news, threatening to dominate yet another part of public life" (p. 127). For many observers, the new communication technologies, the massive coverage of crimes, and the trials that follow have created a public obsession for watching and reading about trials. The nearly three years of O. J. Simpson trials typify this new age of "telelitigation."

This book provides an interpretive and critical analysis of key segments of the O. J. Simpson criminal and civil trials. The focus of the book is on telelitigation, the way that the media has transformed sensational trials with celebrity defendants and victims into telemediated forms. Quite clearly, the Simpson criminal trial is the strongest example of litigation being transformed because of media coverage. From the arrest and live coverage of the chase in the Bronco on June 17, 1994, until the verdict on October 2, 1995, the criminal trial received the most extensive coverage of any event in history. In fact, some scholars claim that the Simpson trials received more media coverage than did the Vietnam War during the actual years the war was being fought. The trial cost Los Angeles County an estimated $9 million and Simpson $10 million. The jury initially composed of twelve regular and twelve alternates was sequestered for 266 days. The prosecution provided testimony for ninety-nine days and the defense for thirty-four ("Simpson Trial Statistics," 1997). Judge Lance Ito's permission for live coverage of the trial in part fostered the intensive media attention.

Even the absence of cameras in the courtroom during the Simpson civil trial did not deter the media from extensive coverage of that case. In fact, one cable channel (CNBC) dramatized replays of the civil trial each day with hired actors to play the roles of O. J. Simpson, plaintiffs, defense attorneys, judge, and witnesses. Both Court TV and the Cable News Network (CNN) featured daily updates on the civil trial and reported what the attorneys, witnesses, and judges said in the trial. All major newspapers gave the case daily coverage. The world wide web indexes list over 3,000 entries on the civil case, including the daily transcripts of the trial. Although Judge Hiroshi Fujisaki banned cameras from the courtroom and imposed gag orders on the media and silence orders on the participants, the media voices of the litigation still surfaced during the civil trial. The theme of this book is that litigation processes of sensational trials, like those of O. J. Simpson, have been altered as a direct result of Court TV and extensive coverage by CNN, and this coverage in turn has created an insatiable appetite for more legal coverage of sensational crimes. This chapter establishes the theme by (1) providing a rationale for study, (2) defining telelitigation, and (3) identifying new media genres created by telelitigation.

Rationale

Since to date, observers and participants in the O. J. Simpson criminal trial have written more than one hundred books on the trial, the question arises—why is there a need for another book? The simplest answer to the question is that even though others have written extensively on their experiences of the case, no analytical and critical book on the trials has yet been published that compares the criminal and the civil trial. Clearly, an academic book that adopts a rhetorical perspective for the analysis of the trials and of the resulting media forms adds an important academic contribution to the literature on the case.

Several other reasons justify a rhetorical-critical analysis of the trials. First, the "trial of the century" was the most covered and watched communication event of the contemporary era. The content of these trials became a common conversational topic with the public. In a strange way, the trials were topics of conversation for people who otherwise had little in common. This book attempts to explain what factors of the case attracted and sustained public attention from the time of the crime, June 12, 1994, until the present; how the media created new types of genres to cover the trials; and why the media information on the trials continues to grow even though verdicts in both trials have been rendered.

Second, the trials served an educative function; people learned information about trial processes that they did not know prior to the Simpson case. Among the lessons learned by the public are explanations of what kind of search warrants are legitimate, what is prejudicial evidence, how investigators search crime scenes, what constitutes definitions of reasonable doubt, how jury consultants work with attorneys, why jurors make decisions, how criminal cases differ from civil ones, and how sequestration affects a jury. This book investigates how the legal procedures and processes, the rhetorical strategies, and the media practices have affected legal and public understanding of the Simpson cases.

Third, the trials provided for discussion of issues that divide the public and, as a result, have forced the public to reflect on these otherwise hidden issues. The primary divisive issue revealed by the Simpson cases is the racial divide in America. Frank Rich, columnist for the *New York Times*, wrote that "for two-and-a-half years, the O. J. case has been a grotesque but nonetheless piercing alarm telling us that there is a racial gap so wide in this country that most white and black Americans view the exact same events, not to mention our civic institutions, in exactly opposite ways" (1997, February 12, p. A8). Another key issue raised by the trials is the issue of domestic abuse. Many attorneys and social workers for victims saw the accusations of domestic abuse against Simpson as a rallying point for their cause. The cases raised questions about domestic abuse as both a legal and a social problem. One entire edition of the *Hastings Law Review* featured a discussion of domestic abuse and the Simpson case. Several television programs and magazine articles used the Simpson trial as a focal point for their discussions of this issue. After the criminal trial, reports from victims of domestic abuse increased. Both Denise Brown, sister of victim Nicole Brown Simpson, and Kim Goldman, sister of victim Ronald Goldman, have become spokespersons for domestic abuse organizations.

Fourth, the trials also raised issues about the use of money in the legal system and hinted at how the legal system works differently for the rich than it does for the poor. Many sources believe that this was the most expensive trial in history for both the State of California and a defendant. Although the exact costs of the case have not yet been published, Simpson attorneys purportedly earned as much as $100,000 per month. One of the expert witnesses for the defense was paid more than $100,000 to testify in the criminal trial. The jury consultant for the defense, Jo-Ellan Dimitrius, earned more than $1 million from the case (Abramson, 1996, pp. 28–29). In the punitive phase of the civil trial, the defense argued that defendant Simpson was broke and could not pay the millions in punitive damages because he had spent his fortune of nearly $10 million on legal fees. The costs of the trial were only one feature of the money and justice debate. Several witnesses were not called to testify at the trials because they were paid by tabloid newspapers and television programs to give their stories prior to the trial. Although the defendant did not testify in the criminal case, he wrote a book that was published prior to trial that told his side of the story and made $2.8 million for his defense fund (Squeezed: Where Did O. J.'s Money Go?" 1997, February 17, p. 30). The issue of money and its uses in the trial remains salient for those who believe that justice should not be for sale.

The Simpson case captured the attention of the public like no other event in media history. A reported 150 million viewers tuned in for the criminal verdict, and hundreds of thousands stayed tuned for the outcome of the civil case. During the civil trial, audiences bought thousands of books about the criminal trial. The media was so interested in the outcome of the civil case that the verdict was broadcast simultaneously with President Bill Clinton's 1997 State of the Union message. For the reasons identified here, the trials are significant communication events worthy of the academic attention of scholars of rhetoric and the media.

The Simpson Trials and Telelitigation

At approximately 10:15 P.M. on June 12, 1994, a vicious killer slashed the throats of Nicole Brown Simpson and Ronald Goldman. In the early morning hours, police found the two dead. Two days after the bodies were found, and after a high-speed chase on the California freeway, Brown Simpson's former husband, sports celebrity O. J. Simpson, was arrested for both murders. The trial started on January 28, 1995, and the verdict was rendered on October 2, 1995. After the jury deliberated less than four hours, millions of people tuned their radios and televisions to hear the verdict of *People v. Orenthal J. Simpson*. As the jury foreperson announced the verdict, "not guilty," women at the Battered Women's Center in L.A. screamed for joy, while at the same time other Americans challenged the verdict as an "outrage" ("The Simpson Legacy," 1995, October 10, p. S5). This "trial of the century" was temporarily over, but its legacy continued in the civil trial, which began in October 1996 and ended on February 4, 1997, with a verdict favorable to the plaintiffs, the Brown and Goldman families. In fact, the jury in the civil trial awarded $33.5 million in compensatory and punitive damages to the Goldman family and to the trust fund of Nicole Brown Simpson's children.

The aftermath of the trials surfaces in the continuing media coverage through television, magazines, and in books even after all of the verdicts have been rendered. Some see the Simpson trials as media circuses that exposed the flaws and the merits of the legal system; others view the trial verdicts as examples of the racial divisions in the country; still others believe the trials are a commentary on domestic abuse. This book views the trials as important texts for analyzing the relationships among rhetoric, media, and law. A summary of the key events of both trials appears in appendix A, and juror profiles for both cases appear in appendix B. All authors used unofficial transcripts from the Internet. These transcripts are referenced as TRC for the trial record of the criminal trial and TRL for the civil trial.

Jury selection in the criminal trial ended on December 8, 1994, and the verdict was announced on October 2, 1995, making it one of the longest trials of the century. Defendant O. J. Simpson was charged with the murder of his ex-wife and of Ronald Goldman. The chief litigators for the State of California were Marcia Clark, Christopher Darden, William Hodgman, Cheri A. Lewis, Hank M. Goldberg, and Brian R. Kelberg. The chief attorneys for the defense were Johnnie Cochran, Robert Shapiro, F. Lee Bailey, Gerald Uelman, Alan Dershowitz, Peter Neufeld, Barry Scheck, Carl Douglas, Robert Blaiser, and Sara Caplan. The prosecution called seventy-two witnesses, and the defense called fifty-four. The jury in the criminal case included nine African Americans, two Anglos, and one Hispanic. After the not guilty verdict was read, the defendant went home. Later, Simpson held a party for the jurors who decided his case.

The civil trial commenced on October 23, 1996, and ended on February 4, 1997. Plaintiffs charged defendant Simpson with civil liability in the wrongful deaths of Brown Simpson and Goldman. The primary attorneys for the plaintiffs were Daniel M. Petrocelli, Peter Gelblum, John Kelly, and Michael Brewer. The attorneys for the defense were Robert Blaiser, Robert Baker, Melissa Bluestein, Phillip Baker, and F. Lee Bailey. The plaintiffs called more than seventy-five witnesses, including the defendant, O. J. Simpson. The defense called forty-five witnesses. The jury consisted of nine Anglos, one of African American and Asian descent, one Hispanic, and one Asian American. The verdict favored the plaintiffs. A penalty-phase hearing followed the verdict. In this phase, jurors awarded $12.5 million to the estate of Nicole Brown Simpson for her children, $12.5 million to Fred Goldman, and $8.5 million in compensatory damages. As this book goes to press, the plaintiffs still have not received any of the money awarded them.

The controversy about the trials is not surprising since the public received more extensive information about the criminal case than did the sequestered jurors. The media system covering the criminal trial included 121 video feeds, 8 miles of cable, 19 television stations, 8 radio stations, 23 newspapers and magazines, 850 telephones, and 2,000 reporters (Darden, 1996, pp. 260–61). The criminal trial created forty-five thousand pages of transcript, and the civil trial produced over eight thousand pages. The civil trial had surprising coverage considering that Judge Fujisaki had gagged the media and silenced the trial participants. Nonetheless, every television network and many cable news programs featured excerpts from the trials with commentary from legal pundits; all of the major newspapers provided extensive day-by-day coverage; and the Internet carried the daily transcripts, public commentaries, news stories, and transcripts of interviews about this case.

In addition to detailing the extensive media coverage of the trials, my purpose in this chapter is to show how the legal processes and procedures create rhetorically persuasive media events and to show how the mass media, through television and its spin-offs in other media, has transformed the legal process. Just as the word *televangelism* represents the transformation of religious discourse into new rhetorical forms mediated by television, *telelitigation* appropriately describes how televisual media transformed the Simpson trial into a media spectacle that altered the legal process. To achieve this purpose, this chapter (1) identifies the characteristics of telelitigation, (2) shows how these characteristics affected other mediated legal discourse of the Simpson trials, and (3) identifies some of the many emerging media genres of discourse that resulted from telelitigation of these two Simpson trials.

Telelitigation

Just as the presence of electronic media in the sanctuary has altered religious discourse, the presence of cameras in the courtroom has popularized litigation and altered its rhetorical content. In 1979, Ben Armstrong wrote a seminal book about popular religion, *The Electronic Church*, in which he lauded the potential of televangelism. He noted the "awesome technology of broadcasting" was "one of the major miracles of the time." He predicted it would revolutionize the churches and bring religion to great masses of the public (pp. 8–9). Armstrong's prophecy about religion also can be applied to law. Before the advent of cameras in the courtroom in many state criminal courts in the early 1980s and prior to the emergence of Court TV in 1991, most of the public paid only passing attention to the participants and processes of the courtroom. They understood the trial through selected reports in the newspapers about the defendants, attorneys, witnesses, and their deeds. But after Court TV and CNN gave extensive coverage to the rape trial of William Kennedy Smith, the sexual mutilation trial of Lorena Bobbitt, and the first trial of the Menendez brothers for the murders of their parents, television brought complete legal proceedings into the homes of masses of people. By showcasing sensational and exceptional crimes, the media transforms the public understanding of litigation. Of course, telelitigation does not occur in every trial, but it does transform the content of those trials where extensive coverage occurs because of the notoriety of the defendants or of the victims or the unusual nature of the crime. In doing so, telelitigation shares many characteristics with televangelism, including faith in technology, emphasis on personality and stardom, dramatic portrayals, and attention to feeling rather than to argumentation.

Technology and the Public's Right to Know

The availability of technology has increased public access to legal information and increased viewers' appetites for more and better legal information. Schultze (1991) identifies several characteristics that apply to the telemediation of both religion and litigation. First, both share faith in technology and the freedoms it promotes. Boorstin (1978) claims that communication technologies are symbols of American progress and achievement. Telelitigation, like televangelism, validates the rights of free press, rights grounded in the First Amendment. Telelitigation reaffirms the "public's right to know," it gives citizens a glimpse of how justice is achieved, and it creates the impression that the public is participating directly in the legal process. This idealistic view has been espoused by Steve Brill, chief proponent of televised litigation. He claims that cameras in the court will educate the public about the justice system and increase public support for the courts. A position paper from Court TV explains its mission:

> Television coverage of trials tells the whole, real, true story about a complicated, often misunderstood and under reported subject. It allows the participants in a democracy to judge for themselves how well the government institution that makes the most fundamental decision that any government makes—liberty or prison—is working. (Quoted in Caplan, 1996, p. 203)

In the Simpson criminal case, the desire of the public to know generated massive information about the case. One result was that Judge Lance Ito decided to sequester jurors to prevent them from getting all the information the public received. In the civil case, the media still produced massive amounts of information even though Judge Fujisaki prevented cameras from being in the courtroom, gagged the media, and silenced the trial participants. The massive amounts of material on the Internet suggest that the public used alternative sources when live television broadcasts were not available. While the civil trial was going on, new books were being published each month on the criminal trial, keeping the public's recollection of that trial at center stage during the ongoing civil drama.

Personality and Stardom

Both televangelism and telelitigation are "personality-led" and have a preoccupation with "stardom and celebrity status" (Schultze, 1991, p. 32). Television gives "authority to the voices and images of certain individuals, making them celebrities" (p. 76). This celebrity status evolves because viewers feel they have a personal relationship with television personalities because the medium communicates the "human face" and creates the illusion of intimacy and friendship (pp. 78–79). Although the friendship is an illusion, in the criminal case, the public and press seemed to believe the illusion when they called the defendant by the familiar "O. J."; referred to the prosecutors as "Johnnie," "Marcia," and "Chris"; and called one of the witnesses "Kato." It was not uncommon for the press and the viewers (as evidenced by the talk shows on radio and television) to be concerned about personal factors, such as the Simpson children, the family dog, the visits of the victims' families to the cemetery, the occupation of Judge Ito's wife, and the hair and the dress of Prosecutor Marcia Clark.

Similarly, in the civil trial, the relational aspects of the case were emphasized by media commentators who noted that Simpson's attorneys were living at his house as they worked with him on the trial. Media audiences also learned about the intense legal battle that was going on between O. J. Simpson and the parents of Nicole Brown Simpson for the custody of the two children at the same time the civil case was going forward. The personal feelings of the Goldman family and their lawyers surfaced as commentary in media accounts. In the absence of live video of the families, the victims, and the witnesses, the television media replayed pictures of the people involved in the first trial at the time they were appearing in the civil case.

Moreover, the attitudes of the litigators seemed to be a major concern of the "media pundits" in their daily assessment of the progress of the trial. Darden (1996) explained that in the criminal trial, "The pundits interpreted every shudder and smirk. If you scowled one day, you were surly. If you frowned, the prosecution's case was in trouble. If you objected too harshly, the strain was wearing on you" (p. 262). The personality of the witnesses, particularly Mark Fuhrman, became the focal point of the first trial.

In the civil trial, the focus also was on the attitudes of the attorneys. It was the Simpson attorneys who were subdued and surly and the attorneys for the plaintiffs who were enthusiastic and committed. At the time that Simpson testified, the media commentators saw him as agitated and nervous, not sure of himself (*Burden of Proof*, 1997, February 11). The focus on personal issues elevated credibility to a major concern and reduced evidence and legal procedures to a lesser role in both the criminal and civil cases.

The Lure of Drama
Telelitigation like televangelism is caught in "the lure of drama"; it amplifies the conflict and adds new dramatic elements (Schultze, 1991, pp. 97–98). The dramatic lure promotes entertainment rather than an informed understanding of the legal process. Just as televangelism depends on novel content "delivered in a dramatic fashion with escalating action and emotion" (p. 109), so does telelitigation require action and emotion in its coverage of legal proceedings. This action and this emotion are promoted by portraits of charismatic characters, contentiousness and

conflict among participants, exaggerated language, and competition among media outlets for air time and profit.

The focus on the dramatic in coverage of the Simpson criminal case concerned Gerald Uelman who argued the defense motions in the case. After the trial, Uelman (1996) labeled the Simpson case "a trial of the century," and he concluded that "adding television cameras in the courtroom" is "like throwing gasoline on a fire. It transforms the proceedings into a sort of 'hype heaven'" (p. 94). The drama of the Simpson criminal case was cast in many charismatic and memorable characters. Defendant O. J. Simpson was a legendary football player and a popular spokesperson for Hertz Rent a Car television advertising. Cochran noted in his closing argument that Simpson "was the best"; he won the Heisman Trophy, which is "emblematic of the best football player in America" (TRC, 1995, September 29). He was an African American millionaire sports celebrity living in an affluent white neighborhood and associating with the rich and famous.

The drama of the civil case centered on two unique features—the testimony of Simpson and the more than thirty photographs of Simpson wearing Bruno Magli shoes. The testimony of Simpson was the dramatic apex of the civil trial, a unique event that set the trial apart from the criminal case. Not only was Simpson forced to testify under the rules of civil procedures, but the preparation and training he underwent for this testimony were also the source of focused attention in the media. As Ganer argues in chapter 5, this testimony was characterized by unqualified denials that Simpson abused his wife, killed her and Ronald Goldman, had bleeding cuts on the night of the crime, wore gloves, owned Bruno Magli shoes, or had a rocky relationship with his former wife Nicole Brown Simpson. The testimony received major scrutiny by the members of the media who commented extensively on how they thought the testimony would affect the outcome of the trial.

The attorneys in both trials held celebrity status. Defense attorneys in the criminal case called themselves the "dream team," analogous to the unbeatable millionaire basketball players who represented the United States in the 1992 Olympics. The dream team was composed of nine active defense lawyers who had achieved their reputations by being lawyers for celebrities. Vincent Bugliosi (1996) points out that with the exception of F. Lee Bailey, few of the lawyers had extensive experience as litigators in criminal trials even though they were well known because of the attention the media had given them in past celebrity cases (p. 38). To the media, the prosecutors were hardworking but not as famous or as competent as were the dream team. Furthermore, the prosecutors were especially flawed because they had let Mark Fuhrman testify and allowed Simpson to try on a bloody glove that did not fit. Additionally, prosecutors tried their best, but they were impeded by personal conflicts. In fact,

Prosecutor Marcia Clark had a major personal distraction because she was fighting her ex-husband for custody of their children, a custody battle in which Clark's ex-husband claimed that the trial had prohibited her from spending enough time with their children.

In the civil trial, the attorneys were not portrayed as celebrities, but as close friends and confidants of the plaintiffs and of the defendant. Instead of the attorneys being allowed to stage their own news conferences and appear on talk shows as they had done in the criminal case, the attorneys were silenced by Judge Fujisaki. This meant that the public knew more about the lawyers' legal credentials and their commitment to their clients than they knew about their ability to talk with the media. In the civil case, Judge Fujisaki, unlike Judge Ito in the criminal trial, was rarely seen by the public and was known only by his name and his rulings in the trial. Whereas Judge Ito was the spectacle ringmaster in the criminal case who was satirized in the weekly broadcasts of NBC television's *Saturday Night Live*, Judge Fujisaki was the stern referee in the civil trial, known to the public only through courtroom drawings and media reports from spectators about his efficient means of running the trial.

Since the civil trial was not televised live, the media commentators were handicapped in their ability to broadcast pictures of conflict. As a result, the media concentrated on some of the controversies occurring outside of the trial, such as the trial in which Brown Simpson's parents were trying to get custody of Simpson's two young children, and the controversies about the first trial that were surfacing in the books and being promoted in the media by the participants in the criminal trial. One way the televisual media added controversy was to place the participants from the first trial (who had published books) in an adversarial dialogue in which they commented on the civil trial. One of these dialogues featured Prosecutor Darden challenging Defense Attorney Bailey; another featured Defense Attorney Shapiro complaining about his co-attorney Cochran's inserting "race" into the case. After the civil trial, several programs featured Detective Fuhrman challenging the investigative procedures of Detectives Lange and Vannatter. In turn, they challenged the credibility and the investigative procedures of Fuhrman, a process detailed in their respective books on the case.

Unlike the criminal trial where many witnesses became media celebrities because of their character traits, the civil trial de-emphasized the personality traits of the witnesses and focused on the evidence they presented. For example, Kato Kaelin, a naive and nervous tenant who lived for free at the Simpson estate, testified at the criminal trial about the normative quality of Simpson's actions before the murder of Nicole Brown Simpson and Ronald Goldman. But after his trial appearance, he stated on television that he thought Simpson might have committed the murder because he was nervous and agitated. Restrictions from the judge prevented Kaelin from commenting on the civil trial while it was in process, but he still appeared in the media and spoke of related events. The media also created villains in both the criminal and civil cases. Mark Fuhrman was the despicable racist cop who found the bloody glove at the murder scene. The bumbling criminalists, Dennis Fung and Andrea Mazzola, lacked knowledge of their jobs and contaminated the evidence that they had recovered. Mark Fuhrman did not testify at the civil trial, and plaintiffs' attorneys condensed the testimony of Fung and Mazzola to minimal details of the investigation. But the plaintiffs clearly cast O. J. Simpson in the role of villain; he was both a murderer and a liar, a fact repeated dozens of times by plaintiffs' attorneys.

The personal disputes among the attorneys also emerged as important to their telelitigated performances in both the criminal and civil trials. In the criminal trial, defense attorneys fought with each other and competed for position in and outside of the courtroom. Lead attorney Shapiro was upstaged by his longtime friend Bailey and overshadowed by Cochran, whom he faulted for "playing the race card" (Schiller & Willwerth, 1996, p. 297). The dramatic conduct of the trial often took front stage, while the legal process appeared manipulated and contrived. At the beginning of the criminal trial, the lead prosecutor was hospitalized, and later he assumed an advisory role in the trial. Lead prosecutors Clark and Darden joined in overt conflicts with Judge Ito over evidence and issues, and the media portrayed the prosecutors as overtly hostile to the defense attorneys. In the civil trial, the media focused on the controversies associated with the adversarial process of cross-examination and refutation of evidence. The animosity appeared in the presentation of the evidence and arguments of the civil trial whereas the animosity surfaced in public displays of anger and public pouting in the criminal trial (Schiller & Willwerth, 1996). Two overt arguments exemplified the animosity between attorneys in the civil trial. One occurred when the defense attorneys tried to challenge the credibility of victim Brown Simpson by trashing her reputation and calling attention to her sexual behavior after the divorce. Another occurred when defense attorneys implied that Ronald Goldman's life was not worth much in monetary loss since he had gone bankrupt. Both of these arguments brought heated objections between plaintiffs' and defense attorneys.

The personalities became so important to the criminal trial that some of the jurors were offended by the participants' focus on their performances. Juror Willie Cravin wrote:

> They were playing to the media. They were playing to the public, and it caused a lot of delays as far as the trial was concerned. I can recall beepers, cellular phones going off in the audience. People were laughing. It was like a show for a while

there. The judge would make comments, and the audience would laugh. Some of the attorneys would make comments, and the audience would laugh. (Cooley, Bess & Rubin-Jackson, 1995, p. 205)

In contrast, the jurors in the civil trial claimed they liked and respected the attorneys on both sides. They observed that defense attorneys had a hard job to do because their client, Simpson, lacked credibility. They commented that they respected the "no nonsense" judge (*Larry King Live*, 1997, February 5).

Feeling Not Argument

Finally, telelitigation resembles televangelism because both mediated processes cater to an audience who wants to "feel" the message rather than understand it. Schultze (1991) explains that televangelists do not speak about "what people ought to hear" but about what they think that people desire to hear (p. 129). Emphasis on emotion permeated opening statements and summations and produced explanations from jurors about their feelings in both trials.

In the criminal trial, the message that succeeded most with the jury, the legal pundits, and the media was the summation of Johnnie Cochran. As the subsequent analysis shows, this message was based primarily on feelings and the inferences these feelings validated about police racism rather than on arguments or legal evidence. Cochran sensationalized trial content by comparing Detective Mark Fuhrman to Adolf Hitler, by telling the jurors that it was their duty "to police the police," and by stressing racism rather than developing a complex legal analysis of the issues. Additionally, Cochran's character attacks and his constant interruptions during the summations of the prosecution heightened the conflict and competitiveness that are necessary for enhancing the feeling of the drama. E. Michael Dyson (1996a) characterized the message of Cochran in this way: "Cochran's gifts spill forth from his golden throat. He is smooth and silky; an orator of great skill whose rhetoric reflects his Baptist roots. . . . He performs the law" (p. 48). Cochran, an effective telelitigator, excelled as a media performer.

In the civil trial, jurors focused on the testimony of O. J. Simpson. The jurors claimed that this testimony "lacked credibility" and "seemed rehearsed" (*Burden of Proof*, 1997, February 7). The focus was on the character of the defendant. Jurors perceived that key evidence—DNA, cuts on his hands, owning Aris extra-large brown gloves, and owning and wearing Bruno Magli shoes—contradicted Simpson's testimony.

In contrast to the criminal trial, where the focus was on the character of Detective Mark Fuhrman, the plaintiffs' attorneys blatantly attacked the character of O. J. Simpson. This intensive character attack is exemplified by these conclusions of Daniel Petrocelli in closing argument:

> Everyone, did you notice by the way, how Mr. Baker referred to Mr. Simpson on the witness stand as O. J. and Juice, even though every other witness was addressed by his or her formal name? . . . I am sure that is no accident. O. J. Simpson has been marketing, manufacturing, packaging and selling his image to the American public for over 30 years. And [you] know what they tried to do in this courtroom, he and his defense team, to sell you an image, O. J., Juice, an image, a personality. I even asked him, are you an actor? He says no, I'm a personality. (TRL, 1997, January 21)

Petrocelli sought to arouse the feelings of the jury about the defendant through these remarks on the superficiality of his character.

Notorious trials, such as the Simpson case, illustrate telelitigation, showing how the public's insistence on participation led to a distorted view of the legal system in which personality overshadowed evidence, feelings dominated over argument, and the media exploited the trial.

New Genres of Discourse

Because of the nature of telelitigation, the trials created new genres of media discourse. The word *genre* means type or kind of discourse. Genres are typically distinguished from one another by "situational," "substantive," and "stylistic" features. Genres have a common "organizing" principle, that is, an "internal dynamic" that links together the common situation, substance, and style of a type of discourse (S. Foss, 1989, pp. 111–12). According to Jamieson and Campbell (1990), the concept of genre "recognizes that while there may be few clearly distinguishable genres, all rhetoric is influenced by prior rhetoric" (p. 340). This brief sample establishes some of "the verbal conventions" of the media spin-offs from the trials as they emphasize the public's right to know, personality, feeling, and drama. The goal here is to identify a few of the diverse media genres that evolved from these trials. Many genres are part of the media legacy of the Simpson trials. These genres include many autobiographical books, journalistic commentaries, videos, games or workbooks for viewing the trial, joke books, and social commentaries.

Simpson's Media Defense

One innovative genre was created as part of Simpson's pretrial media self-defense. Simpson's out-of-court projects for defending himself included his book, *I Want to Tell You*, published during the trial. This work was labeled a "memoir" by his attorneys, and it was published and distributed just as the trial was to begin, the first week of January 1995 (Schiller & Willwerth, 1996, p. 314). The publishers timed the release of the publication so that its content would heighten the drama of the trial and fill the public's need to know about Simpson's side of the story, even though he did not testify at trial. The book appears to be a defense of Simpson's roles as a husband, father, and sports hero. The foreword to the book, written by Lawrence Schiller, explains its purpose: "This book began with 300,000 letters from men, women, and children of all ages, occupations, national and ethnic backgrounds, from all fifty states and many countries of the world, who chose to write to a man they had never met" (Simpson, 1995, p. vii). Schiller reports that the idea for the book came from Simpson's friend Robert Kardashian, who thought that Schiller could help Simpson fashion the letters into a book and make money for Simpson's defense (p. xii).

The content of the book is an attempt at self-defense that emphasizes Simpson's personality and his attitudes and feelings. A second feature that Simpson admits to is that he needs to make money from the book. He responds to one letter in this way:

> Many people think that I am very rich and have access to unlimited funds. This is not the case. I have succeeded and have been able to provide for my family, friends, and loved ones. Some say that I have been too generous at times. The legal system requires that I defend myself in a trial since my statements that I am "one-hundred percent not guilty" have not been accepted by the District Attorney of Los Angeles County. (Simpson, 1995, p. 10)

Simpson used the media in an attempt to influence the outcome of his case even before the opening statements began.

The book consists of more than one hundred letters purportedly written to Simpson while he was in jail awaiting trial, along with his carefully edited answers to the questions. Additionally, the letters represent concerns that the public has expressed about Simpson. The letters respond to the situation of Simpson's arrest, incarceration, and pending trial for the murders of his former wife and Ronald Goldman. The letters cover a broad range of issues, from his role as a sports celebrity, to condemnations of the media, to religious advice. For example, Simpson recorded the content of one letter from a young child. The writer expressed these feelings: "I am 6 years old. I love you—you did not do it. I pray for you." To this letter, Simpson responded, "Now that I think about it, I was never a big letter writer. When I was a kid I don't remember ever writing to anyone to console them about a tragic event, or the death of a loved one" (Simpson,

1995, p. 50). Some of the letters are attacks on the media. For example, Andrea Smith from Fresno, California, opined: "The media is blowing your case all out of proportion. All the coverage isn't necessary. The media acted like a pack of hungry dogs after one dog bone. They should be ashamed of themselves." Simpson responded to this letter claiming:

> At one point, my family was so outraged at what was being said by so many people in the media. I didn't want to fight it out in the press. . . . I wanted to save everything for testimony in court where it would really count. . . . But the jury pool was being poisoned. The press was out of control. . . . They were accusing me of about every bad thing you could think of. (Simpson, 1995, pp. 70–71)

Many of the letters express a religious message. Bill Juarez from Mira Loma, California, noted, "I am sorry for what happened to you, and I pray for you and your family. I believe you didn't do it, and if you have faith and believe in God you can get though this." Simpson (1995) wrote back with this promise: "I know that I will raise my children differently in relationship to God. . . . I'll take them to Johnnie Cochran's church, The Second Baptist Church near downtown L.A. I'm going to take them because their congregation is black and white. I realize now I've got to show them all of their heritage" (pp. 140–42).

Throughout the twelve sections of the book, the majority of the letters continue to discuss the themes of sports stardom, media bashing, and religious reform. Those themes incorporated the key dimensions of telelitigation—the public's right to know and emphasis on personality, feeling, and drama. In most cases, Simpson used the letters as a vehicle for talking about himself, his positive values, and his good character.

The style of the responses to the letters is personal; it mentions himself, his present and past life, his life with friends and Nicole, and his spiritual and religious goals. The organizing principle for these letters is that all of the responses are methods of self-defense. Although the book is self-serving and is a one-sided portrait of the defendant, as many media at the time reported, it met with financial success because the public evidently really did want to know his side of the story. According to the report of his assets in the civil trial, this book made $2.8 million. It is still being sold in major book stores. Schiller and Willwerth (1996) report that when the publication of the book was announced to the defense team, Barry Scheck "exploded" because he was concerned about the subpoenaing of tapes for the book (p. 314); Robert Shapiro thought it "was a disaster" (p. 315); and F. Lee Bailey had read the book and found it harmless (p. 315). Clearly, the book fostered controversy both in and outside of the trial. It was one of Simpson's many attempts to use the very media he deplored to achieve his personal and financial goals, just as televangelists have done for years.

Television Spin-offs

Another spin-off genre is CNN's legal program, *Burden of Proof*, a show that began as a commentary on the O. J. criminal case and continued after the trial. The program began as a half-hour legal commentary on the daily actions of the Simpson trial. The logo for the program was a picture of a female figure holding in her hands the balancing weights of justice, a traditional symbol emphasizing the legal goal of the courts and the adversarial nature of the system of justice. The television program pictured this logo, similar to one found in most federal court buildings, as part of a collage of visuals that included the front steps of the U.S. Supreme Court building, the faces of participants at the Simpson trial, and scenes from other legal proceedings.

Similar to other coverage of the Simpson trials, the program emphasized the dramatic and the controversial. In fact, the show began by using footage of a controversial segment of the trial. Some days this footage featured a ruling by Judge Ito; other days testimony by witnesses such as Kato Kaelin; other days an outburst by Marcia Clark; and other days visual charts of DNA evidence. During the civil trial, still photos or drawings of the participants were shown with excerpts from their testimony superimposed over the pictures. The opening footage showed visuals pertaining to the particular people and content upon which the program would focus. The footage usually emphasized some personality features of the judge, attorneys, or witnesses; and the program drew inferences about the feelings and issues that a particular trial participant was presenting.

After the opening footage was played, the two co-hosts, both lawyers, Greta Van Susteran and Roger Cossack, commented on the controversial segment from their perspective as former trial lawyers. The emphasis of the commentators was on their personalities and experiences as veteran lawyers with "real" courtroom experience. Then the two lawyers interviewed other lawyers-turned-journalists, some who attended the trial, and others who did not, about their opinions of the controversial segment featured for the program. Van Susteran and Cossack frequently disagreed about the legal content and social effects of a trial segment, a rhetorical technique for fostering conflict and enhancing the dramatic. Frequently, they interviewed a panel of several experts who disagreed with each other. Many of the experts they interviewed were media personalities, such as legal commentators for CNN's live coverage, and others were from Court TV. In order to get a cultural cross-section of interviewers, some of their weekday shows featured journalistic and legal personalities from the African American community, the feminist community, and families of the victims. They ended their program by saying, "Stay tuned for continuing developments in the Simpson Case."

The style of the commentators was one of seriousness and intensity. They constantly tried to develop a controversial angle about the day's events, to use interesting personalities, and to uncover the intense feelings of those they interviewed. Some of their reporters' angles were trivial and personal as were their comments about Marcia Clark's haircut; others were as substantive as whether Mark Fuhrman's penalty for perjury is legitimate. The organizing principle of *Burden of Proof* is a talk show combined with a news format. This format fosters debate about the legal and social issues; at the same time, it presents a daily commentary on the trial news.

The program continued during the civil trial using the same format. However, since visuals were not available, the program used video footage from the criminal trial and made it appear as if the witnesses and the evidence of the civil case were the same as those of the criminal. The program continues today with updates on contemporary legal proceedings, such as the federal cases against Timothy McVeigh and Terry Nichols for the bombing of the Oklahoma City federal building or the emerging investigation of the death of six-year-old JonBenet Ramsey, the daughter of a wealthy businessman from Boulder, Colorado. *Burden of Proof* seems to be one of several successful media spin-offs from the Simpson case that embodies the principles of telelitigation—the public's interest in trials, the focus on feeling and personality, and the tendency to create new and compelling dramatic portrayals of the events happening at trial.

Many other media genres evolved as part of the case. Faye Resnick produced yet another genre with her book, *Nicole Brown Simpson: The Private Diary of a Life Interrupted*. The book is a diary of Nicole Brown's life written, not by Brown Simpson, but by a loyal friend. In this diary written in narrative form, Resnick accuses Simpson of domestic abuse against his ex-wife. Other genres emerged on the Internet. For example, several Web sites provided discussions of the guilt or innocence of Simpson, and others provided a forum for legal discussions of the case. One innovative company produced a daily trial companion complete with answer sheets and daily workbook exercises for watchers of the Simpson trial (Roberts, 1995). A computer software company (*People v. O. J. Simpson*, 1994–95) produced trial transcripts and pictures of evidence along with a set of instructions for evaluating the evidence and the witnesses in the case. Because of the lack of live coverage in the civil trial, a proliferation of Internet sites provided transcripts and commentary on the trial.

Still another genre emerged after both trials, in the form of contentious books by Detective Mark Fuhrman (1997) and by Detectives Philip Vannatter and Tom Lange (Moldea, 1997). The books defend the detectives' own investigations of the criminal cases. They also malign each other's investigative procedures. Several autobiographies by Shapiro (1996), Cochran (1996), Dershowitz (1996), Darden (1996), Clark (1997), and Petrocelli (1998) discuss their roles in the trial and tell about their personal lives. Additionally, legal writers, who achieved fame in other cases, such as Vincent Bugliosi, wrote their own commentaries on the trial. All of these books fostered television appearances and reviews in the media that added to the telemediated legacy of the Simpson trials.

Telelitigation uses old and new communication technologies to enhance the public's right to know about crime, criminal investigations, and legal proceedings. Telelitigation and its media spin-offs, like their predecessor televangelism, focus on the personalities of the participants of an investigation and trial, stress conflict and the dramatic elements, and capitalize on the feelings of the public about the participants in the trial, the legal issues, and the social issues raised by the trial. One of the legacies of the O. J. Simpson cases is that they have created new genres of legal discourse that reflect telelitigation qualities, and therefore the trials have altered the way that the media likely will cover popular trials in this decade and into the next century.

2

The Media Spectacle and the O. J. Simpson Case

Diane Furno-Lamude

TELELITIGATION BOTH CREATES AND IS CREATED BY the media spectacle. The media reputation of O. J. Simpson in combination with the events surrounding his arrest contributed to the telelitigation of the trials. The spectacle also created the telelitigation by setting the agenda, combining news with entertainment, and fostering media access and competition. Examining this case as a media spectacle illuminates the characteristics of sensational trials as well as highlights what drew the media to the Simpson cases.

The power of the media is well documented. Maxwell McCombs (1994) emphasizes, "Not only do the news media largely determine our awareness of the world at large, supplying the major elements for our pictures of the world, they also influence the prominence of those elements of the picture!" (p. 4). One way the media influences is through the spectacle. The dictionary definition of a spectacle is "a public show or exhibition on a grand scale"; it is also a pair of spectacles, that is, "something through which one views things, or something that influences, colors, or biases one's views or ideas." Metaphorically, the O. J. Simpson trial may be equated with a spectacle, and media coverage of the trial, to a pair of spectacles through which the public sees, interprets, and translates information presented as news.

The purpose of this chapter is to develop a model for analyzing the media spectacle as it applies to the O. J. Simpson criminal trial. To accomplish this goal, the chapter (1) defines media spectacles, (2) investigates the texts, such as the Bronco chase, that shaped the spectacle, (3) describes the components of the spectacle and develops a theoretical model of media spectacles, and (4) explores policy issues raised by the O. J. Simpson spectacle. One reason for developing a model is to provide a representation of media processes and effects involved in this sensational case. McQuail and Windahl (1993) claim that "so much of the subject of communication has to be dealt with within verbal abstractions that it is an aid and a relief to have at least something fixed in graphic form, however much of the element of abstraction may remain" (p. 4).

The Media Spectacle

The O. J. Simpson criminal case offers an illuminating example of the study of a media spectacle because this story dominated the nation's news media and its national consciousness in a way unrivaled since the Lindbergh case of more than sixty years ago. The O. J. Simpson story is one that "hijacked America" (Shaw, 1995, October 9, p. S1). The study of the media in the Simpson case is important because it demonstrates the pervasiveness of media and its effect on the public's knowledge about crime and the legal system.

First, the media are not neutral, unobtrusive social agents providing simple entertainment or news; their pervasiveness alone makes their influence extensive. More specifically, in a typical American home, television is on for more than seven hours a day. The public listens to radio about three to four hours daily on the average. The circulation for daily newspapers is more than 50 million, and 400 million copies of magazines are purchased annually (Dominick, 1996, p. 137).

The social policy implications provide a second reason to study media and the Simpson case. The trial raised issues about money and its impact on the judicial system. The media have helped to push the California taxpayers' tab for the case to nearly $10 million because of the complexity of the trial and the spectacle it became. The trial also raised questions about interracial marriage, domestic abuse, and police ineptitude.

Third, amidst all of the commotion surrounding the effects of the media, the study of the Simpson case offers a unique opportunity for increasing understanding of how media influences society and affects public knowledge about crime. Although the mass media are only one source of the public's knowledge about crime and justice, they are the most common and pervasive source of shared information on this subject. For example, one study found that the media provided 95 percent of the information the public receives about crime (Graber, 1979, p. 179).

Over the years, many news events have been identified as media spectacles. In the past decade, for example, various new occurrences have led some scholars to identify numerous stories as media spectacles. However, the term *spectacle* has been used loosely to define stories that range from the movie rendition of John F. Kennedy's death, to the changing representations of black and gay characters in popular film (Garber, Matlock & Walkowitz, 1993).

Although numerous events are identified as media spectacles by different scholars, no attempt has been made to illustrate any defining characteristics or identifiable patterns in media coverage of these spectacles that would differentiate them from other news events. In one study, Jun and Dayan (1986) defined media events as news events that interrupt regularly scheduled programming on the major television networks and dominate news coverage. These authors described media events as having these traits: (1) they are planned and scripted by the media; (2) rival networks broadcast them simultaneously; (3) viewing of these events becomes a group activity; (4) television treats them as serious and nearly sacred; (5) they involve "larger than life" characters; (6) they are broadcast live; (7) they interrupt normal programming; and (8) they draw large viewing audiences (p. 74).

According to these defining characteristics, the O. J. Simpson case fits all of the characteristics of a media event. These characteristics are perhaps more useful for describing news occurrences such as John F. Kennedy's funeral, the moon landing, Anwar Sadat's peace trip to Israel, Indira Ghandi's funeral, and the death of Princess Diana. These characteristics need modification if they are to explain the complex news spectacle of the O. J. Simpson cases. The remainder of the chapter elaborates and expands the characteristics of a media spectacle as it applies to this sensational trial.

The Simpson case demonstrates several unique qualities that differentiate it from a media event, including the proliferation of media texts and innovations, as well as the complexity and variety of the media coverage of the trials.

Media Texts

To be identified as a spectacle, a particular event must receive a great deal of attention from all forms of the mass media. This attention creates a myriad of texts, and each important text sets part of the agenda for how the public should perceive the trial. According to agenda-setting research, the mass media have a powerful impact on the public agenda (Rogers, Dearing & Bregman, 1993). The public agenda set by the media ordinarily consists of compelling and unresolved social issues. The more compelling a specific issue becomes, the more apt that other concerns will become less important to the public (Fan, Brosius & Kepplinger, 1994). Clearly, the Simpson case set the agenda for the public about issues related to spousal abuse, police malfeasance, and the lives of the rich and famous. Live television coverage of Simpson combined with extensive newspaper coverage contributed to the development of a spectacle. In the *Los Angeles Times*, the Simpson story appeared on the front page for more than three hundred days after the murders. Additionally, when the criminal trial began, every local Los Angeles station except one carried it live. The major network evening newscasts devoted more air time to the Simpson case than they had given to Bosnia and the Oklahoma City bombing combined ("The Simpson Legacy," 1995, October 9).

From the day of the crime, the media texts proliferated. The media spectacle began with the nationally televised, low-speed chase of Simpson's white Bronco on June 17, 1993, five days after the murder of his ex-wife, Nicole Brown Simpson, and Ronald Goldman. A spokesperson for the Los Angeles Police Department (LAPD) held a news conference to inform the media that O. J. Simpson was fleeing his arrest after he had agreed to turn himself in to the police that day at noon. Late that afternoon, at 5:00 P.M., one of O. J. Simpson's attorneys held a news conference to read aloud an apparent suicide letter that Simpson had left, thereby adding yet another text and contributing to the growing media spectacle. In that letter, O. J. Simpson sent his love and thanks to some twenty-four friends, teammates, golfing buddies, and girlfriend Paula Barbieri. He also criticized the press for their negative reports about his relationship with Nicole Brown Simpson. In this letter, Simpson tells this version of his story through the media:

> Unlike what has been written in the press, Nicole and I had a great relationship for most of our lives together. Like all long-term relationships, we had a few downs and ups. . . . Please, if I've done anything worthwhile in my life, let my kids live in peace from you [the press]. I've had a good life. I'm proud of how I lived. . . . Nicole and I had a good life together. All this press talk about a rocky relationship was no more than what every long-term relationship experiences. All her friends will confirm that I have been totally loving and understanding of what she's been going through. At times, I have felt like a battered husband or boyfriend but I loved her, make that clear to everyone. Please think of the real O. J. and not this lost person. (Bugliosi, 1996, pp. 307–8)

Almost an hour after the letter was presented publicly, the LAPD located Simpson's white Bronco, driven by Al Cowlings, on a Los Angeles freeway. Countless police cars and helicopters from local television stations took up pursuit. One dramatic text followed another as television news persons and legal analysts commented on the chase. The commentaries added intensity to the spectacle of the chase as it was unfolding. Also, the commentaries added intensity by focusing attention on the accused and his motives.

The Bronco chase created media innovations. The three major networks and the Cable News Network (CNN) interrupted all regular programming to go to live television coverage of the police chase of the white Bronco. At the time, NBC television was covering the National Basketball Association (NBA) championship series game between the New York Knicks and the Houston Rockets. When television news helicopters picked up the Simpson chase, the game was boxed off to one corner of the television screen, while the main picture focused on the police chasing the Bronco. With this technological shift, ninety-five million people (Nielsen, 1994) were viewing the chase live, not knowing how it would end. Most people watching were wondering if O. J. Simpson would commit suicide, be arrested, escape, or engage in some kind of violent confrontation. Whatever might ensue, the shared adventure gave millions of viewers a vested interest, a sense of participation, a feeling of being on the inside of a national drama in the making.

The Bronco chase was a text of major significance to the media spectacle because it focused attention on Simpson and on the media's approach to reporting crimes related to celebrities. According to Andrea Ford (1995, October 9), the Bronco chase was "the defining moment. It locked people into this common emotional experience" (p. S3). This shared forum of television was the arena for the declaration and confirmation of the "reality" of events (Meyrowitz, 1985, p. 88) taking place with Simpson. Shaw (1995, October 9) reported that this case eventually became such a compelling shared news spectacle that a Chicago-based human resources group claimed that employers all across the United States collectively lost an estimated $40 billion in productivity during the course of the trial (p. S3).

After the Bronco chase, public interest and involvement in the case heightened, and media coverage increased. Meyrowitz (1985) identifies one reason for this escalating interest. He claims that nineteenth-century life entailed many isolated situations and sustained many isolated behaviors and attitudes that are gone in today's world. As a result, the contemporary public has different needs. He further explains:

> Our own age . . . is fascinated by exposure. Indeed, the act of exposure itself now seems to excite us more than the content of the secrets exposed. The steady stripping away of layers of social behavior has made the "scandal" and the revelations of the "deep dark secret" of everyday occurrences. Ironically, what is pulled out of the closets that contain seemingly extraordinary secrets is ultimately, the "ordinariness" of everyone. The unusual becomes the usual: famous stars who abuse

their children, Presidents who have hemorrhoids, Popes who get depressed, and congressmen who solicit sex from pages. (p. 311)

As a result, many behaviors that at one time were private and isolated were opened to public view because the media continued to report backstage or private behavior.

On the date of the Bronco chase, the public was fascinated by the exposure of Simpson's emotions as they appeared in the media text of the chase, the news conference, the publication of the suicide letter, and the arrest of Simpson at his home in the Brentwood area of Los Angeles. It was apparent to the media that this news event was unfolding as a mystery revealing secrets, a compelling element of this media drama.

At the same time as these texts surfaced, pseudo events or staged media events also appeared, paradoxically causing the coverage of front-stage behavior (Goffman, 1959). Front-stage behavior is formal, planned, and performed in professional and public settings. Staged media events are visual and appear spontaneous but are scheduled and planned to meet the electronic media's need for news. The long-term trend in both the print and the electronic media is toward more and more intensive coverage of backstage behavior (Meyrowitz, 1985; Surette, 1992). Backstage behavior usually consists of unplanned, private actions that are not normally expected to be observed by anyone but the individual's intimates. Up to this point in the spectacle, the backstage actions of O. J. Simpson were events that went on during the police chase and the behind-the-scene investigations that led to his arrest.

These pretrial texts also included many news conferences by the attorneys for the defense; a book and a videotape by O. J. Simpson (1995); a book by Nicole Brown Simpson's friend Faye Resnick; live coverage of the preliminary hearing; legal and social commentaries by trial spectators; and extensive print news and features about the defendant, the victims, and the trial participants. These texts increased in quantity even further once jury selection for the criminal trial began and its live coverage saturated the airways and the print media. The verdict in the criminal case did not end the extensive media coverage; rather, the coverage changed in focus from the drama of the trial and its outcome to justifications and explanations of what happened in the trial. The emergence of dozens of books by participants in the criminal trial and the drama of the civil trial in 1996 continued to create texts (see chapter 1).

Components of Media Spectacle

The Simpson media spectacle consists of several components—agenda setting, celebrity involvement, dramatic media events, coverage by multiple media outlets, and access of cameras to the event. These components extend the characteristics of telelitigation presented in chapter 1, as well as illuminate the features that create media spectacles.

Agenda Setting

The media persuades by conferring attention and status on individuals and by setting the agenda on how the public should perceive these individuals. The fact that certain individuals or issues receive media attention means that they achieve a certain amount of prominence. Sociologists call this process "status conferral." At the basis of this phenomenon is a rather circular belief held by audiences that "if you really matter, you will be at the focus of mass media attention, and if you are the focus of media attention, then you really matter" (Dominick, 1996, p. 37). Numerous studies (Rosengren & Windahl, 1972; Levy, 1979; Rubin, Perse & Powell, 1985; Conway & Rubin, 1991) have found that individuals are likely to respond to media messages according to the degree of involvement that individuals have with media sources. Rubin and Perse (1987) classified two conceptualizations of involvement in their research: (1) a motivational state that reflects the attitudes that people bring with them to the communication situation; and the (2) cognitive, affective, and behavioral participation induced by the media during media exposure (p. 246).

Celebrity Involvement

Involvement with a celebrity, such as O. J. Simpson, may be defined as a psychological variable that represents a person's motivational state toward the celebrity created by repeated exposure to that celebrity through the mass media. O. J. Simpson was a national icon and a hero. His background as a professional football player earned him the Heisman Trophy for his outstanding play at the University of Southern California. Next, he broke several records while he was a running back for the professional football team the Buffalo Bills. Simpson also acted in several movies, and he was liked and remembered for the commercials he did for the Hertz rental car company. He appeared on many television shows and served as a sports commentator for football games for the NBC network.

Social science research reports on the impact of this kind of celebrity status on products. Atkin and Block (1983) note that celebrity endorsements generally receive high ratings and promote more favorable images of products than do those without benefit of the celebrity. This persuasive impact is even greater when there is a "match" between the celebrity and the product being endorsed (Kahle & Homer, 1985). Simpson's popularity in endorsing products and as a football commentator ensured his status as a celebrity. There is no question that because of his celebrity status created by his role as a football hero and an outstanding athlete, O. J. Simpson's status conferral was high at the time he was charged with two brutal murders. According to a recent study (Brown, Duane, & Fraser, 1997), celebrities who are at the center of criminal trials attract an inordinate amount of media coverage that invariably affects public attitudes, beliefs, and behavior.

Not only was Simpson a celebrity himself, but others of high status appeared in the courtroom during the trial. For example, two well-known authors, Dominick Dunne of *Vanity Fair* and novelist Joe McGinnis, were in the courtroom. Other celebrity appearances were made by actors James Woods and Richard Dreyfuss; former baseball star Steve Garvey; playwright Anna Deavere Smith; and media personalities Barbara Walters, Larry King, Diane Sawyer, Jimmy Breslin, and Geraldo Rivera. In addition, lawyers for the defense gained even more celebrity status with their daily presentations for the nightly newscasts. All these celebrities added notoriety to the trial and added to the perceived importance of the event for the public, thereby conveying status to the trial.

Dramatic Media Events

Media events have entertainment functions, high levels of involvement, re-current entertainment themes, sensational personalities, scripts created in process, attention from print media, and competition between media outlets.

According to Bloom (1996), the Simpson case had all of the ingredients of a media event, particularly in an atmosphere where the media already had developed an obsession with the trials of William Kennedy Smith, the Menendez brothers, and Rodney King. Surette (1989) has defined a "media trial" as a regional or national news event in which the media co-opt the criminal justice system as a source of high drama and entertainment. It is, in effect, a dramatic miniseries built around a real criminal case. One of the primary factors behind the development of media trial events is that the news organizations competing over ratings structure broadcast news as entertainment, presenting it within themes, formats, and explanations originally found only in entertainment programming (Comstock, 1980). Consequently, fast-paced, dramatic, and superficial presentation with simplistic explanations has become the norm. As Surette (1989) sees it, as this trend developed, some criminal trials came to be covered more intensely, and organizations expanded their coverage from "hard" factual to "soft" human interest news to emphasize the extra legal processes and the human interest elements. This process has culminated in the total convergence of news and entertainment in the "media trial" (p. 68).

Entertainment function. The cases that become media trials contain the same elements popular in entertainment programming. For example, a media trial may contain human interest bordered with mystery, sex, bizarre circumstances, and famous or powerful people (Roshier, 1981,

p. 47). Media trials are distinguished by massive and intensive coverage that begins with either the discovery of the crime or the arrest of the accused. In the case of O. J. Simpson, massive and intensive coverage started with the Bronco chase, continued with the arrest and trial, and culminated with the civil case and the damages awarded to the plaintiffs.

Media involvement. The O. J. Simpson criminal case offers a perfect representation of a media trial, considering the extensive amount of media involvement. Barber (1987) explains the characteristics of "media trials":

> The media cover all aspects of the case, often highlighting extralegal facts. Judges, lawyers, police, witnesses, jurors, and particularly defendants are interviewed, photographed, and frequently raised to celebrity status. Personalities, personal relationships, physical appearances, and idiosyncrasies are commented on regardless of legal relevancy. Coverage is live whenever possible, pictures are preferred over text, and text is characterized by conjecture and sensationalism. (pp. 112–14)

Recurrent themes. In ways similar to the entertainment domain, recurrent themes dominate media trials and depiction of crime. Surette (1989) identifies three typical themes: (1) the abuse of power and trust by participants in trials, (2) the exposure of the foibles of the sinful rich, and (3) the presence of evil strangers (p. 68). These three themes help audiences to understand the content of the coverage by structuring it to promote perceptions that the rich are immoral in their use of sex, drugs, and violence; that people in power are evil and greedy; and that the public authorities should not be trusted. In the Simpson case, these factors surfaced when the defense alleged that the police abused their power and planted evidence; the prosecution claimed Simpson was a wealthy man concerned with his image; and the defense claimed that evil strangers, like the drug cartel, may have committed the crime.

These entertainment themes correspond with how the media often portray business people and high government officials (Bortner, 1984; Lichter & Lichter, 1983). They also portray strangers or outsiders with different lifestyles or values as inherently dangerous. Media trials fit with the "abuse of power and trust" theme (Surette, 1992, p. 71) when the defendant occupies a position of trust, prestige, or authority as O. J. Simpson did. The general rule is the higher the rank, the more interest the media will have in the case. "Sinful rich" media trials include cases in which socially prominent defendants are involved in bizarre or sex-related crimes. These trials have voyeuristic appeal and are covered in such a way as to persuade the public that it is being given a rare glimpse into the backstage world of the upper class. These factors contributed to the appeal of the O. J. Simpson case.

Sensational personalities. Other factors related to interesting person-alities also characterize media trials. Love triangles and inheritance-mo-tivated killings among the jet set are primary examples. The category of "evil strangers" can be considered as comprising two subgroups: "non-Americans" and "psychotic killers." The media trial theme of the non-American evil stranger may involve immigrants, blacks, socialists, union and labor leaders, anarchists, the poor, members of the counterculture, members of fringe religious groups, political activists, crusaders, or ad-vocates of unpopular causes. Several examples in this category apply to the cases of Albert DeSalvo, the Boston Strangler; Richard Speck, a mass murderer; Sacco and Vanzetti, Italian immigrants accused of robbery and murder in the 1920s. The Simpson trials fit most clearly with the themes of "abuse of power" and the "sinful rich." At the time of the murders, Simpson occupied a position of prestige and authority. In addition, he was socially prominent because of his wealth and status as a sports hero and media commentator. Graham (1995) reflected that Simpson "is the first defendant I ever saw who literally had the presumption of innocence . . . and the only defendant I ever heard of who was so highly regarded by the public" (p. S3). Simpson's visibility and social prominence were greater than those of any other defendant in this century. The impeach-ment trial of Bill Clinton featured a defendant with comparable promi-nence and a media spectacle of equal excess to that of the telelitigation of the Simpson trials.

Scripts in progress. The defining characteristics of a media event as proposed by Jun and Dayan (1986) are limited in explaining the O. J. Simpson case for several reasons. First, as a news event, the Simpson case was not planned and scripted by the media. Scripting is a key ingredi-ent, according to Steven Brill, president and chief executive officer of the Court TV network. He says everything on television is scripted except for sports. However, he notes, "With trials people never know what will happen" ("The Simpson Legacy," 1995, October 9, p. S5). In the Simpson trial, the case was a constant script in progress with Simpson, his friends, his attorneys, and spectators adding to the script on a daily basis.

Print media attention. Although the O. J. Simpson case, as a news event, was broadcast live to interrupt normal programming, which drew a large viewing audience, the trial also received an enormous amount of atten-tion through other media. The Simpson story appeared prominently in newspapers, magazines, books, radio talk shows, and on the Internet (see chapter 1). The print media devoted proportionately as much space to the Simpson trial as did the electronic media. Yet the definition of "me-dia events," as described by Jun and Dayan (1986), is focused on the electronic media, while it overlooks newspaper and magazine coverage. The extensive coverage of the print media contributed to the spectacle of the trial. For example, *Newsweek* magazine published six cover stories about the Simpson criminal trial in a ten-month period. Major mainstream newspapers ran more than one thousand stories on the case in the sixteen months after the murders: For example, the *Boston Globe* ran 102; the *Philadelphia Inquirer* ran 121; the *Dallas Morning News* ran 123; the *Atlanta Journal and Constitution* ran 126; the *Miami Herald* ran 129; the *Los Angeles Times* ran 398; and *USA Today* ran 143 ("The Simpson Legacy," 1995, October 9, p. S4). Dominick Dunne (1995, February) gives reasons for the prominence of the Simpson case in print media: "The Simpson case is like a great trash novel come to life, mammoth fireworks display of interracial marriage, love, lust, lies, hate, fame, wealth, beauty, obsession, spousal abuse, stalking, brokenhearted children, the bloody knife-slashing homicides, and all the justice that money can buy" (p. 48). Other journalists referred to the Simpson case as "a national, real-life, cross-channel soap opera" ("The Simpson Legacy," 1995, October 9, p. S4).

All of the above-mentioned features of media events combine to create dramatic elements that are appealing to a broad public audience. It is no wonder that a great many people were riveted by the story. The more dramatic the elements included in a news story are, the more it is likely to become a media spectacle. If people are interested in a story, it is likely they will want to hear and read more about it. This interest and involvement by the public may spell out higher ratings and/or higher circulation for the media. Hence, prolonged coverage is another dimension of a media spectacle. Network news commentators, including Dan Rather and Peter Jennings, agree that the battle for ratings is responsible for much of the "wretched excess" of the media in regard to the Simpson case. More specifically, as Jennings put it, this story was regarded as "a very effective commercial device by a lot of broadcasters and newspapers . . . to improve circulation and ratings" ("The Simpson Legacy," 1995, October 9, p. S5). CNN reported on several occasions that when they tried to cover other important events by breaking away from the Simpson proceedings, the phones at CNN headquarters in Atlanta jumped off the hook with calls from outraged viewers ("The Simpson Legacy," 1995, October 9, p. S5).

Media Competition

For the media, this extensive coverage led to a competitive impulse. In order for the print and electronic media to be first and to get credit for being first, they had to continue covering the Simpson story. With this particular story, the mainstream press found that it was competing with the tabloids to be first with a breaking report. In the past, the mainstream press generally picked up stories after they were reported by the tabloids.

However, with the Simpson case, the mainstream press shifted, and in the process, the tabloids gained newfound credibility with many of the major print media. The *National Enquirer* beat the established media on several Simpson stories. The *New York Times* expressed what many in the media began to realize, when they noted that "*The Enquirer* has probably shaped public perceptions of the case more than any other publication" (p. 4). Shaw (1995, October 9) concluded that "the lines between the mainstream news media and the print and electronic tabloids were blurring for a couple of years, but in the Simpson case, the overlap was greater than ever. Whatever, it is clear that many media professionals and the general public are perceiving the tabloids differently" (p. S5).

Media Access

Multiple media outlets foster competition. Thus, another component for consideration in defining a spectacle is that day-by-day there are many more and diversified media outlets. The primary venues for the Simpson case included Court TV, CNN, the tabloids, the weekly television magazine shows, the tabloid television shows, the nightly talk/interview programs, and the Internet. Some of these media outlets did not even exist ten years ago. It is no wonder then that the O. J. Simpson case has remained on the media agenda as long as it has. According to Shaw (1995, October 9), there are so many media outlets that in sheer volume, "[n]o story has ever received anywhere near the prolonged pervasive attention across so broad a media spectrum as that accorded the Simpson trial" (p. S4).

In media trials, the key to access is the presence of cameras in the courtroom. In order for a news story to become a spectacle, the trial judge must permit television cameras in the courtroom. Television cameras are permitted in the trial courts in forty-seven states, but only at the discretion of the presiding judge. Federal courts restrict the use of cameras. Judge Ito's authorization to allow cameras in his courtroom in the criminal trial meant that everyone talked longer. For example, the exposure of the many lawyers, witnesses, and family and friends of the victims translated into many independent stories. This component is one way the media were able to set and extend the agenda of the Simpson case. The civil trial had extensive coverage without cameras in the courtroom, but the lack of cameras did limit the amount of live coverage.

The key components for a media spectacle are the opportunity for the media to set the agenda, confer status on celebrities, and create dramatic news through live television coverage in the courtroom. All of these components increase the degree of public involvement with the trial process, the participants, and the social and legal issues.

Model of a Media News Spectacle		
Components		**Effects**
▶ agenda setting ▶ dramatic media events ▶ multiple media outlets	**leads to**	major news event
plus		
▶ celebrity component ▶ dramatic component ▶ media accessibility ▶ media innovations and shifts	**leads to**	media news spectacle

The table shows the main components that create the effects of a spectacle news event. Deutsch (1966) notes three advantages of the use of models in the social sciences. First, they have an organizing function; second, they explain what occurs; and third, they make it possible to predict outcomes. The model described in this chapter rests on a relatively simple version of the selected aspects of news events that turn them into news spectacles. This model does revise and expand Jun and Dayan's description of a media event by representing the process by which news develops into major events and even media spectacles. Effective use of this model for explanation and predictions depends on a few basic propositions about the way these components, alone or in combination, affect whether an event develops into a spectacle: the celebrity factor, the dramatic point of view inherent in the story, the accessibility of the media, and the attitudes of those who read and view the media.

Celebrity Component
A major component that determines a news spectacle is the "celebrity factor." An event is more likely to draw media and public attention if a celebrity is involved. If the news story is about wealthy and socially prominent people, then a regular news report may emerge as a major event. Also, if many celebrities are involved in the news story, then the event increases public interest and involvement, calling forth the media to deal with the conflict and intrigue caused by the celebrities. Research studies (Atkin & Block, 1983; McCracken, 1989; Ohanian, 1991) have demonstrated that people are likely to respond to media messages according to the degree of involvement they develop with media sources.

Besides O. J. Simpson, numerous people involved in the case became celebrities, including members of the victims' families; lawyers for the defense and the prosecution; Judge Lance Ito; witnesses, such as Kato Kaelin and Mark Fuhrman; seated jurors; dismissed jurors; and friends of the victims. The celebrity factor in the model extends from low-interest news events to high-interest spectacles. As the news-factor component moves from low-interest news to a news spectacle, both the media's and the public's agendas widen and increase.

Dramatic Component

The dramatic component operates in a way similar to that of the celebrity component. That is, as the dramatic elements increase, the entertainment dimension widens, and the news story becomes increasingly more of a major news event or spectacle. It depends on the number and kinds of elements included. For example, the more a news story contains elements of murder, sex, love, lust, lies, fame, wealth, beauty, obsession, bizarre circumstances, or societal ills—such as spousal abuse, stalking, and brokenhearted children—the more likely this component grows, as does the scope of the media news spectacle. This "info-tainment," a hybrid of news and entertainment, has become the mainstay of television programming.

Media Accessibility

Another component important to the spectacle news event is the access the media have to the event. The more available it is to the media, the more the public is exposed. In the case of the criminal trial, access was nearly wide-open when television cameras were allowed in the courtroom and the public had available gavel-to-gavel coverage of the proceedings. The courtroom television cameras encouraged media coverage, public interest, and involvement and promoted more stories about this news event. The extensive coverage prolonged the media spectacle even into the civil trial and beyond the verdict.

Media Innovations and Shifts

Finally, this model identifies several media innovations and/or shifts that may occur with a spectacle. For example, with the Simpson news spectacle, television coverage was live to millions of viewers through CNN and other major networks, which interrupted the reporting of regular news for their coverage of trial events. Other stations created innovations, such as boxing off the Bronco chase during a major sporting event to provide simultaneous coverage of both events. No incident in the past has received the immediate, widespread, and simultaneous attention that the Simpson Bronco chase and the subsequent verdict received.

Changes in the media may occur as innovations or as shifts in attitudes among spectators. Attitudinal changes concern modifications of public attitudes about social issues or shifts in media attitudes about their focus of coverage. For example, battered women were an issue that had the potential for changing peoples' attitudes about spousal abuse. During the Simpson case, a shift of attitude occurred in the print media when the tabloids gained respect from the mainstream press. Many other examples can be drawn from the Simpson case for both shifts in public attitudes about the issues that the case raised and the media practices concerning coverage of trials with this amount of exposure.

Issues Raised by Trial

The news spectacle model, as proposed in this chapter, clarifies some of the components that were present in the Simpson criminal trial and raises issues about current and future trials. The Simpson trial possessed all of the components needed for a media spectacle. It contained compelling texts, beginning with the Bronco chase and temporarily ending with the verdict and its aftermath. Moreover, the media coverage was marked by agenda setting, celebrities, and a dramatic media event that was enhanced by live television coverage, creating high levels of public involvement. For these reasons, the criminal trial was clearly a media spectacle.

The civil trial had some of the celebrities and was a dramatic media event, but it lacked the live television coverage and the media access of the criminal case. The comparison of the two trials shows that judges can limit the degree to which a trial becomes a spectacle by taking legal measures to limit media access. Judge Hiroshi Fujisaki used some of these measures in the civil trial when he gagged the media, silenced the courtroom participants, and banned cameras from the courtroom. Although these restrictions limited the coverage, the media found ways to circumvent these limitations by bringing news about the trial to the public, who continued to have high levels of interest in its outcome. Among the innovations used by the televisual media were dramatic reenactments of the trial, which were presented daily from the court transcripts with professional actors. This innovation was used by CNBC. Other innovations included showing live pictures and testimony of witnesses who testified at the criminal trial on the days they actually were testifying at the civil trial. The media presented these recycled pictures with new captions from the civil trial followed by legal commentaries. Some commentators were present in the courtroom of the civil trial, and others just drew inferences from their observations of the criminal trial. Additionally, the proliferation of books by participants in the criminal trial permitted new and evolving commentary for the television and print media that was applied to the civil trial (see chapter 1).

This chapter raises media issues, such as how the media sustain long-term and extensive coverage of a single event and maintain an interested reading and viewing audience. I believe the components of the media spectacle permit this kind of massive and effective coverage. Although this spectacle can be reduced in its scope by the judge—as occurred in the Simpson civil case and later in the Timothy McVeigh trial—the coverage cannot be suppressed totally because the media use innovations to make the information available to the public. Judge Fujisaki attempted to do this when he banned television cameras from the civil trial. His ban included the following analysis:

> The Court has concluded from the experience of the criminal trial of this defendant concerning the same essential factual circumstances, that electronic coverage of the trial significantly diverted and distracted the participants therein; it appears that the conduct of witnesses and counsel were unduly influenced by the presence of the electronic media. This conduct was manifested in various ways, such as playing to the camera, gestures, outbursts by counsel and witnesses in the courtroom and theater outside the courthouse, presenting a circus atmosphere to the trial. This detracted from the integrity of the trial process and the dignity of the courtroom. The trial process requires that the evidence be presented to the jury undistorted by these extraneous influences. The intensity of media activity in this civil trial thus far strongly supports this Court's belief that history will repeat itself unless this Court acts to prevent it. ("Judge's Order," 1996, August 23)

Clearly, Judge Fujisaki feared that a media spectacle would occur in the civil case and applied many of the legal measures available to him to prevent it.

This chapter also raises issues about how spectacles may contaminate jurors, especially when the pretrial coverage is as extensive as it was in the Simpson trials. Of course, judges use juror questionnaires and rigorous *voir dire* to reduce the effect of juror contamination by the media, but totally erasing this media information from the decisions of jurors seems unlikely. Criminal defense attorneys, such as Robert Shapiro, seem to believe that they can have an impact on jurors even after the case is in progress. Shapiro purportedly said that he would try to affect the sequestered jurors in the criminal case by showing them movies of people being framed by the police, such as *Twelve Angry Men* (Schiller & Willwerth, 1996, p. 161).

Finally, this chapter offers explanations of media effects of telelitigation by showing the media's power to set the agenda for the public, to confer status on principal participants in these events, and to solicit public attention to social issues such as spousal abuse and police malfeasance. The trial is an attractive media vehicle because it is real life rather than fictional, and the outcomes are unknown until the process is completed. As the Simpson trial indicates, the media sustained interest in the case even after the civil trial by reporting Simpson's actions on the golf course and his financial woes. Just like sensational trials of the past, those of Bruno Richard Hauptmann in the Lindbergh kidnapping and Sam Sheppard in the murder of his wife (Schuetz & Snedaker, 1988), the media never really ends their coverage of trials. Instead, the public continues to show interest in the celebrities who appeared in the trials and to follow the effects the trial has had on participants. During the other celebrated trials of this century, Court TV, cable television, and the Internet did not exist. The existence of these new media significantly contributed to the spectacles of the Simpson cases and to their telelitigated content.

3

Opening Statements: Lasting Impressions

Lin S. Lilley

BY THE VERY NATURE OF THEIR DIFFERING burdens of proof, audiences would expect criminal and civil trials to contain different rhetorical appeals. But, as this chapter will show, the differences between the opening statements in the Simpson criminal and civil trials go beyond the difference in legal standards. This chapter illustrates how the attorneys, particularly in the criminal trial, merged trial facts with media appeals and attempted to affect the court of public opinion in addition to the opinions of jurors. The characteristics of telelitigation affected the strategy, the content, and the style of opening statements. In the civil trials where the appeal was to the cameras in the corridors, the effect was more subtle. By contrast, the cameras inside the courtroom during the criminal trial encouraged attorneys to adopt a sophistical verbal style and supplement it with extensive visual aids. At the same time, the attorneys' awareness of the media subverted some legal procedures.

One of the original jurors in the Simpson criminal trial, Tracy Kennedy, remembers the openings this way: "The prosecutors outlined evidence that seemed overwhelming. It was a double-barreled attack. As Darden talked about why O. J. Simpson did it, Clark explained how it was done. . . . The next day the defense got its shot. And Johnnie Cochran was magnificent" (Kennedy & Kennedy, 1995, p. 145). As Kennedy, who was dismissed two months into the trial when accused of using his laptop computer to keep notes for a book, sees it, trial delays gave Cochran the advantage of time to review the prosecution's opening and to "shoot holes" in their case. Kennedy believes that Cochran planned the delay to seize the advantage (p. 146). Indeed, a detailed defense opening, delivered during two days of a six-day period, appears to have siphoned off the momentum that prosecutors usually would have had going into testimony.

In the civil trial, both sides gave detailed opening statements. Attorneys for the plaintiffs—Daniel M. Petrocelli for Fredric Goldman, Michael A. Brewer for Ron Goldman's mother, Sharon Rufo, and John Quinlan Kelly for Louis Brown—organized a triple-barreled attack. Robert C. Baker answered on behalf of O. J. Simpson. In the second trial, the defense had no timing advantage, and, what is more significant, each side knew what the other would say. As a result, the civil trial began with more balanced opening statements. By contrast, in the criminal trial, Cochran delivered a long and aggressive opening statement, one especially designed for cameras in the courtroom.

Courts allow some latitude in the content and presentation of opening statements, but attorneys are proscribed from arguing the facts or the law of the case (Markus, 1981, p. 119). These limits explain why opening remarks are labeled as a "statement," while closing comments are referred to as an "argument." Although judicial rule makers have not clearly articulated why they forbid argument in opening statements, Lind and Ke (1985) suggest it is likely that early rule makers worried that jurors would "be overly susceptible to arguments offered prior to the presentation of evidence" (p. 231).

But successful advocates have learned to push the envelope and to use rhetorical techniques to persuade without seeming to break the court-imposed rules against argument. The analysis focuses on the transcripts of the opening statements in both trials and on the way the attorneys set about to persuade jurors. This chapter answers the following questions: How did the opening statements reflect adaptation for telelitigation? What techniques—choices of language, organization, or content—did the attorneys employ to enhance the persuasiveness of their openings and to play to the media audience? Did any of the attorneys push the envelope too far and break the legal standards for opening statements? Which of the opening statements were the most powerful and persuasive? To accomplish this goal, the chapter (1) provides a rationale for studying opening statements, (2) describes legal standards, (3) explains how attorneys use indirect argument, and (4) suggests implications for understanding the other segments of the Simpson trials.

Rationale for Analysis of Opening Statements

An analysis of opening statements illuminates the centrality of this part of the trial. In 1983, the Speech Communication Association and other professional organizations sponsored a conference on communication strategies in the practice of lawyering. The consensus in the sessions dealing with opening statements was that, while lawyers regularly stress the value of opening statements, little had been done to study how to make opening remarks more effective (see, for example, Benoit & France, 1983,

p. 384; Starr, 1983, p. 424). In 1991, Ronald J. Matlon, one of the con-
veners of the 1983 conference, reported little progress in applied communication research focusing on opening statements (p. 67).

To fill the gap, attorneys routinely resort to learning from the "mas-
ters" (e.g., Purdue et al., 1996). Lawyers regularly write how-to books
and articles (Julien, 1982; Auerbach, 1990), but the advice dispensed is
largely anecdotal, based on the attorney's attempt to generalize from her
or his personal successes. Although there appears to be considerable
agreement among lawyers on how to develop openings, there is still ample
room for systematic analysis.

One way communication scholars can extend the scope of current
writings about opening statements is through case studies. Even though
case studies enjoy less prestige because they are qualitative rather than
quantitative, Buchanan (1983) suggests, "[E]ven that disadvantage can
be somewhat offset over time if one observes enough cases" (p. 458). Trial
consultants are in the unique position to observe large numbers of opening
statements, and it is that perspective that I bring to this analysis of the
openings in the Simpson trials.

Legal Standards for Opening Statements

This section identifies and defines the major legal constraints attorneys
face in developing opening statements and examines how the criminal
and civil attorneys in the Simpson cases either adhered to or attempted
to bypass each constraint.

Ban Against Arguing the Evidence and the Law

As noted above, attorneys are not permitted to argue the evidence or the
law. In particular, they are cautioned against "encouraging inferences or
conclusions from abstracted data until the abstracted data have been
actually adduced in the trial event" (Markus, 1981, p. 119). Some judges,
in the absence of objections by opposing counsel, are allowing attorneys
some leeway in interpreting this standard.

The lead attorney in Simpson's civil trial, Robert Baker, objected to
Daniel Petrocelli's attempts to precondition jurors by talking about
Simpson's defenses. In the following segment excerpted from the side-bar
dealing with this issue, Judge Fujisaki shows himself to be a strict inter-
preter of the standards for opening statements:

Baker: It's my position, in opening statements, they can show what their
   evidence is going to present. . . . Opening statement is what their case
   is, what their evidence is going to prove, what they have a burden of
   proving. It is not to rebut what our position may or may not be at the

time of trial. And for him to do that, it then becomes argument. And he's got to, in my opinion, save that for the conclusion of his case.

Petrocelli: A good part of my opening is going to be devoted to addressing the defense contentions. One is that there's a long struggle. . . . In this case, they're going to put on an expert that will say that the struggle took 15 minutes.

Court: Mr. Baker may decide not to call this man at all. . . . I'm a sympathetic person to the defense position. You're trying to shape his argument and shape his presentation of his case and I don't think that's appropriate. . . . You can save it for closing argument. You . . . want to explain to the jury what evidence you are going to offer, you may. And you can state it for the purpose of showing that the struggle lasted only such and such a minute. But your [*sic*] front loading this, and I don't think that's appropriate because we haven't heard any evidence yet. (TRL, 1996, October 23)

Forewarning jurors, as Petrocelli attempted to do, is a favorite tactic. Sometimes neither opposing counsel nor judges recognize the tactic as a form of argument. If successfully introduced, such forewarning helps jurors resist subsequent persuasive appeals. Psychological research demonstrates that people resist later persuasive attempts to a greater degree when they have been forewarned (McGuire, 1964). The concept is similar to being inoculated for a disease. If you inoculate or forewarn against an upcoming argument, individuals start to develop counterarguments for what they anticipate hearing (McGuire & Papageorgis, 1962; Petty & Cacioppo, 1977 & 1979). Exposing individuals to the opposing side's major themes or arguments and then going on to refute them can result even in greater resistance to persuasion (Cialdini, Petty & Cacioppo, 1981).

In the criminal trial, the prosecution took the so-called ethical high road and did not attempt to characterize the defense's evidence. However, Clark briefly touched on the defense's contamination theme: "Now, the defense is going to speak to you at length about contamination and all the problems that could ensue in testing, but I will simply say this at this point: There are safeguards built into the DNA tests" (TRC, 1995, January 24). In hindsight, Clark would have been more persuasive if she had offered a more thorough explanation. For example, it is well within accepted legal standards to summarize briefly your own key witnesses' testimony. By reviewing the testimony of key prosecution scientific witnesses, Clark could have stayed on the ethical high road and yet familiarized jurors with favorable DNA explanations that potentially could have inoculated jurors and the media audience against anticipated defense attacks on DNA evidence. For Clark to have glossed over the discussion about DNA seems particularly inexcusable. Perhaps she was too cocky in assuming that the scientific evidence would prevail, perhaps she was not accustomed to having adversaries who could present strong arguments against the reliability of DNA, or perhaps she just wanted to keep the opening statement shorter, less technical, and more focused on the amount of blood evidence rather than on the mechanisms for analyzing the evidence.

When it comes to arguing the law, some judges once again allow leeway and permit attorneys to offer a few general instructions. For instance, Judge Ito let Marcia Clark generally address the concept of reasonable doubt. Cochran went further and actually displayed the wording of the jury instructions on witness credibility, alibi testimony, direct and circumstantial evidence, presumption of innocence, reasonable doubt, and burden of proof (TRC, 1995, January 30).

None of the attorneys in the civil case chose to talk about specific jury instructions in opening statements, perhaps because their burden of proof was substantially reduced in the civil proceeding, but more likely because of Judge Fujisaki's strict interpretation of the contents of opening statements.

Admissibility of Evidence

Richard Crawford (1990) argues that, because some judges are moving away from such strict interpretation of standards for opening statements, "[t]here is actually an opening statement evolution/revolution in full bloom" (p. 227). Crawford (1989) is in the forefront of teaching attorneys to "immediately take your best shot, so fire your silver bullets" (p. 110). For Crawford (1990), the only "hard and fast rule" is that "you can point to anything if it is anywhere in the written or testimonial evidence to appear during trial" (p. 228). Klonoff and Colby (1990), former assistant U.S. attorneys, who have written a popular how-to book on trial strategy, emphasize that the American Bar Association Standards mandate that "the advocate should obviously not identify any testimony or piece of evidence unless he is certain that he *can* and *will* introduce it. Indeed, it is improper for an advocate to refer in opening statement to evidence that he does not intend to introduce or that will be ruled inadmissible" (p. 165).

Different admissibility rulings in the two trials meant that the civil and criminal trial stories were somewhat different. In the criminal case, weeks before opening statements, the prosecution waged an important battle over the admissibility of domestic abuse evidence. Although prosecutors in murder cases are not legally required to prove motive, the prosecuting attorneys felt it essential to build a case against Simpson. Prosecutor Scott Gordon expressed it this way: "The public believes that Simpson was a friendly, affable, peace-loving guy. Not the type of guy that's going to commit murder. If we can't get in motive evidence, that erroneous perception of his character will win the day" (Goldberg, 1996, pp. 16–17).

Prosecutors submitted their motion on domestic abuse, citing "sixty-two separate instances of abuse, manipulation, and threats by Simpson" (Darden, 1996, p. 217). Judge Ito ruled, on what Hank Goldberg—who argued the prosecution motion—called a "meticulous and well-reasoned order," that all of the statements Nicole made to other people and in her diary were inadmissible (Goldberg, 1996, p. 39). Although Ito excluded some important evidence, the prosecution felt his "ruling left Chris Darden sufficient latitude to accurately and meaningfully characterize the nature of the relationship to the jury" (Goldberg, 1996, p. 40).

Different rules of evidence in the civil arena meant that much of the domestic abuse evidence, deemed inadmissible in the criminal proceeding, would be fair game in the civil lawsuit. Petrocelli, Brewer, and Kelly would find it much easier to explain why a smiling, successful O. J. Simpson would commit such heinous murders.

On the domestic abuse issue, the prosecutors faced a further constraint. They could not introduce expert testimony to explain Simpson's conduct and state of mind. Assistant Los Angeles prosecutor Lydia Bodin explains that under Evidence Code section 1107(a) they could bring in an expert on domestic abuse only "to refute certain myths and misconceptions if the defense raises them. But we can't introduce the evidence to show that Simpson fits a batterer's profile. The reason for this law is that we don't want an expert coming into court and saying the defendant is in fact a batterer" (Goldberg, 1996, p. 18).

However, Cochran spent a significant amount of time in his opening talking about the defense's world-renowned expert on battered women's syndrome, Dr. Lenore Walker. Because the prosecution was restricted from using an expert in the field, Darden later writes:

> We were salivating for the chance to question Walker. Apparently, she had given Simpson a number of tests, and if she was called, the information in those tests would be fair game for us to question her about. And so evidence that might otherwise be lost as hearsay—for instance, Nicole Brown's diary and her frantic telephone call to the Sojourn shelter—would be opened up for questioning. But the defense never called her either. And the only thing the jury knew about her would come from Cochran's wild opening. (1996, p. 227)

Most admissibility issues were handled pretrial, as would be expected, but some hotly contested issues still arose during Cochran's opening statement. Two admissibility concerns raised in Cochran's opening seemed particularly egregious and caused Judge Ito to delay the completion of

Cochran's opening. First, Judge Ito ruled Cochran out of bounds after Cochran tried to display an envelope to jurors (TRC, 1995, January 25). The implication was that the murder weapon was in the envelope. Cochran explained to Judge Ito that he merely wanted to display the envelope and "allude" to its contents without describing them. Although Ito did not allow Cochran to display again or to "allude" to the envelope, the judge did allow Cochran to talk about how the police searched Simpson's home and the surrounding area and never found a knife (TRC, 1995, January 25).

Second, Cochran introduced highlights of several witnesses' testimony in his opening even though their statements had not been turned over to prosecutors during discovery. Because Judge Ito perceived the defense's actions as a blatant attempt to gain tactical advantage, the judge granted "the highly unusual remedy" (Ito's own words in TRC, 1995, January 30) of allowing the prosecution to re-open at the close of the defense's opening statement. Ito, in fact, could think of only one civil case where this sanction previously had been allowed (TRC, 1995, January 30). Further, Ito gave jurors a detailed instruction about the defense's transgression:

> The laws governing criminal procedure in California require that each side disclose and give to the other side the names of the persons they intend to present as witnesses and any written record or recording of the statements made by these witnesses. The law also requires the disclosure of any real or tangible evidence . . . be made before trial. . . . During the course of opening statements defense counsel mentioned witnesses who had not previously been disclosed to the prosecution or whose written statements were not given to the prosecution before trial, as required by law. This violation of the law— this was a violation of the law and one of the causes of the two-day delay, including the absence of Mr. Hodgman [a lead prosecutor who was hospitalized after Cochran's first day of opening]. Keeping in mind that statements by the lawyers are not evidence, you are directed to disregard the comments of defense counsel during his opening statement as they pertain to the following potential witnesses: Mary Anne Gerchas, Michelle Abudrahm, Mark Partridge, Howard Weitzman, Skip Taft, Christian Riechardt. If and when these witnesses are presented to you during this trial, you may consider the effect of this delay in disclosure, if any, upon the credibility of the witnesses and give to it the weight to which you feel it is entitled. Please note, however, and this is important, please note that the failure of the defendant's attorneys to comply

with the law is not evidence of the defendant's guilt and should not be considered as such by you. (TRC, 1995, January 30)

Did Ito take such an unusual step because he was concerned about his own media image? Was he worried about being perceived as too lenient toward the defense? Prosecutor Hodgman had made repeated objections about admissibility issues specifically relating to the witnesses named in Ito's cautionary instruction. The jury was not privy to the nature of the objections, but the media audience was. Interestingly, many advocates of televising criminal trials argue that opening the process to the television audience lessens the likelihood that a judge will act like an arm of the prosecution (Shoop, 1995). Given the latitude Ito allowed the defense, it appears that the media presence indeed had an ameliorating effect.

Cochran took a chance in his opening, and he may well have been rewarded for his risk taking. Judge Ito restricted Clark to a ten-minute re-opening statement and specified what she could do with the time. In addition, by the time the defense actually presented its case, most of the jurors probably had long forgotten Judge Ito's admonition. But the jurors would remember the impression that the prosecution was hiding something because Clark and Darden never told jurors about these witnesses at any point during the trial. As the old lawyer's saying goes, once the jury hears something, "You can never unring the bell." Research on cautionary instructions is mixed, but more studies validate that jurors are likely to disregard the judge's instructions than to follow them (see, for example, Sue, Smith, & Caldwell, 1973, and Kassin & Wrightsman, 1979).

Ethical Obligation to Stick with the Facts

In the wake of the Simpson criminal trial and the first trial of the Menendez brothers, the public is waking up and beginning to complain about so-called smoke-screen defenses, such as the "race card" or the "abuse excuse," which focus on peripheral issues rather than on the facts of the case. Judges and attorneys also are questioning whether zealous advocacy is truly a justification for "making arguments that confuse material issues or trigger jurors' prejudices on subjects such as race, sexual orientation, ethnicity and religion" (Curriden, 1995, p. 57).

Rule 403 of the Federal Rules of Evidence and its state law equivalents provide the standard for deciding what evidence should be excluded, and Judge Fujisaki religiously adhered to the standard: "Although relevant, evidence may be excluded if its probative value is substantially outweighed by the danger of unfair prejudice, confusion of the issues or misleading the jury, or by considerations of undue delay, waste of time or needless presentations of cumulative evidence" (quoted in Curriden, 1995, p. 58).

Newman Flannigan, executive director of the National District Attorneys' Association, believes that, although the evidentiary rules preclude bogus defenses not supported by the physical evidence, judges continue to let them in because "judges are afraid of being reversed, so they let anything by the defendant in. When that defendant is found not guilty, there is no appeal, so no precedent is set" (quoted in Curriden, 1995, p. 58).

Immediately prior to Petrocelli's opening in the civil trial, Judge Fujisaki ruled that the defense could not make references to Detective Fuhrman's testimony in the criminal trial nor to his perjury. Further, although the defense had some indication that Fuhrman would testify voluntarily, Fujisaki precluded Baker from telling the jury about this in opening statements.

Even without Fuhrman's criminal case testimony, Petrocelli was justifiably concerned about police-bashing and police-planting defenses. As a consequence, Petrocelli closed the introductory portion of his opening statement with this persuasive appeal:

> And finally, ladies and gentlemen, we will show that when faced with the truth of his blood, his hair, his clothing, his gloves, his shoes, his Bronco, his rage, his motive, his words, and his actions, you will see how Mr. Simpson in this trial will resort to theories of police conspiracies, frame-ups, cover-ups and incompetence, to try to explain away all of the incriminating evidence. And we will show you that there is not one ounce of evidence, not one ounce of proof, and not one ounce of truth to any of these things. We will demonstrate to you that far from these theories born out of desperation, there is only one—[objection by Baker]. (TRL, 1996, October 23)

Baker objected to Petrocelli's "argument," and Fujisaki sustained the objection. For the fifth time in the first ten minutes of Petrocelli's opening, Baker had lodged an objection claiming that his opponent was arguing. Petrocelli pushed the envelope on the legal constraint against argument in order to keep the focus on the plaintiff's version, physical evidence pointing to Simpson's culpability, rather than on the defense's smoke-screen conspiracy theory, which had been so convincing in the criminal trial.

Techniques for Indirect Argumentation

Every attorney's goal in the opening statement is to convince jurors of the superiority of his or her case. Even given the legal constraints discussed in the last section, attorneys still have powerful persuasive tools. Crawford (1990) reminds us that "in ordinary and nonlegal decision-making forums, an 'argument' can be defined as any communication act which substantively or psychologically advances a position, a case, or a cause" (p. 228). By contrast, "prohibitions against using arguments or being argumentative during an opening statement are based on the more narrow legal definitions of argument which center on drawing the final inference, characterizing the evidence, becoming inflammatory, and the like" (p. 228). Indeed, courts may ignore communication techniques that inherently have the effect of argumentation. These techniques, which function as argument, but generally fit within the legal standards, are the focus of this section.

Themes

Gerry Spence (1995), a longtime regular on the attorney-lecture circuit and now a frequently seen television legal commentator, has for years advocated the use of a theme, phrase, or "slogan that represents the principal point of our argument." The theme can summarize a story and can stand for "the ultimate point we want to make, a saying, as it were, that symbolizes the very heart of the issue" (p. 77).

Matlon (1993), who has compiled the only serious compendium of research on opening statements, recognizes the usefulness of themes. Matlon encourages attorneys to provide a single theme or a few themes. He notes, "Too many themes (or too many defenses) bog a case down and confuse the audience" (p. 11). Themes are easy to remember, and once in our memories, they provide a framework for organizing new information and for retrieving that information at a future time. Themes become more important when a trial is lengthy or complicated, especially if note-taking is prohibited. Although note-taking was allowed in both trials, all attorneys on both sides employed themes, perhaps because related research such as Pyszczynski and Wrightsman (1981) indicates that trial verdicts tend to favor the side that creates a thematic framework over the one that does not.

Obviously, the theme or themes must fit the evidence, and they must be simple. Matlon (1993) reminds us that attorneys need to embed the theme "in the minds of the judge and jury in the opening statement, emphasize it throughout the questioning of witnesses, and stress it once again in summation" (pp. 13–14). In chapter 6 of this volume, Schuetz examines the summations in the Simpson trials and identifies the prime storytellers in the criminal trial as Darden and Cochran and in the civil trial as Petrocelli and Baker. As the following analysis of themes will show, these were also the attorneys who made the most systematic attempt to develop themes in their opening statements.

Theming is essentially condensed storytelling. A few words call forth a full story. By the end of the first day of Cochran's opening (TRC, 1995,

January 25), jurors had been bombarded with both the police's and the prosecution's "rush to judgment" and their "obsession to win at any cost and by any means necessary." Cochran easily weakened Clark's one and only theme about the "trail of blood" leading to the defendant (TRC, 1995, January 24). According to Cochran, "What [Clark] did not tell you is that there are trails that lead toward innocence and they were not pursued" (TRC, 1995, January 25). Cochran did not stop there. In day one of his opening, he pounded the prosecuting attorneys themselves with fifteen separate accusations of withholding evidence. He assured the jury that "all of us [lawyers] have an obligation to share with you and be as honest and forthright as we can," and "I want to keep the faith with you about being as accurate as I can." Cochran goes on to imply, yet another time, that the prosecutors are withholding evidence from the jury, evidence that would show Simpson's innocence.

Vincent Bugliosi (1996), a former Los Angeles prosecutor in the Charles Manson case, believes there is one cardinal rule for prosecutors: "The prosecution should *always* convey to the jury that as representatives of the people they *want* to present all the relevant evidence on the issue of guilt" (p. 107). Cochran made Fuhrman into an issue partly because the prosecutors chose not to even mention his name in opening statements. Clark's allusions to Fuhrman's role were so oblique, in fact, that she resorted to passive voice as she showed a picture with Fuhrman pointing out the glove: "And there is the glove where it was found in the very same location where it was found that night right next to the air conditioner on that narrow path" (TRC, 1995, January 24). Earlier, Clark avoided saying Fuhrman's name by pointing out the path in a picture and indicating where "they" went, when in actuality it was where Fuhrman, by himself, first went. Cochran clearly made her rue the omission as he talked about the prosecution's "trying to hide Fuhrman."

Fuhrman is not the only witness Cochran accused the prosecution of hiding: "They never once mentioned their coroner . . . these two excellent lawyers . . . he is another mystery witness they don't want to talk about" (TRC, 1995, January 25). One of the first things Cochran spoke about in the body of his opening was the prosecution's withholding of witness testimony:

> The evidence will show that the prosecution in this case has enlisted the services of many, many police agencies across the United States, the FBI, many local police agencies. They have gone around the world talking to witnesses. But the evidence will show they failed to go next door to Mr. Simpson's house and talk to a witness [Rosa Lopez] that they knew about who provided him with an alibi, and there are other witnesses like

that and we will have to only ask ourselves why. (TRC, 1995, January 25)

Cochran bashed the prosecutors and the Los Angeles Police Department (LAPD) unmercifully about hiding certain witnesses. Ordinarily, such blatant bashing, if even allowed, is reserved for closing argument when attorneys actually can talk about which witnesses did not appear.

The extent of Cochran's thematic harangue raises serious questions: Why did the prosecutors fail to inoculate in some fashion against the onslaught of witnesses whom they had interviewed and chosen not to use? But also, why did Darden and Clark eliminate two significant pieces of evidence so entrenched in the public's minds—the low-speed Bronco chase and the "suicide" letter? Clark admits that she worried about whether to introduce the low-speed chase, but, based on the general responses to the juror questionnaires, she decided that the replay of the chase would create increased sympathy for Simpson (1997, pp. 190–91). Yet every time they objected to some reference to the chase or the letter, the district attorneys came across—as Johnnie Cochran first depicted them throughout most of day one of his opening statement—as prosecutors "who didn't tell you about" critical evidence.

Perhaps Clark and Darden followed one of the new trends in litigation, something called the "sponsorship theory of evidence." Klonoff and Colby (1990), two former prosecutors who proposed this "theory," advocate that attorneys should introduce only evidence that favors their side and never should talk about "less-than-strong evidence" in opening statements or anywhere else in the case (pp. 166–67). This flies in the face of traditional recommendations, which include talking about the weaknesses in your case and putting your own spin on them before the other side interprets them unfavorably (Haskins & Gardner, 1990, p. 53; Matlon, 1993, p. 23).

Cochran did not stop his attacks on the LAPD with the "rush to judgment" theme. He went on to lambaste the LAPD lab as a "cesspool of contamination" with "covered-wagon collection techniques." "Who," but this lab, "has the opportunity to contaminate [the Bronco evidence], or compromise it or in any way corrupt it?" (TRC, 1995, January 30). Cochran repeated the three C's—"contaminated, compromised, corrupted"—until they were secure in the jurors' minds along with the phrase "you put garbage in, you get garbage out" (TRC, 1995, January 30). Criminal defense attorneys frequently devote one or more of their themes to attacks on the prosecution's evidence, and, where possible, they develop a theme devoted to the positive depiction of their client. In developing a theme to describe Simpson, Cochran chose to speak positively about Simpson's "circle of benevolence" (TRC, 1995, January 25), which extended not only to Nicole but also to her family and to charitable organizations through the gifts that he gave them.

When it came to theming or building condensed stories, Darden was not nearly as masterful. One of his themes seemed to work: the image of Simpson's "public face, public persona" and of exposing this "face" at trial (TRC, 1995, January 24). Clark reiterated this theme when she referred to "the other side of the smiling face in the Hertz commercial" (TRC, 1995, January 24). Darden got even more mileage from the public face theme by indicating, "Domestic violence happens where the public can't see . . . in bedrooms, in homes." Also, when Darden talked about Simpson's need to explain the domestic violence of 1989 "to the media and the public," he made sure to point out that Simpson's "public" characterization of the incident was a so-called "mutual wrestling match" (TRC, 1995, January 24).

Darden unsuccessfully attempted to use the word *control* and its variants—*controlled, controlling, in control*, and *out of control*—as a theme. In all, Darden repeated *control* or one of its variants forty-five times in just over an hour. The repetition did not cure the problem of using the control concept as a key theme. Without expert testimony to lay out a pattern of domestic violence as control, this most likely was lost on the jurors. Further, so many repetitions without an understanding did seem to make Darden strident, and thus Darden made himself especially vulnerable to Cochran's claim that the prosecutor was engaging in "character assassination" (TRC, 1995, January 25).

Plaintiff attorneys split their opening statement assignments three ways. Petrocelli led off with how all of the physical evidence pointed to Simpson's guilt. Next, Brewer briefly told about the low-speed chase and the so-called suicide note and how they, too, indicated Simpson's guilt. Finally, Kelly talked about motive and Brown's and Simpson's relationship and how, as "the passion died . . . , the anger, hostility and resentment grew" (TRL, 1996, October 23).

Obviously, the attorneys involved in the civil trial benefited from theming efforts in the first trial. Marcia Clark once mentioned near the close of her opening statement that "the evidence will consistently point to the guilt of only one person" (TRC, 1995, January 24). Petrocelli and Brewer seized upon this theme. In the beginning of his opening statement, Petrocelli asserted that "all of the evidence points to O. J. Simpson" and proceeded to outline all of the evidence that pointed to Simpson and to no one else (TRL, 1996, October 23). Brewer echoed this by contending that the "evidence undeniably points to the responsibilities of Mr. Simpson" (TRL, 1996, October 23). Petrocelli again borrowed from Clark: "In his extreme panic and hurry, Mr. Simpson left behind a trail of incriminating evidence, starting right at the murder scene and leading right into his bedroom" (TRL, 1996, October 23).

Thanks to the deposition of Simpson taken after the criminal trial in preparation for the civil lawsuit, Petrocelli could add "lies and deceptions" to his themes. Petrocelli referred to three other themes: "He has no alibi"; he "had the opportunity and the time to commit the murders"; and "his actions indicated a consciousness of guilt" (TRL, 1996, October 23). Brewer reiterated the consciousness of guilt theme in his mini-opening. Both men used the concept to indicate that Simpson "did not act and behave like an innocent man." It was Brewer's job to tie the low-speed Bronco chase and the so-called suicide letter to consciousness of guilt. Brewer stepped out of bounds and was reined in by Fujisaki when he said: "And I'm going to even title my discussion as it relates to the event of June 17, 'Mr. Simpson's flight from justice'" (TRL, 1996, October 23).

In the third plaintiff opening, Kelly focused on the "outer veneer of Mr. Simpson . . . the charismatic individual, the impeccable dress, irresistible smile. But then the evidence and the testimony will take you beneath the polished veneer to a sometimes dark and a violent and frightening world of uncontrollable rage" (TRL, 1996, October 23). Kelly also talked about "the dark side of Mr. Simpson" and the "dark, black mood" Simpson was in the day of the murders (TRL, 1996, October 23). The wisdom of Kelly's description of Simpson's personality as "dark" and "black" was questionable, given at this stage of the civil trial there was still potential for race to become an issue. Clearly, though, Kelly had learned from Darden's focus on "control" that the plaintiffs needed a better way to argue motive.

Although Brewer's and Kelly's thematic efforts were marginal, Petrocelli greatly improved upon the prosecution's attempts at using themes. However, Baker displayed none of Cochran's finesse. He principally used theme reversals rather than trying to establish his own independent themes. As a consequence, Nicole Brown became the one who was controlling, and she became the one who was "out of control" and surrounding herself with prostitutes and drug users. In a separate theme reversal, Baker declared that Simpson's acts in volunteering to be interviewed by police without a lawyer present, to give blood, and to hire the world's best detective and best blood scientist showed "consciousness of innocence" and "not a consciousness of guilt" (TRL, 1996, October 24). Baker dropped all of Cochran's catchy phrases except for once when he referred to the LAPD lab as a "cesspool of contamination." Baker replaced Cochran's themes with difficult phrases such as "besides the tampering and moving of pieces of evidence, [there was] a failure [on the part

of the LAPD] to collect evidence that could have exculpated my client"
(TRL, 1996, October 24).

Order and Organization

Ordering effect. Jurors heard Darden's potentially unsatisfying explanation about why Simpson committed the crimes before they learned just
how heinous the crimes were and how much physical evidence pointed
only at Simpson. Did this lead jurors to discount the domestic abuse
theory from the very first? In research relating to the story model of juror decision making, Pennington and Hastie suggest that the most acceptable story to jurors is the one that covers the greatest amount of evidence.
As Pennington and Hastie (1993) see it, "An explanation that leaves a
lot of evidence unaccounted for is likely to have a lower level of acceptability as the correct explanation" (p. 198). In this instance, the story's
coverage may have been poor for two reasons. First, the prosecution
would never get the chance to put an expert on the stand to explain just
how significant the control issue is in domestic violence cases. Second,
the control theme did not account for Simpson's lawyers presenting the
other side of the story for each domestic abuse incident. The theme of
control was ineffective because it focused on equivocal or arguable evidence and took the emphasis away from the seemingly indisputable physical evidence.

Kelly's motive was the least effective theme offered by the three plaintiff
attorneys, but it was stronger than Darden's attempts to portray the relationship between Brown and Simpson, probably in large part due to
Kelly's speech being the last of the plaintiffs' opening statements rather
than the first, like Darden's.

Parallel action. Other authors in this volume address narrative as argument (see Schuetz, chapter 6, and Burnett, chapter 7). Therefore, this
chapter emphasizes only one aspect of storytelling, an organizational
approach for describing parallel action. Customarily, this technique is
used to describe how the victim and the accused start from two separate
places and times. Matlon (1993) notes that each of the two background
scenarios is established independently and suspense builds as they move
toward the location in which the crime is committed (p. 38). Largely
thanks to an exhibit that showed what was happening at five-minute
intervals, Cochran developed a masterful story of parallel action simultaneously illustrating what was happening at Bundy and what was happening at Rockingham. Jurors found it easy to follow this type of timeline,
where the scenes and times were pictured side-by-side. In addition,
Cochran had separate conventional timelines for the collection of evidence
relating to the socks and to the Bronco. Clark, Petrocelli, and Baker tried

to weave their timelines orally. Unfortunately, because of all the details, they often found themselves backtracking.

Focused lists. Petrocelli excelled at pulling all of the evidence together and indicating what it would show. For example, within the first five minutes of his opening, Petrocelli listed nineteen items of blood, hair, or fiber evidence "undeniably pointing to O. J. Simpson" (TRL, 1996, October 23). Petrocelli asked jurors, "What will Mr. Simpson say about what he was doing during this time [the one hour and twenty minutes in which the murders were committed]?" After a list of eight things Simpson supposedly did, Petrocelli warned jurors to expect inconsistent testimony because they would "hear Mr. Simpson say a lot of other things about where he was during that time" (TRL, 1996, October 23). But perhaps the most significant list of all was Petrocelli's explanation of why the police would not and could not have planted the evidence. Marcia Clark certainly could have benefited from such focused lists, especially on the police-planting issue.

Word Choice

Some words have, as Ng and Bradac (1993) noted, "an extraordinary ability to evoke a particular structuring of beliefs and emotions" (p. 136). Loftus and Palmer (1974) researched how some words, such as *smash*, *bump*, and *collide*, can actually distort the memories of eyewitnesses.

Lawyers have long been wordsmiths, even if they were not aware of the research on emotive words. In a case where an auto hits a child following a ball onto a roadway, the plaintiff, for instance, may talk about a "playing child," the defense, about a "darting child." The idea is to condense a story into a few words.

What words did these attorneys use to talk about race issues? What beliefs and emotions did their words evoke? Not surprisingly, Cochran made the most, though still a very limited, mention of race. Cochran began his opening this way: "You hear a lot about this talk about justice. I guess Dr. Martin Luther King said it best when he said that injustice anywhere is a threat to justice everywhere, and so we are now embarked upon this search for justice, this search for truth, this search for the facts." He immediately followed this with a quotation from Abraham Lincoln about jury service being "the highest act of citizenship" (TRC, 1995, January 25). After that, Cochran launched his attack against the police and the prosecutors for telling only part of the truth.

As Cochran talked about the "circle of benevolence," he referred to "a spindly leg youth from San Francisco who suffered with rickets . . . who grew up to become the greatest running back in the history of the National Football League." Cochran further noted that, because of commercial endorsements, Simpson has a calendar filled with activities such as in "March when you find that he was in New York, he was doing Bryant Gumble's charitable golf tournament" (TRC, 1995, January 25). Finally, Cochran invoked the name of Martin Luther King when he apologized for having stated that one of the defense's experts was a Nobel Prize winner: "I notice that I misspoke when I said at one point that Dr. Cary Mullins had won, I think I said, the Noble [*sic*] peace prize, and I think I must have had Dr. Martin Luther King on the mind when I talked about him. He won the Noble [*sic*] prize for chemistry" (TRC, 1995, January 30).

Darden alluded to race when he employed metonymy, a figure of speech wherein the name of one thing is used for that of another with which it is associated. Darden told jurors that "my people up in Richmond, California, and friends in Fayetteville, Georgia, and all across the country" want to know whether O. J. really killed Nicole Brown and Ron Goldman (TRC, 1995, January 24). The implication of "my people" was that black people across the country were wondering about Simpson's guilt. In the introduction of his opening statement, Cochran attacked Darden personally when he retorted:

> Mr. Darden said yesterday that in Richmond, California, and some place in Georgia people were asking questions. Well, I would like to think that in my hometown of Shreveport, Louisiana, my mother-in-law in New Orleans, Louisiana, and other places throughout this country, that they are asking why did Mr. Darden spend all that time on domestic violence if this is a murder case? (TRC, 1995, January 25)

Although Cochran was indignant before the jury as he chastised Darden, the first real battle over race occurred before opening statements during pretrial arguments relating to Detective Fuhrman. Darden argued that "Fuhrman's racial views, whatever they were, were completely irrelevant" (Clark, 1997, p. 260). Darden went on to contend that "when you mention that word to this jury or to any African American, it blinds them" (Clark, 1997, p. 261). As the whole nation watched, Cochran launched into a response: "His remarks this morning are perhaps the most incredible remarks I've heard in a court of law in the thirty-two years I've been practicing law. His remarks are demeaning to African Americans as a group. And so I want to apologize to African Americans all over the country" (Clark, 1997, p. 262). At this point, Ito ruled that Fuhrman's animus could not be introduced unless the defense could show proof he had planted the glove (Clark, 1997, p. 263). Only later, after the Laura Hart McKinny tapes emerged, would Ito's ruling change.

When you remove the two black attorneys who were key players in the first trial, the references to race, as seen in the civil case, are virtually nonexistent. Baker used a single reference to race when he accused a police officer from the 1989 incident of being "totally abusive to O. J. Simpson" (TRC, 1996, October 24). Baker indicated that this officer was mentioned in the Christopher Commission report, and Baker assured jurors that he would question the officer about this connection. The implication, of course, is that this LAPD officer has a "record" of abusing blacks. Thus again, Baker attempted a role reversal.

Kelly attempted to defuse the race issue by indicating that there were black people who loved Nicole Brown and there were black people whom she loved, as well as white people. Kelly also reflected that Simpson's children Sydney and Justin were "growing up color blind" (TRL, 1996, October 23).

Nonverbal Considerations

Sometimes, a picture is truly worth a thousand words. Dismissed juror Tracy Kennedy noted that "for most of the time that Cochran was speaking we were looking at an enlarged photograph of O. J. and his daughter, Sydney, taken on the day of the killings. In the photo, O. J. was smiling" (1995, p. 145). The trial transcripts proved Kennedy's recollections. During most of the first day of Cochran's opening, this picture was before the jury. After this picture came another "smiling" photo of Simpson and Paula Barbieri at an Israeli benefit. Then, once again, Cochran placed the picture of Simpson and Sydney before the jury (TRC, 1995, January 25). The prosecutors never objected, perhaps because they already had made numerous objections. Their silence followed the general legal how-to advice that attorneys should limit their objections in order to avoid appearing like they are blocking the truth. Since one of Cochran's first orders of business was to accuse the prosecution of withholding evidence and of hiding the truth, prosecutors likely tried to limit their objections, not thinking this territory was worth the battle.

As Clark reviewed the evidence, especially the blood evidence, she relied on photograph after photograph. For Clark, the effect was to portray the abundance of evidence, and indeed the photographs made it seem as if the prosecutors had all the evidence needed to convict Simpson. But in the process of displaying all the visuals, Clark lost control of the story. Jurors may have found it difficult to understand how each photograph pointed only to Simpson as the murderer. When Cochran settled into a review of the evidence, he, too, began an extensive display of exhibits, and, like Clark, at times lost focus. Both Clark's and Cochran's presentations of graphics seemed in large part for the benefit of the external audience. Since television viewers generally saw long stretches of an attorney standing at the lectern and nothing else, the visuals gave welcome relief. The jurors, by contrast, had all of the energy and activity of the courtroom to keep them attentive.

While Clark's and Cochran's presentations became top-heavy with visuals, Darden's was without visual aids. The transcripts also reflect that Brewer and Kelly did not use visuals. Petrocelli, seemingly borrowing from Cochran's bag of tricks, left the victims' pictures before the jury for an extended period before later turning to a map and a diagram of Rockingham. Baker borrowed one of Petrocelli's maps and then used a handful of other exhibits, including a smiling Simpson picture and an exhibit relating to the Bruno Magli shoes, which Baker claimed showed that the negative had been duplicated. The contrast was stark. Clark's and Cochran's openings became high-technology laser shows, while the civil case depended on old-fashioned easels. Although the trend is to use more and more exhibits in the courtroom, here the use of visuals seemed as much dictated by the cameras as by the need to make the story clear for jurors.

Association/Dissociation

Each of the previously discussed techniques for indirect argumentation generally fits within the confines of legal standards. However, one final technique operates largely outside the bounds of legal acceptability. Cochran, in a bold approach clearly beyond the normal scope of opening statements, accused the prosecutors of character assassination. He said,

> And so Mr. Darden kind of apologizes at the end and says this isn't character assassination. . . . That is exactly what he had done for an hour to O. J. Simpson. He is not charged with any domestic violence. This is a murder case. And in their pursuit to win, they are trying to dredge up some theory to give you a motive, because they don't have a motive. (TRC, 1995, January 25)

In asserting that "this should not be a case of character assassination" (TRC, 1995, January 25), Cochran encourages listeners to anchor their beliefs in Simpson's outstanding past record. It is important for Cochran to discount any theories of domestic violence, and hence of motive, and to leave audience members "feeling" that prosecutors have tainted the reputation of a great man. This is certainly not a typical legal approach but, rather, one couched in the precepts of telelitigation with its emphasis on personality, stardom, and celebrity status. Cochran associates Simpson with the positive nature of celebrity and dissociates Simpson from the negatively perceived beliefs on domestic violence. This does not arrive at the level of logic, but many people—whether largely uneducated jurors or ordinary television viewers—can be influenced by considerations such as credibility. The central idea of Cochran's association/dissociation discussion is to have the audience remember Simpson as a hero. Under ordinary circumstances in a murder trial, jurors could be offended by an assertion so contradictory to the evidence of a heinous murder and so dependent on feelings rather than logic. Was this a risk worth taking because Simpson was likely a hero in the eyes of many jurors? Did the broader media audience relish the drama of the assertion and, in the heat of the drama, simply overlook the illogic of Cochran's assertion? Through this approach, Cochran went on the attack and deliberately challenged the prosecution's claims about domestic violence. Since Cochran could not overtly deny what sounded to most like acts of domestic violence, he chose this technique to reframe and thereby minimize the prosecution's claims.

Such a tactic exceeds the constraints of the evidence, but Cochran rolled over the prosecution's objections with Ito's blessing. Was this, then, another example of how Ito reconciled the conflicting needs of broad public access and criminal justice? Two things are for certain. First, a less tolerant judge would have curbed Cochran's dramatic portrayal of Simpson as the victim of character assassination. Second, outside the spotlight of the in-court camera, the prosecution's objections likely would have been sustained.

Implications

This chapter posed the following question: How did the opening statement reflect adaptation for telelitigation? In other words, given the limited strategic options available due to the strength of the evidence, what choices did attorneys make in their openings seemingly to reach the broader media audience? Were the defining characteristics of telelitigation present in the civil trial even though the camera was in the corridor and not the courtroom?

The Simpson cases took the role of celebrity to a new height in forensic rhetoric. Given the celebrity aspect and the sensational nature of the murders, there continued to be a media circus even after Judge Fujisaki banned cameras from the courtroom. Absent the in-courtroom cameras and given Fujisaki's iron-fisted control of the courtroom, attorneys gave relatively traditional opening statements. Although they used several of the indirect techniques for argumentation and refined some of the themes from the criminal trial, Petrocelli's, Brewer's, and Kelly's openings appeared constrained by and focused on the evidence. The personality and credibility issues so salient in defining the genre of telelitigation largely are missing. Baker tried to emphasize Simpson's celebrity status, but he succeeded only in recounting Simpson's rise from rags to riches and his "circle of benevolence" without being able to connect these descriptions to the rest of his opening. However, Baker took the risky approach of role reversal as he attempted to portray Brown Simpson and a police officer who answered a domestic violence call as "scoundrels" in this story. Whether this was a juror or a media ploy is unclear. Disparaging the victim is a familiar legal tactic, and the transcripts give no hint that Baker employed the tactic to appeal to the cameras in the corridors.

By contrast, the opening statements in the criminal trial demonstrated a bolder form of rhetoric. Cochran, particularly, came across as innovative and risk-taking, as willing to challenge and hence to protect Simpson's status rather than to acquiesce to the prosecution's portrayal of Simpson as a domestic abuser. Cochran catered to an audience who wanted to "feel" his message rather than merely understand it. Clearly, Cochran wanted to reach his immediate audience, the jurors. He chose his words carefully to identify himself as one of them, a thinking black man attempting to get to the truth. But Cochran also appeared to have been concerned about involving the broader media audience, as time and time again, he pushed against and tried to engineer his way around the limits imposed by the strength of the evidence.

This analysis demonstrates that Cochran's go-for-broke approach deliberately and repeatedly exceeded the generally accepted standards for opening statements. Of course, the very nature of criminal defense issues the license to take more risks. There is no appeal if the defendant is acquitted. But, even given that license, Cochran pushed further than many legal observers deem ethical. Did Cochran do this to further the one-two punches he and the "dream team" liked to deliver: the first in the courtroom during the day; the second on the courthouse steps each afternoon for the benefit of the media? In all likelihood, the answer is yes. Even if this goal was unintentional, what better way could Cochran enhance the conflict and make good news?

However, it is difficult to believe that Cochran structured his opening unintentionally. Rather, Cochran seems to have been cognizant of the broader media audience and to have chosen to make his opening statement into a rhetorically persuasive event. Cochran made his opening into a prime example of telelitigated address when he elevated Simpson's celebrity status through association and dissociation and thus reduced the power of the evidence relating to domestic abuse. He capitalized on the lure of the drama and enhanced it by suggesting that he was providing "the rest of the story," left untold by prosecutors. Finally, add the appeal to feelings and emotions over logic, and the result is telelitigation.

By contrast, the prosecutors were cautious and restrained. After a July 19, 1994, meeting with black community leaders about the issue of fairness in the Simpson case (Schiller & Willwerth, 1996, pp. 152–53), Gil Garcetti made it clear that he expected the assistant district attorneys handling the Simpson case to take the high road. Darden's and Clark's opening statements reflected Garcetti's dictates and indicated how they would try the case—conservatively.

The second question this chapter examined was, What rhetorical techniques did the attorneys use to enhance the persuasiveness of opening statements? Even though Cochran played "down and dirty" in some respects, this analysis points to his absolute command of rhetorical strategies. No other attorney in either trial was better in establishing themes or presenting the chronology and the parallel action of the night of June 12, 1994. However, Petrocelli displayed the most prowess in being able to organize the evidence and focus the jurors' attention to reach the exact conclusions he felt they should reach from the upcoming evidence. Both Cochran and Petrocelli constructed stories clearly designed to fit their different tasks as attorneys and to appeal to their different juries.

Finally, which of the opening statements were the most powerful and persuasive? The two most powerful opening statements were delivered by Cochran and Petrocelli. The degree of persuasiveness depends, in part, on how much significance can be assigned to opening statements. For years, attorneys lecturing on opening statements have mistakenly contended that the Chicago Jury Studies show that 80 percent of jurors make up their minds after hearing opening statements. Unfortunately, the Chicago research did not even talk about opening statements, and it took almost thirty-five years to debunk the myth (Zeisel, 1988, p. 17). More recent research points to the opening statement as an important factor, even if it is not the deciding one, in the outcome of trials.

In the Simpson trials, the opening statements may not have been the "turning point" for jurors. Perhaps the die was cast with Cochran's particularly aggressive opening, or perhaps it was cast with the Fuhrman testimony and subsequent perjury about the so-called n-word. Schuetz, in chapter 4 of this volume, and Burnett, in chapter 7, suggest that the true turning point in the criminal trial was the controversy surrounding Detective Fuhrman. Ganer, in chapter 5, and Burnett believe the die was cast in the civil case with the apparent deceptions arising from Simpson's own testimony.

One thing is for sure. Cochran, especially, delivered some potent persuasion. Now his efforts remain to be judged for their ethics. This chapter will not be the final analysis of Cochran's rhetorical efforts—only the opening salvo in the debate.

4

Detective Mark Fuhrman:
The Race Card

Janice Schuetz

THE ISSUE OF RACE CREATED DRAMATIC CONFLICT in the criminal trial of O. J. Simpson and contributed to the telelitigated drama and performance of the attorneys and witnesses involved with it. The testimony of Detective Mark Fuhrman made race a central issue in the trial. Eric Dyson (1996b) emphasizes that "when the not guilty verdicts in the O. J. Simpson double-murder cases were handed down, the compass of race went haywire. . . . The case has rudely reminded us of a gigantic and numbing racial divide" (p. 12). Most spectators of the trial also agree that the defense did use race as a predominant countertheory in their case. Bugliosi (1996) concludes, "There is no question that Mark Fuhrman, was defamed, vilified, maligned, and slandered far more at the trial than Simpson, who was accused of a brutal and gruesome double murder" (p. 133).

The sources of racial issues in this case are multiple. Prosecutor Christopher Darden claims that the focus originated with Defense Attorney Johnnie Cochran who used race from the beginning (Darden, 1996, p. 162). Others argue that it was not until the cross-examination of Fuhrman, when Judge Lance Ito allowed the so-called n-word into the testimony, that the content of the trial shifted from the legal indictments to the social issue of race (Fuhrman, 1997). Still others assert that the racial nature of the case began with the selection and composition of the jury (Toobin, 1996). Whatever the case, race had an important role in the trial and the posttrial discussions of the case. Dyson (1996a) notes that "the 'race card' invariably related to Johnnie Cochran's introduction of race as a factor in Simpson's trial. It referred especially to the defense's intended blasting of Mark Fuhrman, and to Cochran's statements outside the court about the persuasive nature of race in our nation" (p. 40).

This chapter examines the issue of Detective Mark Fuhrman and the question of racism as it developed in the criminal trial through Fuhrman's own testimony and in others' accounts of race after the trial. To accomplish this goal, the chapter (1) shows the importance of Fuhrman's testimony to the trial; (2) explains the characteristics of accounts; (3) shows how accounts are used in the social construction of reality through denials, apologies, justifications, and excuses; and (4) explains the implications of this analysis for the study of the Simpson trials.

Fuhrman's Testimony and the Race Card

Several reasons point to the important effect that Fuhrman's racism had on the content of the trial and on its dramatic presentation in the media. One reason was that racial issues appeared in the trial process early on. In one way, this had to do with the crime itself. An African American man, who had been married to a white woman, was charged with her murder and that of one of her white male associates. From the time that the district attorney decided to try the case in Los Angeles, media pundits expected that the makeup of the jury would be predominantly African American; their predictions were accurate. Early jury consultation processes conducted by Decision Quest concluded that the African Americans felt sympathy for defendant Simpson. In the mock juries conducted prior to the trial for the prosecutors, Toobin (1996) reports that black women gave Simpson very high scores of approval in contrast to those they gave to victim Nicole Brown Simpson, who received low scores. Furthermore, black women gave high scores to defense attorneys and very low scores to Prosecutor Marcia Clark. Moreover, the public likely remembered the Rodney King case, the predominantly white jury, the verdict, and the race riots that followed. Finally, Defense Attorney Cochran had a reputation for using the "racist bad cop" theory in other cases that he had defended (Darden, 1996). Even before the opening statements were delivered, racial content seeped into the trial. Long after Fuhrman testified, race took center stage in media accounts about the trial.

A second reason for studying the racial perspective of the trial is that the defense had leads early in the case about racial problems in Mark Fuhrman's background. Prior to Fuhrman's testimony, Bailey and Clark argued motions outside of the hearing of the jury. Bailey urged Judge Ito to admit the testimony of Andrea Terry to corroborate the testimony of Kathleen Bell; both related incidents pointing to the racism of Fuhrman. Bailey claimed:

> Andrea Terry . . . allegedly met Kathleen Bell at Hennesseys
> where Kathleen Bell introduced her to Mark Fuhrman and
> . . . at that time [Bell] allegedly made a comment that she
> was attracted to Marcus Allen. And [then] allegedly Mark
> Fuhrman, in a response, in this crowded bar, said, "I think
> that interracial couples are a crime against nature." . . .
> [A]nd [then Fuhrman stated] that "if he saw a black and
> white couple together in a car he would find a reason to
> pull them over." (TRC, 1995, March 14)

The prosecution knew at the time Fuhrman testified that others would impeach his credibility by claiming he had used racial epithets in the past. However, the potency of the race issue surfaced after an article, written by Jeffrey Toobin (1996, September 9) in the *New Yorker Magazine*, exposed Fuhrman's background. More specifically, Toobin discovered that the detective had filed a lawsuit against the City of Los Angeles, asking that he be allowed early retirement because of his psychological problems related to racial incidents. This article created extensive media commentary. For example, Larry King announced this finding as a major break in the case noting, "The charge is simple and stunning, and it's already touched off a fresh round of fierce debate. . . . The claim from the defense, made public today though a pair of respected magazines, is this: O. J. was framed, set up by a . . . racist cop, who planted one of the famous bloody gloves at the Simpson mansion" (*Larry King Live*, 1995, July 18). Toobin (1996) himself acknowledged the importance of the story: "Robert Shapiro had a parochial, if not accurate, reaction after the Fuhrman-as-racist-villain theory appeared in my story. On the day that the issue of the *New Yorker* appeared, Shapiro called F. Lee Bailey in London and said 'I won the case'" (p. 157).

A third reason is the emergence of evidence that contradicted the testimony of Fuhrman and brought about the dramatic turning point in the trial. This evidence, twelve audio tapes of interviews with Fuhrman conducted by Laura Hart McKinny, surfaced in July, more than six months after opening statements began. After the tapes became public, the last few months of the trial focused almost entirely on Fuhrman and on the defense's racist-cop-conspiracy theory. McKinny notified the defense about the existence of these tapes, claiming Fuhrman had used the n-word forty-two times. The defense first subpoenaed the tapes and later succeeded in getting Judge Ito to allow them to play a very short segment to the jury. However, extensive segments of the tapes were played in the courtroom outside the hearing of the jury and were broadcast and published. In late August, McKinny testified about the tapes; she demonstrated that Fuhrman had lied during his court testimony in March about his use of the n-word. Andrea Terry, Natalie Singer, Kathleen Bell, and Roderic Hodge also testified that they had heard Fuhrman use racial epithets.

The taped conversations with Fuhrman, heard by the attorneys, the judge, and the public, had significant impact on the trial. The slurs on the tapes were delivered in a calm and matter-of-fact tone, and they proved conclusively that Fuhrman used the n-word. Defense Attorney Gerald R. Uelman (1996) emphasized the impact of these tapes: "The lesson of the Fuhrman tapes will resound in the American courtroom. . . . The lesson is that racism is alive and well, and it does affect the way citizens are treated by police officers" (p. 154). From August until the October verdict, the content of the trial, the media coverage, and the public discussion of the Simpson case focused more on Mark Fuhrman than it did on the defendant.

The testimony of Fuhrman and the emergence of the tapes containing his racist remarks created a turning point in the trial drama. Schiller and Willwerth (1996) described the beginning of this testimony as high drama: "The defense wants the jury to see Fuhrman as a man desperate to stay in the case, desperate to be a star, desperate to punish a black man who flaunted his sexual involvement with a white woman. Today, Bailey wants to show the jury that Fuhrman was a bad cop promoted to a bad detective" (p. 402). At the time of the testimony, most commentators, including Defense Attorney Uelman, described the testimony as a letdown for the defense and for media spectators. Uelman (1996) concluded: "F. Lee Bailey's cross-examination of Detective Fuhrman was widely regarded as ineffectual. . . . He hammered away, and Fuhrman never wavered. He testified like a choir boy, looking Bailey in the eye and flatly denying the accusations of racism and the suggestions that he may have planted evidence" (p. 134). The expected drama was disappointing, but its importance became known when the tapes surfaced. Then the content of Bailey's cross-examination of Fuhrman seemed brilliant because he had forced Fuhrman to say he had not used the n-word in the past ten years.

Together, the trial location, the relationship between defendant and victims, the investigations of Fuhrman's background, and the emergence of the McKinny tapes contributed racial content to the trial. These factors made Fuhrman's testimony and the testimony about him decisive to the outcome of the criminal trial.

Trial participants socially construct reality through their presentation of accounts and account repairs. In telelitigation, the quality and complexity of a sensational trial are complicated by the variety and quantity of accounts—accounts by attorneys and witnesses, accounts about accounts in the media, and accounts among members of the multiple audiences. This chapter examines accounts relating to Mark

Fuhrman's racism. These accounts include statements he made during direct and cross-examination, statements fellow detectives and trial attorneys made about him, and posttrial statements he made in his book, *Murder in Brentwood* (1997).

The term *accounts* has legal origins. Erving Goffman (1971) explains that the term always has been considered "by students of law in connection with the issue of defenses, pleas, mitigating of offenses, and the defeasibility of claims. Law . . . provides the beginning of analysis" (p. 109). A general understanding of accounts, as they concerned Fuhrman, requires a look at their characteristics, strategies, and types.

Characteristics of Accounts

In their simplest form, accounts are descriptions or explanations of events that others have called into question. People offer accounts because they want others to view their behavior in a positive way. Accounts are most likely to occur, according to Benoit (1995), when someone attributes responsibility for undesirable or offensive behavior to another person. The person deemed responsible then seeks options for repairing his or her credibility by offering accounts of why the undesirable behavior occurred. This broad definition of accounts applies to a wide variety of communication taking place in and outside of a trial. Accounts can be offered by participating attorneys, witnesses, judges, jurors, and an infinite number of spectators. In a highly publicized trial with a well-known defendant, such as the Simpson criminal case, the number of accounts of those not involved in the courtroom proceedings is likely to exceed that of the actual trial participants.

Scott and Lyman (1968) identify several characteristics associated with accounts (p. 46) that call attention to Fuhrman's role in the criminal trial. First, accounts are explanations about conflicts between a person's behavior and audiences' expectations of what that behavior should be. Several distinct accounts surfaced in the Simpson trial and its aftermath. Some accounts given by Fuhrman focused on his investigation of the crime scene and especially on his finding of the bloody glove at the Simpson estate. Other accounts concerned his credibility as presented through his testimony, particularly his racism. Still other accounts included what he said about himself and what others said about him after the criminal trial was over.

Second, others understand accounts according to the status of the account giver (Scott & Lyman, 1968, p. 47). Direct examination usually features voluntary accounts in which witnesses, through dialogue with their attorneys, create positive explanations about themselves and their own behavior. The goal of these accounts is to establish the facts of the case and to bolster the credibility of the account giver. During the direct examination of Fuhrman, Clark tried to build his reputation as a skillful detective by eliciting information about his extensive experience. Fuhrman testified that he had nineteen and one-half years of experience as a detective, had investigated 250 to 300 crime scenes, and had been the first officer to arrive at a homicide scene ten to fifteen times (TRC, 1995, March 9).

Third, the testimony elicited during cross-examination creates involuntary accounts in which opposing attorneys seek to weaken or destroy the credibility of the account giver. They do this by prompting witnesses to make incriminating statements and to reveal negative aspects of their past behavior. As an example, Defense Attorney Bailey's cross-examination attacked the credibility of Fuhrman by implying that he was a reckless detective who did not follow orders.

Bailey: When the others went to Arnelle's room at Kato's suggestion, I take it you stayed behind?
Fuhrman: Yes.
B: Had anyone directed you to stay and question Kaelin?
F: No.
B: This is something that you decided to do on your own, is it not?
F: Yes.
B: Did you go to the lead detective, or any of them, since they were all your superiors, and ask permission to interrogate Kato Kaelin?
F: No. (TRC, 1995, March 14)

By showing that Fuhrman disobeyed some orders, this account suggested that he also may have disobeyed other standard police procedures.

Next, Bailey elicited accounts from Fuhrman to raise the jurors' consciousness about his alleged racism, a fact Bailey knew other witnesses would substantiate.

Bailey: Did you tell the lawyers in that room that you never used the word "nigger"?
Fuhrman: It was never asked. . . .
B: Do you use the word "nigger" in describing people? . . .
F: No, sir.
B: Have you used that word in the past ten years?
F: Not that I recall, no.
B: You mean if you called someone a "nigger," you have forgotten it?
F: I'm not sure that I can answer the question the way you phrased it. . . .
B: And you say under oath that you have not addressed any black person as a "nigger" or spoken about black people as "niggers" in the past ten years, Detective Fuhrman?
F: That is what I am saying, sir. (TRC, 1995, March 15)

In this segment of cross-examination, Bailey associated Fuhrman with racist language and forced him to deny facts that later in the trial were contradicted by the testimony of Kathleen Bell, Valerie Singer, and others.

After the trial, Detectives Vannatter and Lange (Moldea, 1997) gave their reaction to the Fuhrman tapes. They claimed that Fuhrman had told McKinny on July 28, 1994, that he was the "key witness" in the O. J. Simpson case and that the glove meant "everything" to the case. At that time, the two investigating officers realized that "Fuhrman lied to them and concealed his clear-cut history of fanatical racism." They further recognized that Fuhrman had "completely exaggerated his importance to the investigation" (p. 275). After the trial, Vannatter and Lange expressed their lack of respect for Fuhrman and, by doing this, tried to discount the importance of his role in the criminal investigation.

Accounts as Strategy

Accounts are part of a strategic process of attributing responsibility. This process is judged according to the norms or rules of a community or culture. Heider (1958) explains the strategic process in this way. Actions represent choices, and each action has a number of effects. Audiences observe actions and make inferences about the intentions of the person performing the act. Audiences then judge these acts according to common rules and conventions for behavior. Then they attribute responsibility for that behavior to others. The process of attributing responsibility to Fuhrman for flawed investigative procedures is complicated because the process has many stages, beginning with observations that police detectives write as notes, followed by explanations of what they observe. These explanations justify the police procedures that follow. Investigators then use their notes and explanations of procedures as the basis for their depositions and testimony. Finally, this information is crafted by attorneys into questions that elicit testimony from them when they appear as witnesses.

During Fuhrman's testimony, the attorneys shaped the accounts by the questions they asked; next, the legal commentators construed the testimony and second-guessed the questions used by the attorneys; then other witnesses gave different accounts of the same events. The public observers of the trial made judgments and even offered new interpretations of their own. After the trial, participants and audiences both elaborated upon the explanations given during the trial and constructed new accounts. Many of these accounts affirmed or denied Fuhrman's responsibility for racist words and behaviors. Fuhrman was in a classic double bind; that is, if he accepted responsibility for the accusations made, the public would likely see him as a bad cop and an impediment to the case of the prosecution. But if he denied responsibility, he risked perjury, harm to the prosecution's case, and an end to his career.

The courtroom elaborations about Fuhrman's use of racial epithets show the complexity of the process of responsibility attribution. For example, the facticity of the account of Fuhrman and his use of the n-word changed considerably as the trial progressed. In direct examination, he denied knowing Kathleen Bell and using racist language. On cross-examination in March 15, 1995, Bailey asked Fuhrman: "So that anyone who comes to this court and quotes you as using that word in dealing with African Americans would be a liar, would they not, Detective Fuhrman?" Fuhrman responded: "Yes, they would" (TRC). He denied using words and phrases that denigrated African Americans. By September 1995, the testimony given in March was impeached by other witnesses. When Defense Attorney Cochran asked Laura Hart McKinny about Fuhrman: "During that time that you talked with Mr. Fuhrman, during this ten-year period of time, did he ever use a racial epithet, which I will call the n-word, during the course of your conversations with him?" McKinny attributed responsibility to him, saying, "Yes, he did." Cochran continued: "And in the course of your preparation of your testimony here today, can you tell the jury how many times you counted that he used that word?" McKinny responded: "42 times" (TRC, 1995, September 5). Additionally, Valerie Singer claimed that she had heard Fuhrman make racist statements. Bailey asked her: "Can you tell us what he said? You may use the n-word if you wish." She worried: "Is it okay to say that?" And later she informed the jury that Fuhrman had said, "The only good nigger is a dead nigger" (TRC, 1995, September 5). Both witnesses claimed Fuhrman made racist statements, leading the attorneys for the defense to conclude: If he engaged in racist behavior and denied it under oath, then he likely was lying about other things, such as planting evidence.

After witnesses testified against him, Fuhrman returned as a defense witness and took the Fifth Amendment. During closing arguments, Clark agreed with the defense attorneys' assessment of Fuhrman: "The fact that Mark Fuhrman is a racist and lied about it on the witness stand does not mean that we haven't proven our case beyond a reasonable doubt" (TRC, 1995, September 26). In this way, the prosecution confirmed part of the defense's theory: Fuhrman is a racist. Defense Attorney Cochran expanded the argument. He emphasized that Fuhrman's racism was the motive and that he had the opportunity to participate in a police conspiracy to frame Simpson. After the trial, attorneys for both sides of the case claimed that the testimony against Fuhrman was the turning point in the trial (Darden, 1996; Dershowitz, 1996; Shapiro, 1996; Uelman, 1996; Clark, 1997). In his rebuttal, Darden tried to dissociate the "fact" of Fuhrman's racism from the issues in the case. He reasoned:

> Don't let these people get you all riled up and all fired up
> because Fuhrman is a racist. Racism blinds you. . . . Mr.
> Fuhrman was exposed to be what he is. . . . We ought to put
> a big stamp tattooed on his forehead 'racist.' . . . They want
> you to become impassioned, to be upset, and then they want
> you to make quantum leaps in logic and judgment. (TRC,
> 1995, September 27)

Darden concluded by explaining that the responsibility for one action, such as using racist epithets, does not necessarily mean responsibility for an unproven and unrelated action, such as planting the bloody glove. The in-court arguments showed how the strategies used by attorneys to construct a reality fit with their respective theories of the case. These prosecution accounts attributed responsibility to Fuhrman for racist behavior but denied his responsibility in any police conspiracy. The defense argued that Fuhrman's racism proved he conspired with other police and that he planted evidence. Which arguments the jurors and the public believed depended on their social knowledge and experience.

Nearly a year after the verdict, Fuhrman pled no contest to perjury charges resulting from his lying about his use of the n-word. He received three years of probation and a fine of $200. In the eyes of the public, he admitted responsibility for offensive behavior. In his 1997 book, Fuhrman apologized: "My immature, irresponsible ramblings with the screen writer were never intended to be heard by anyone but the two of us" (p. xxi). The choices Fuhrman made created social conflict by violating the rules of propriety and political correctness, social standards for proper behavior in American society. He used other accounts after the trial to explain these choices.

Accounts have long-term consequences in highly visible trials because they are reported and rehashed by media commentators. Harvey, Weber, and Orbuch (1990) explain that accounts provide a "sense of immortality to us as being cognizant of our own relatively imminent demise" (p. 107). In the courtroom, the enduring quality of accounts is associated with their surprising content, their evidentiary impact on jurors, or the attention they receive by media commentators. The accounts of Fuhrman's racism received attention in all three categories. The initial impact came from the shocking content. Uelman (1996) explains the immediate and enduring impact of the tapes on the courtroom audience (excluding the jury):

> I offered one excerpt after another, a total of sixty-one excerpts. The effect was stunning. The courtroom was absolutely silent as everyone strained to hear the words. As the depth of hate and bigotry they conveyed seared into the consciousness

of the courtroom audience, one could sense a heavy resigna-
tion in the air. It was truly Los Angeles's worst nightmare,
indisputable proof that all the years of abuse that Los Angeles blacks had endured at the hands of rogue police were not
figments of overactive imaginations. (p. 150)

Uelman believed that the tapes had enough surprise evidentiary and media
content to be a significant factor in the trial. For him, this proof of police
racism was the first step in showing the police could have framed O. J.
Simpson. Even though serious gaps appeared in the logical connections
of Uelman's reasoning, most observers agree with the conclusion that the
evidence affected the trial's drama and its verdict.

It is not surprising that Fuhrman saw the need to tell his version of
events after he had been demonized by the media, rejected by the prosecutors, and vilified by the defense. Fuhrman cites the personal consequences of the trial: "My personal and professional reputation is damaged beyond repair. Few people seem to realize that I'm not the rogue
cop they wanted me to be. I'll have to live with this my entire life. I think
about it all the time. I spend hours asking myself, what if . . . ?" (Fuhrman,
1997, p. 318). This account tried to redeem his reputation and blame
others for the charges made against him.

The Fuhrman-racist-cop issue illustrates that accounts are caused by a
conflict between action and expectation, affected by the status of the
account giver, used as strategic processes for attributing responsibility, and
instrumental in participants' and observers' interpretations of the trial.

Types of Accounts

Accounts of witnesses presented in the courtroom differ from public
accounts given outside of the trial in several ways. Accounts given in the
courtroom are presented in a dialogical form. They are constrained by
the questions of advocates, which are designed according to legal standards and norms; by the rulings of the court that their accounts must be
material, relevant, and proper; and by the evidence that the witnesses offer
to support or deny legal issues. Accounts given inside the courtroom report past observations and behaviors, but the personal accounts given
outside of court construct future perceptions of self by redefining and
reconfiguring definitions others have presented. In contrast to legal accounts, personal explanations are presented in a narrative form in which
the account giver is both the creator and the editor of the account. Unlike legal accounts, which are governed by the rules and norms of the
courts, personal accounts reconcile the alleged offenders with their de-
tractors and permit them to save face with the public. Whereas the goal
of legal accounts is to report the facts as they are recalled, the goal of
personal accounts is to rebuild reputation and save face.

The legal accounts the prosecution gave outside of the hearing of the jury hinted at the anger and mistrust that the prosecution had for the defense. This anger was particularly apparent during the bench conferences between the opposing attorneys and Judge Ito. Many of the emotionally charged accounts concerned the credibility of Mark Fuhrman. Marcia Clark demonstrated her animosity toward opposing counsel in these remarks:

> The people respectfully submit to the court that what we have here is not a defense; it's a smear campaign, and there is not any of it relevant to the detective's credibility. . . . And all we are going to do here is engage in a smear campaign so that the jury will forget that we have two people murdered and an officer who found key evidence. . . . So I submit to the Court respectfully that this is the Court's opportunity to keep this trial on track and prevent counsel from engaging in a smear campaign that will mislead, confuse, and inflame the jury. (TRC, 1995, March 14)

These courtroom accounts made outside the hearing of the jury seemed more like personal than legal accounts because the rules of evidence did not apply and because the account givers attempted to save face for themselves and their witnesses.

In bench conferences, some of the defense attorneys severely criticized Fuhrman and thus increased divisiveness between themselves and the prosecution. For example, Defense Attorney Barry Scheck demonized Fuhrman in this motion to admit additional evidence by portraying the detective as a Nazi: "We have an incident here where Detective Fuhrman is alleged to have put a swastika on the locker. . . . My understanding of Nazis is that they don't like Jews, they don't like Blacks, they take law into their own hands. . . . When you look at those tapes, you know that is exactly what Mark Fuhrman might do" (TRC, 1995, March 7). Although motions are typically legal accounts, Scheck's explanation was personal; it attempted to destroy Fuhrman's credibility more than it established legal facts relevant to the indictments.

Fuhrman's posttrial personal accounts of what went on in and outside of court were an attempt by Fuhrman to save face:

> The defense needed to portray me as a racist in order to float their bizarre conspiracy theories. . . . As the hysteria grew and attention increased, people came forward with lies and allegations about me. Unfortunately, they were given the benefit of the doubt, while those who told the truth about me were either shouted down or simply ignored. (Fuhrman, 1997, p. 120)

With his explanation of the courtroom procedures, Fuhrman tried to preserve his reputation after it had been severely damaged through the accounts of other witnesses and the defense attorneys.

Even though legal accounts differ from personal ones according to the forum in which they are presented, the content of these accounts is often similar. In the Simpson criminal case, several types of accounts appeared both in and outside of the legal forum, including denials, apologies, justifications, and excuses.

Denials

One common account is denial, which occurs in several forms. For example, the accused claim that they did not commit the alleged offensive acts; witnesses deny their involvement with the illegal actions or with questionable actors; attorneys deny the relevance of opposing counsel's arguments; and judges deny motions and objections. Benoit (1995) identifies several forms of denial: The account giver denies that (1) the act occurred, (2) the alleged actor committed the act by claiming mistaken identity or offering an alibi, (3) the evidence presented is truthful, (4) the offender has responsibility through implicating another person, (5) the account giver is credible, or (6) the evidence presented applies to the offensive actions at issue (p. 75).

Some denials have more than one form. For example, Prosecutor Clark denied both the evidence and the credibility of the account giver. When Bailey asked Judge Ito to admit evidence from witnesses who had charged Fuhrman with racial slurs, Clark argued: "These allegations get more outrageous by the minute, and I'm stricken again by the preposterousness of the claims of the defense. . . . What we have here is a false offer of proof by the defense, an offer that they are going to use to slur Mark Fuhrman again unfairly in the eyes of the jury" (TRC, 1995, March 14).

Denials also occur during the cross-examination of witnesses. Evidence constructed through cross-examination can deny that the offensive action ever occurred, deny the evidence presented by others, or deny information about the defendant's or other witnesses' credibility. One example occurred when Bailey tried to impeach Fuhrman's credibility by bringing up the name of Kathleen Bell. He asked whether the prosecution had prepared Fuhrman to answer questions. Although Bailey wanted Fuhrman to tell the jury that his attorneys told him what to say regarding Kathleen Bell, the detective denied it. Bailey inquired, "Were you told what to do or not to do when questions were put to you?" Fuhrman responded, "No." Bailey continued, "Did any of the questions contain the name 'Kathleen Bell?'" Fuhrman answered, "I don't believe it did. No" (TRC, 1995, March 15). This denial led to a sequence of questions about whether he had used the n-word as Kathleen Bell alleged. During the entire cross-examination, Fuhrman denied that he had committed any offensive acts.

Denials also appear in motions made by attorneys concerning what testimony is admissible. In this case, attorneys argue that judges should deny the motions of opposing counsel. When Prosecutor Clark argued that Judge Ito should not instruct the jury about Fuhrman's invoking the Fifth Amendment, she gave the following account:

> We have Mr. Fuhrman making remarks to the screen writer for the purpose of creating a fictional work. . . . Miss McKinny testified before this court that there was no evidence made to fact check anything that he said because it didn't matter. It didn't matter whether it was true or not. . . . It was information she could use to make a work of fiction. (TRC, 1995, March 7)

Clark's account denied the relevance of the evidence and convinced Judge Ito to withhold jury instruction about Fuhrman's use of the Fifth Amendment.

Posttrial personal accounts of witnesses and attorneys explain and elaborate the denials. After the trial, Fuhrman denied he was a racist and implied that he had been permanently harmed by these charges. He noted: "A criminal suspect like O. J. Simpson gets presumption of innocence in the court and in the media. But a person who is charged with racism is considered guilty until proven innocent. Since you can't prove a negative, it's almost impossible to convince people that you aren't a racist. Therefore the charge often sticks" (Fuhrman, 1997, p. 131). In her posttrial book, Prosecutor Clark (1997) stressed that she lacked any knowledge of the McKinny tapes. She claimed that Fuhrman had never told the prosecution about the tapes, despite the fact that he had talked with McKinny as recently as July 1994, immediately after the murders of Nicole Brown Simpson and Ronald Goldman. She reflected about the tapes in this way: "The two of them had agreed to lie low until the case was over; then they'd make the sale and Mark would get a percentage." She elaborated, "After the tapes came out, I got a lot of criticism for having 'embraced' Fuhrman. . . . I never had any choice about calling him as a witness. And it was Mark Fuhrman's job to inform us of anything that might be used against him" (p. 439). Elaborations of in-court denials, like those used by Clark, are remnants of telemediated trials. Since participants achieved celebrity status because of the trial, the public wanted them to talk about their trial experiences long after the verdict was decided. Thus, it is not surprising that over a dozen trial participants have written detailed books about their role in the Simpson criminal trial and appeared on television to give accounts about what they said in these books.

One of the unique features of this trial was that the media often provided testimony that they believed to be legitimate for the public to consider even though this information never was presented to the jury. The prosecution understandably called no witnesses to deny Fuhrman's racism since he was not on trial. Nonetheless, several of his allies came forth with their supportive testimony in the media. Several examples of such accounts appeared in the *Los Angeles Times*. For example, Roberto Alaniz, an LAPD officer and former partner of Fuhrman, denied that Fuhrman was a racist: "The person that the world knows . . . on the tape . . . is a racist who made terrible remarks, who probably represents the filth the world has to offer. . . . The Mark Fuhrman I know is not that. He's not a racist" (quoted in Fuhrman, 1997, p. 283). Denials like this one validated Fuhrman's posttrial accounts.

Apologies

Another type of account is an apology. According to Goffman (1971), "[a]n apology is a gesture through which an individual splits himself into two parts," the part that is "guilty of an offence and the part that dissociates itself" from the defect and "affirms a belief in the offended rule" (p. 113). In his posttrial accounts, Fuhrman made an apology for his behavior. He said: "The mistakes I made and the pain I inflicted on myself, the citizens of the country, and the people I love will forever haunt me. This is not a book of justifications or excuses, but one of truth. . . . An apology for the racial unrest I caused seems painfully inadequate" (Fuhrman, 1997, p. xxi). This apology affirmed his knowledge about the norms of political correctness; that is, racial epithets are inappropriate types of communication because they violate social norms.

Apologies take several forms. They can merely express embarrassment, clarify right conduct, repudiate the negative behavior, vilify self, or make restitution (Goffman, 1971, p. 113). Fuhrman (1997) clarified right conduct when he explained: "Many will say my words of apology stem from the mere fact that I was caught on tape. This is not the case. In my heart, I always knew it was wrong, even if I said them only to create a fictional story." Then he vilified his behavior: "My first failure was the lure of greed, and the second was my lack of compassion. There is nothing in life that comes free. I failed myself, my friends, and my family when I grabbed the chance to make money" (p. xxi). In this prologue from his book, Fuhrman repudiated his offensive behavior and took responsibility for his racist remarks.

Since an apology is an "account repair," it should consider the point of view of the offended (the public) and make amends to them. Semin and Munstead (1983) explain that the apology should "convince the audience that the offense is not typical of the offender's behavior" (p. 73).

Fuhrman clearly tried to make amends to those offended when he said: "There are no words for what I want to express. No thought can describe the remorse I feel for the people I wounded. No story that can begin to excuse my insensitivity . . . but in this case, it comes from the depths of humility: I am sorry" (p. xxii). It is not at all clear that he succeeded with his intended audience because he used the public forum of a best-selling book and television appearances, and he never directly addressed those whom he had offended. His apology took less than two pages. However, his justifications and excuses consumed most of his book and were the focus of most of his media appearances promoting the book.

Justifications

A justification occurs when someone who is accused accepts responsibility for that offense but denies the evil associated with it. Criminal and civil trials use many justifications. Judges justify their rulings; attorneys justify their motions, objections, and evidence; witnesses justify their perceptions of events; defendants justify their behaviors associated with alleged crimes; investigating officers and criminalists justify their procedures; and expert witnesses justify their technical evidence. In fact, justifications are so common that they constitute much of the content of any trial and most of the content of posttrial explanations.

Fuhrman's posttrial accounts included justifications for his investigation of the crime scene. A controversial feature of the police investigation was that the LAPD entered the Simpson estate with a questionable search warrant, and then detective Fuhrman found a wet, bloody glove. Fuhrman took responsibility for finding the bloody glove at the Simpson estate, but he denied that he planted the glove. He justified the action this way: "We entered the property because we were presented with circumstances over which we had no control, and [we] were obligated to investigate further to make sure that no one else was hurt and that the suspect was not hiding somewhere nearby. That's all we did" (Fuhrman, 1997, p. 98).

Justifications are socially acceptable reasons for questionable behavior. One controversy was whether Fuhrman found the bloody glove or whether he planted it. During direct examination, Clark prompted Fuhrman to give socially acceptable reasons for his actions at the Simpson estate by questioning him about why he searched for evidence behind a wall where houseguest Kato Kaelin lived:

Clark: And then after you passed through that second gate area, you saw the wall that appeared to match Kato's wall?
Fuhrman: Yes.
C: Then what happened?

F: I continued walking down the path, and when I got approximately fifteen or twenty feet away, I saw a dark object and I continued to walk forward towards that object. . . .

C: And how close did you get before you could tell what it was?

F: Several feet, maybe three or four, I'm not sure. At some point, I could tell it was a glove. . . .

C: And then when you were able to tell what it was, then what did you do?

F: Well, I walked closer to look at it. . . . I didn't touch it. I looked at it. I didn't know what the significance of it was.

C: Can you please describe the appearance of the glove, Sir? . . .

F: It appeared [to be] a dark leather glove. It appeared to be somewhat moist or sticky. (TRC, 1995, March 13)

Clark asked Fuhrman to justify his actions by showing that they were reasonable. First, her questions allowed him to explain that his actions were motivated by the alarm of Kaelin about the sounds he heard against his wall. Second, she permitted Fuhrman to explain how he proceeded cautiously to the area where the sound originated. Third, her questions resulted in his explanation of his surprise at finding the glove. Justifications are also reasonable to the extent that they point to norms associated with social knowledge and expectations (Scott & Lyman, 1968, p. 46). Through her questions, Clark elicited information from Fuhrman showing that he was both cautious and surprised, two norms that would fit with social expectations about accidentally discovering key evidence.

In contrast to Clark, Bailey pointed out that the finding of the glove was not reasonable. In fact, his leading questions in cross-examination attempted to expose Fuhrman's accounts as unreasonable:

Bailey: So you proceed along the walkway pausing to look at the structure, what you called indentations?

Fuhrman: Yes.

B: And you come upon a glove?

F: Eventually, [y]es.

B: You told us that you learned in school that footprints not visible to you might be raised by a criminalist, true?

F: That is possible, [y]es.

B: When you saw the glove did it occur to you that there could be in that area, whether where you had just gone or in the other direction, some footprints that could help identify the person who may have dropped it there. . . .

F: That wasn't on my mind at that time, [n]o. . . .

B: Did you ever for one minute, Detective Fuhrman, while looking at that glove, think, gee, some victim may have dropped this here? . . .

F: I can't say for a hundred percent that it would be [a] suspect, so there is a small percentage I said it is a possibility. (TRC, 1995, March 14)

In this segment of cross-examination, Bailey pointed to Fuhrman's ulterior motives by showing he did not have a proper flashlight, did not have assistance from other officers, conducted the search in secrecy, and violated police procedures. All of these attributions suggest his actions were planned rather than accidental.

At the time of the trial, this justification was effective to the extent that it questioned Fuhrman's credibility. Prior to the emergence of the McKinny tapes, the defense argued that the planting of the glove was possible. After the McKinny tapes surfaced and damaged Fuhrman's credibility, the defense insisted that the planting of the glove was plausible since a person who lies about his racism is likely to lie about planting evidence.

Excuses

In contrast to justifications, excuses are ways of relieving self of responsibility for actions. Typical account givers justify their actions by offering socially acceptable reasons for why they acted a certain way. Account givers who offer excuses do not accept responsibility for their actions but instead place blame on other persons or external occurrences. Both legal and personal offenders can repair their reputations by offering explanations that reduce their responsibility for an offense. Standard legal explanations that diminish responsibility are incompetence, drunkenness, youthfulness, senility, passion, and lack of training. Personal accounts often minify the offense by claiming it was an accident, a joke, or an unforeseen consequence. Goffman (1971) explains that "the offender can agree that the act occurred and that he did it, but present the mitigation that he was ignorant and unforeseeing, exuseably so, and could not reasonably be asked to have acted so as to forestall it" (pp. 110–11). More simply, the account of mitigation acknowledges that an offensive act occurred but claims the account giver was not at fault or his or her action was unintended. Excuses typically are more common in civil rather than in criminal trials. Nonetheless, many excuses were offered by Fuhrman.

Personal excuses tend to be of three types (Scott & Lyman, 1968). The first is an accident, an offensive action or irregularity created by external factors out of the control of the account giver. Much of Fuhrman's explanation of his finding of the bloody glove implied that his actions were caused by others and were therefore accidental rather than intentional. Several accidental occurrences led to his finding of the glove. For example, he claimed that an interview with Kaelin called his attention to a hard thumping sound outside of the wall, and this unusual sound prompted his search there for evidence. He did not need proper permission because the investigation was legally justified. Fuhrman (1997) re-marked: "When I found the glove behind Kato's [Kaelin] bungalow, I was looking for a suspect or victim, not evidence. I believed we had probable cause in entering Rockingham" (p. 98).

A second kind of excuse is scapegoating, an explanation where the account giver claims his or her actions were caused by the actions of others (Scott & Lyman, 1968). Fuhrman blamed other police officers, the media, and the prosecution for the failure of the state to convict O. J. Simpson. One source of scapegoating was to blame the problems with the investigation of the crime scene on the two principal investigators, Detectives Philip Vannatter and Tom Lange, rather than to accept blame himself. He said that his investigation of the crime scene was professional and complete and faulted them for sloppy investigation. Specifically, he blamed other detectives for improper evidence gathering, failing to in-spect a bloody fingerprint on the back gate, issuing an incomplete search warrant, contaminating Simpson's Ford Bronco, and neglecting appro-priate supervision of the work of criminalist Dennis Fung. He concluded: "The mistakes made by the investigating detectives seriously undermined what should have been an easy case. They contaminated evidence and mishandled the crime scenes" (Fuhrman, 1997, p. 58). Fuhrman excused his own behavior by making it seem like his work was compromised by others at the crime scene.

Another type of scapegoating is blaming the media or some institution or nonpersonal entity for the outcome of the trial. Fuhrman (1997) re-called: "The entire Simpson trial was not a search for the truth or a jour-ney to justice or any other courtroom cliché. It was theater, or more ac-curately, television. If O. J. Simpson wasn't a millionaire celebrity and the trial hadn't been televised, then nobody would have thought twice about Mark Fuhrman" (p. 309–10). Fuhrman was not alone in blaming the media for the outcome of the trial, but he took little responsibility for encouraging that media coverage and contributing to the dramatic climax of the trial. Fuhrman explained, "A lot of people in the media and in Los Angeles blamed me for the verdict. But the people who knew me . . . didn't blame me" (p. 304). Of course, after the trial, Fuhrman used the media to add more conflict and drama to the posttrial discussion of the case by blaming others for the failure of the prosecution to win the case.

A final type of scapegoating is blaming persons who have power and authority. In this case, Fuhrman blamed the prosecution for not defend-ing him and for losing the case. The disgruntled detective (1997) said Clark "not only indicted me, but she also tried, convicted, and figura-tively sentenced me to death" (p. 295). Clearly, Clark vilified Fuhrman when she said: "Did he lie when he testified there in the courtroom say-ing he did not use racial epithets in the last ten years? Yes. Is he a racist?

Yes. Is he the worst that LAPD has to offer? Yes" (TRC, 1995, September 28). In fact, after the McKinny tapes were offered into evidence, the prosecution rejected both Fuhrman and his behavior. For example, in his cross-examination of Kathleen Bell, Prosecutor Darden highlighted rather than refuted the defense's claims about the racist language:

Darden: I take it that you understand it, that this word, this epithet is the most vile word in the English language?
Bell: Yes. . . .
D: And when you heard Detective Fuhrman use this word, you were offended?
B: Yes. . . .
D: And you were frightened of him because of his use of this word? (TRC, 1995, September 5)

These excerpts suggest that the prosecution shared responsibility for Fuhrman becoming the focus of the trial. Of course, Fuhrman was not alone in blaming the prosecution for an ineffective strategy; others— Bugliosi (1996), Toobin (1996), and Dershowitz (1996)—also blamed the prosecution. Often, the scapegoats created by the media are the same ones used in personal accounts.

Implications

The defense and prosecution, as well as Fuhrman himself, played the race card in their interpretations of trial. This race card became the key conflict in the drama of the trial and added to the media's desire to cover the trial and its aftermath. If Cochran dealt the hand, then the McKinny tapes were the bluff that forced Fuhrman to show his cards. This chapter shows that the complex moves of the trial participants take the form and content of accounts. The controversies surrounding Fuhrman's investigation of the crime scene and the revelations in the McKinny tapes ruined his credibility by calling the jurors' and the public's attention to his offenses. These controversies provide informative legal and personal texts for discussing the role of accounts.

This chapter illuminates the role of accounts by looking at Fuhrman's role in and outside of the trial, by identifying the characteristics of accounts in this controversy, and by explaining how the trial and its aftermath were constructed using denials, apologies, justifications, and excuses. Further, this analysis shows how the notoriety of O. J. Simpson, the racist history of Mark Fuhrman, and the media's extensive coverage of the criminal trial affected the quantity and content of these accounts.

After the criminal trial, Bugliosi (1996) commented on the Fuhrman fiasco, claiming: "After the Fuhrman tapes surfaced, the prosecution stayed away from Fuhrman the way the devil stays away from holy water. He was a leper, a pariah to the prosecution. As for the defense, they couldn't get enough of him. They loved him. He was like the manna, miraculously supplied to the Israelites from the wilderness" (p. 129). The role of Fuhrman was so powerful in the criminal case that he did not appear in the civil case as a witness. Some commented that the absence of Fuhrman was indeed a strength for the plaintiffs, as validated by their success in proving the preponderance of evidence that Simpson was liable for the deaths of Nicole Brown Simpson and Ronald Goldman. Fuhrman's physical absence in that case is one of the reasons why the turning points in the civil trial drama were distinctively different from those in the criminal trial. Because Fuhrman did not appear, the racial issue was significantly diminished. The focus of the civil case was on the accounts of O. J. Simpson and his alleged offensive acts rather than those of Fuhrman.

This analysis of accounts and account givers shows the variety of explanations that appear in and outside of the courtroom in a highly publicized trial. The procedures that control the content of the legal accounts made in front of jurors are absent when attorneys argue motions before the judge or when any trial participants or commentators present personal accounts. The personal accounts parallel the traits of other telelitigation. They quench the public's thirst for information about the trial; and they emphasize personality, center on the dramatic, and appeal to the feelings associated with the telelitigated trial discourse.

5

The Credibility of O. J. Simpson: "If the Shoe Fits . . ."

Patricia M. Ganer

JUST AS THE TESTIMONY OF AND ABOUT MARK FUHRMAN was the turning point for the criminal case, the testimony of O. J. Simpson served this dramatic function for the civil case. The public wanted to hear his story, and the media responded with extensive excerpts of testimony and media commentaries. Interviews with friends and family of the defendant and participants from the criminal trial infused the media commentaries with strong negative and positive feelings about his credibility. At the time that he testified without cameras in the courtroom, the media recreated Simpson's testimony so that it appeared live. They showed pictures of him from the criminal trial, from his arrest, and as a celebrity spokesperson for Hertz rental cars. They superimposed the words of his testimony in the civil trial on these old media images from the criminal trial to create the qualities of telelitigation—personality, stardom, feeling, and conflict.

The setting on the day of the civil trial was almost surreal. Television cameras were set up in the Capitol, ready to air the State of the Union address of the newly reelected president of the United States. But three thousand miles away, cameras also were gathering around a nondescript courthouse in Santa Monica, California, ready to air the civil verdicts against this former star football player. The results of the two cases were different, the criminal jury finding Simpson "not guilty" of the crimes of which he was accused, and the civil jury finding him liable in the death of Ron Goldman and the beating—and by extension, the death—of Nicole Simpson. Much speculation has been offered as to the reasons for the different verdicts. Reasons offered have included differences in the quality of the teams of attorneys, the personality and rulings of the judge, the lack of cameras in the courtroom, the appearance of new evidence, and the nature of the juries. *USA Today* ("Trials Have," 1997, February 5) outlined twelve key differences between the civil and criminal trials focusing on the shoes, the police statement, the writings of Nicole, the emotional triggers, the lie-detector test, the violence, the slow-speed chase with Al Cowlings, the increased use of scientific evidence, the race card, the blood, the gloves, and the appearance of Simpson on the stand (p. 5A).

Although one may never be able to ascertain the precise impact of such differences, one must weigh heavily the fact that the defendant, O. J. Simpson, was required to testify in the civil trial and, because of Fifth Amendment protections, did not have to do so in the criminal trial. That testimony would be critical to assess the differences in the two trials. This chapter examines the testimony of Simpson in the civil trial by (1) showing the centrality of his testimony, (2) investigating how the testimony affected his credibility, and (3) analyzing the strategies of image restoration used by him and his attorneys.

Centrality of O. J. Simpson's Testimony

The plaintiffs speculated that the ability to question Simpson would be a central organizing principle for the building of their case. That orientation included both the importance of the pretrial depositions and the testimony during the trial itself. Daniel Petrocelli indicated the importance he placed on the depositions in this report from *Time*: "As a civil lawyer, he rooted much of his strategy in the concept of the pretrial deposition and the opportunity it gave him to question witnesses under oath, to trip them up and to use their conflicting statements to impeach their credibility on the witness stand" (Lafferty, 1997, February 17, p. 31).

The process of taking depositions in California is unique to civil trials; no such opportunity exists in the criminal system. The opportunity to examine an individual twice under oath gives the attorney the possibility of exploiting inconsistencies, a central element in the process of impeaching the witness. As Richard Rieke and Randall Stutman (1990) noted, "The most common impeachment strategy is to show a prior inconsistent statement by the witness. This inconsistency renders the current statement incredible by exposing the witness as dishonest" (p. 171). It was a tactic that would prove extremely effective for the plaintiffs, not so much because Simpson would contradict his depositional statements on the stand, but more because they would be able to hold him accountable for statements he had made and force him to repeat them. Such repetitions would prove dangerous in light of additional evidence that would surface.

Despite the apparent danger of having Simpson testify, the defense attorneys had suggested that they were confident that O. J. Simpson would make an excellent witness on his own behalf. That process began even during the criminal trial when several of Simpson's attorneys expressed both their desire to call Simpson and their confidence in the testimony that he would present to the jury. There had been considerable discussion among the attorneys with both Johnnie Cochran and F. Lee Bailey publicly expressing their beliefs that Simpson should take the stand (Schiller & Willwerth, 1996, pp. 209, 598). However, through the course of the trial and a mock cross-examination, conducted using San Francisco attorney Christine Arguedas (pp. 409–92), they were convinced that putting him on the stand would be a massive error. Schiller noted that "Dershowitz had also told Kardashian that if O. J. testified, every one of his lawyers should be disbarred. At this point in the case, no thoughtful lawyer would let him get within a mile of the witness stand" (p. 598).

In the civil case, of course, the decision was not an option open to the defense: Simpson's testimony was mandated by legal procedure. Nonetheless, even then his attorneys expressed great confidence in his ability to handle the questioning. Lafferty (1997, February 17) reported that "one of the greatest potential resources for the defense was O. J. Simpson himself. Says Phillip Baker, 'O. J. is intelligent. He knows the case better than anyone else'" (p. 35). Whether those were the defense's true feelings or whether it was a statement based on bravado is irrelevant. The fact remains that, publicly, the defense was committed to the position of welcoming the opportunity for O. J. Simpson to testify.

Certainly, the media was tuned in to the importance of Simpson's testimony. As Simon (1996, September 18) indicated, "Seventy-two news organizations asked for seats in the courtroom, seven more than during the criminal trial, court officials said" (p. A10). Because cameras were not allowed in the courtroom, the television media lost some of their ability to focus on the case. But attention skyrocketed when Simpson was on the stand. For example, KNBC, a local station that had offered a nightly half-hour wrap-up each day of the criminal trial, resumed such coverage for the time Simpson was on the stand during the civil trial. Much of the coverage in newspapers that had been relegated to the back pages was once again on the front page. Simpson's testimony was the subject of the lead story on several national network news programs. Clearly, the lack of cameras in the courtroom did not preclude coverage of Simpson's testimony. It was central to the media's coverage of the civil trial.

There is little doubt that such testimony also was important to O. J. Simpson himself. He had long proclaimed his desire to be able to offer his side of events. While in jail and pending trial, Simpson authored his book *I Want to Tell You* (1995). While it did not deal with much of substance in the case, the title revealed that Simpson believed he could set matters straight by speaking out on the subject. After his acquittal, he also participated in a videotape production that gave him an opportunity to speak out once more. In the criminal trial, Johnnie Cochran had requested that Simpson be allowed to address the jury for one minute during Cochran's opening statement, an extraordinary request that Ito denied. Later, in another amazing action, when Ito asked Simpson to waive his right to testify, Simpson said, "As much as I would like to address some of the misrepresentations made about myself and my—and Nicole concerning our life together, I am mindful of the mood and stamina of the jury" (TRC, 1995, September 22). His phone calls to Larry King and other reporters shortly after the criminal trial verdict also indicated that Simpson had faith in the fact that he could convince others of his innocence.

Ultimately, the testimony was most important to the jury in the civil trial. It was the members of the jury that would have to weigh the testimony of Simpson and evaluate his credibility. If they believed him, he would be free of the claims against him; if they did not, he would be indirectly branded a murderer and would stand to lose a great deal of any remaining personal fortune he had. While Rieke and Stutman (1990) note that "[t]he general impact of a defendant's testimony is in dispute" (p. 151), the postverdict statements of the jury in the civil case indicate that they weighed Simpson's testimony heavily.

In short, the stakes involving Simpson's testimony were extraordinarily high for all participants in the trial. It is for that reason that further examination needs to be given to the impact of O. J. Simpson's testimony.

Centrality of Credibility in Court Cases

A person's credibility is a major factor that determines his or her persuasiveness both in society and in the courtroom. As John Reinard (1991) notes, "What receivers think of arguers strongly affects the persuasiveness of arguments. Indeed, there may be no more influential element in the argument's persuasiveness than source credibility, at least in the short term" (p. 351). In the legal context, Rieke and Stutman (1990) suggest that

> few legal practitioners presume that messages would have the same effect regardless of who delivers them. Communicators are as vital to persuasion as the content of the messages they impart, and a litany of evidence suggests that a communicator accorded high credibility will exert more influence than will one with low credibility. (p. 116)

There is little doubt that in assessing the case, a jury, faced with the presence of O. J. Simpson on the stand, would focus on issues of his credibility, including many extrinsic and intrinsic factors.

Extrinsic Factors of Credibility

A variety of factors contribute to the assessments receivers make of a source's credibility. Rieke and Stutman (1990) note that "courtroom actors carry with them an assortment of extrinsic factors—such as status, physical appearance, age and general reputation—that influence credibility judgments" (pp. 126–27). It may be that these factors were more important in the criminal trial since the jurors had no opportunity to assess Simpson's credibility directly. This may help explain some of the reasons for the different verdicts. Simpson clearly had some extrinsic credibility in his favor that might hold more importance in circumstances where his own intrinsic credibility was not on view for the receivers.

One extrinsic factor of credibility is physical appearance. Rieke and Stutman (1990) conclude that "the general physical appearance of a defendant may also influence attributions of guilt. . . . Jurors hold stereotypic notions about the appearance of criminals and generally assume that people who commit crimes maintain similar appearances, usually possessing aberrant features" (p. 129). O. J. Simpson hardly fits the stereotypical appearance that most expect from criminal defendants. A physically imposing man, very good-looking, immaculately and expensively tailored, Simpson certainly seemed the ideal corporate spokesman rather than a common street thug.

Another potentially critical external factor of credibility is status. Rieke and Stutman (1990) indicate that

> status is an individual's relative position in a prestige hierarchy. People learn through everyday experiences that certain characteristics are associated with status, and as a result they develop expectations that affect behavior even in situations where status is not an issue. . . . In addition, although there is not a direct link between status and credibility, persons of high status are generally rated higher in credibility than are low status persons. (p. 139)

Obviously, Simpson, based on his football records, his broadcasting and film career, his corporate roles, and his wealth, enjoyed a great deal of status.

Because the criminal jury did not have any opportunity to hear from the defendant himself, their perceptions of Simpson's credibility may have been influenced by the only available cues they had, the extrinsic factors. In this sense, it is not surprising that they might view him as an individual incapable of committing the heinous crimes of which he was accused. However, the civil jury viewed not only the extrinsic facts but also the intrinsic characteristics of credibility as they heard O. J. Simpson testify.

Intrinsic Factors of Credibility

Intrinsic factors of credibility are those the person brings to a situation that reflect his or her personal characteristics. Richard Rieke and Malcolm

Sillars (1993) suggest that the four major factors of credibility are competence, trustworthiness, goodwill, and dynamism (pp. 170–72). Individuals need not be high on all areas to be regarded as credible—situations may focus on specific elements—but all four are considered in assessing an individual's overall credibility.

In a case where a defendant is testifying, the trustworthiness of the individual is obviously going to be the key factor. However, the factors of goodwill and dynamism also enter into the picture and need to be considered independently. Competence may be considered an important characteristic for witnesses and occasionally for the defendant. In the Simpson criminal case, however, competence is not a factor with significant implications for the trial's outcome.

Goodwill. Goodwill, or the likability of the individual, proved important to the civil trial. In the case of O. J. Simpson, it is certain that this may have been a critical factor in terms of his defense in both the criminal and civil trials. Beginning as a Heisman Trophy–winning popular football player at the University of Southern California, continuing as a professional football player, and becoming a broadcaster and film actor, O. J. Simpson had achieved and cultivated a positive image, particularly in the Los Angeles area. Jeffrey Toobin (1996) notes that "the creation of a public image—that is, defining what 'being O. J.' meant—had been Simpson's life work. . . . Simpson for many years had enjoyed a clean-cut and lovable image" (p. 45). Leola Johnson and David Roediger (1997) went further and noted, "If not quite interplanetary, Simpson's aura of greatness and goodness was distinctly Supermanly and that aura suffused accounts of his image as being above the racial fray" (p. 218). When he was arrested in the double murders, many individuals were unable to imagine Simpson as a homicidal maniac. That image posed difficulties for the prosecution in the criminal trial. Marcia Clark (1997) referred to his appearance at the preliminary hearing as "the O. J. You Know and Love, Falsely Accused. And no Shakespearean actor would play this one better" (p. 99). Such a persona made it difficult for individuals to denigrate him in the criminal trial.

Johnnie Cochran, during his opening statement to the criminal jury, spent a considerable amount of time reinforcing the image of O. J. Simpson as a wonderful human being. Stressing the "circle of benevolence" that the defendant conferred upon others, Cochran was able to reinforce the image of Simpson that had existed prior to the murders (TRC, 1995, January 25). That process continued throughout the trial, particularly in calling family members as witnesses—Eunice Simpson, Arnelle Simpson, and Shirley Baker. Cochran took opportunities to reinforce the goodwill most people held for the defendant.

Surprisingly, the prosecution did not attack that image with their full might. Darden said, "I'm not afraid to point to him. Nobody pointed him out and said, 'He did it.' I'll point to him. Why not? The evidence all points to him." But the reluctance to attack was also evident in some of Darden's final comments in his summation to the jury. When Darden concluded that he "was glad it was not his decision to make" (TRC, 1995, September 27), he signaled to the twelve jurors that convicting such a well-known defendant was almost unthinkable. This was hardly a stirring attack by the prosecution.

In the civil trial, Petrocelli was not as loathe to take on a popular figure. He made a point of saying in the civil trial, "[T]here is a killer in this courtroom" (TRL, 1997, January 21). As Dominick Dunne (1997) noted, "Petrocelli did not treat Simpson with kid gloves as some sort of fallen hero because of his celebrity. He treated him as if he were just another defendant on trial for a couple of murders. He called him a liar over and over again" (p. 14). Obviously, one of the main tasks of the plaintiffs was to undermine that sense of goodwill that individuals felt toward Simpson.

Even when Simpson did have an opportunity to refurbish his reputation, the plaintiffs cut him short. After reading from Simpson's letter left before the infamous Bronco chase, attorney Michael Brewer cited the line where Simpson beseeched people to "remember the real O. J., not this lost person" and asked, "Mr. Simpson, who is the real O. J.?" Simpson responded, "I like to think I was a guy, including Nicole when we were together and when we weren't, people could come to. I liked to think I treated everybody the way I wanted to be treated. My basic philosophy was 'do unto others.'. . . I treated everybody the way I wanted to be treated. I'd like to think I was a good friend." Brewer followed with, "And this 'lost person,' Mr. Simpson, is a double murderer" (TRL, 1996, November 26). While no one expected Simpson to agree, the direct confrontation was still a potentially powerful aspersion on the defendant, directly questioning his good will.

After his testimony, Simpson had little success in rebuilding his golden image. Simon (1996, December 9) noted,

> So far, Simpson has not had much opportunity to turn on the charm in court. But his lawyer has promised to put him on the stand for hours of friendly questioning. If so, Simpson could get a chance to do what he does best: to win people over. To reveal, in the words of one analyst, all those qualities "that cause people to believe this kind of evil does not exist in him." (p. A28)

Such an attempt was made. After having been called by the defense to the stand on January 10, 1997, Simpson was led by his attorneys through a recitation of the honors and awards he had won during his career. As one CNN reporter noted, "He was guided by gentle questioning from defense lawyers bent on rehabilitating the ex-football star in the eyes of the jury at the wrongful death trial" ("Simpson Portrays," 1997, January 10). When asked to describe his relationship with his ex-wife, Simpson responded, "We were very much in love" (TRL, 1997, January 10). His answer lacked believability because Petrocelli's cross-examination focused on a litany of accusations of brutality during the marriage.

Simpson's goodwill seemed to diminish as the trial continued. After the civil verdict, *USA Today* ("The Verdict Arrives," 1997, February 9) summed up the public's attitudes: "The public came to see Simpson as something of a Jekyll and Hyde. By day, a gracious and graceful athlete, actor and TV pitchman. By night, a serial wife beater" (p. 14A). That changing perception of goodwill made it easier for the jury to conceive of Simpson as a murderer.

Dynamism. Rieke and Sillars (1993) discuss dynamism in terms of "showmanship" (p. 117). They consider qualities of dynamism in terms of composure, sociability, and energy (p. 117). It may be more inclusive to regard it as an aspect of presentational skills, that is, showing how the person comes across to receivers as they assess credibility. It is in this area that Simpson may have had his greatest success in both the criminal and civil trials.

The sense of charisma, which had been Simpson's bread and butter during his postfootball career, continued in the criminal trial. Numerous commentators pointed out that his mere presence in the courtroom commanded the attention of all those in it. While he never spoke orally in the presence of the jury, his actions spoke when he showed them his scarred legs and when he tried to put on the gloves. These certainly were among the dramatic highlights of the criminal case.

In the civil trial, when Simpson was out of jail and could come and go as he pleased, that dynamic persona became more pronounced. As Dunne (1997) indicated, "Right up to the end, when his world came crashing down around him, the sheer stardom of Simpson prevailed. . . . He was always in character, demanding our attention, sometimes waving, sometimes not, sometimes limping, sometimes not, knowing exactly how much of himself to share with the public on any given day" (p. 136). He still remained a commanding figure with strong dynamism.

During his testimony in the civil trial, the persona changed. But even then Simpson hit the right notes in terms of presentational skills. He neither got rattled nor became overly dramatic in his responses. Instead, Simpson remained supremely calm, perhaps the best possible approach he could have taken. As Rieke and Stutman (1990) explain, "Research to date implicates the adverse effects of a strident denial by the defendant. In other words, an outburst of self-proclaimed innocence may sometimes do more harm than good" (p. 151). Simpson did not react with any type of outburst. Despite withering questioning from the plaintiffs, Simpson maintained his composure. CNN noted that Simpson "appeared poised and confident" ("Simpson Portrays," 1997, January 10). Moreover, Dunne (1997) emphasized, "As Daniel Petrocelli pounded away at him with his questions, sometimes standing only inches from his face, Simpson maintained confidence, assurance, even dignity during a cross-examination that would have felled a lesser mortal" (p. 137). Dunne further stated that "each time Simpson left the stand, there was no sense that he was ready to collapse into his lawyers' arms for solace, like a fighter at the end of a round, needing pats on his back and water on his face until he can regain himself. He stopped to speak to this person and that person, smiling, jovial, seemingly carefree" (pp. 138–39). He projected the image of a man in control, hardly the image of a man given to murderous rages.

The disputed issue, though, that had to be determined was whether that image was real. Clearly, individuals such as Dunne felt Simpson was hiding behind the mask of his image. As Dunne claimed, "He has been a public personality for most of his life. He is used to being stared at, and he knows how to present his public persona no matter what is going on in his private life. Image is a thing he understands perfectly" (p. 137). Thus, the dynamism that Simpson projected was useful only if he was also seen as trustworthy, perhaps the most important credibility factor at stake in the civil trial.

Trustworthiness. The trustworthiness of O. J. Simpson was the major test of credibility in the civil trial. Unlike the factors of goodwill and dynamism, where he earned average or better-than-average grades, this was the test he failed. Much like his abysmal score on the polygraph test— which was controversially introduced into the court proceedings— Simpson had trouble convincing the jurors of his honesty.

Numerous studies explain the difficulties of a jury—or any group of individuals—incorrectly assessing whether a person is telling the truth. As Rieke and Stutman (1990) conclude, "Although observers are known to encode those cues that reflect deceptive behavior, remarkably they are not very accurate in detecting deception perpetrated by strangers" (p. 126). However, what is important in court is the jury's perception of the defendant's trustworthiness; as far as the court decision is entailed, their perception is the reality.

Simpson's credibility was impugned largely through the painstaking process of depositions engineered by Daniel Petrocelli. He put Simpson on the record on a wide variety of issues, such as giving inconsistencies in his prior statements and making inaccurate statements that contradicted other existing evidence. The depositions led Simpson into a hole that he could never dig out of. As Petrocelli indicated in *Time*, "We pinned him down. It is a perfect illustration of how the deposition process can work. We had no photos. But Simpson lied and lied and lied. He committed himself. Whatever happened, it was important to pin him down on the lies, because we knew we would have an opportunity to confront him on the stand" (Lafferty, 1997, February 17, p. 31).

Much of Simpson's difficulty during the civil trial could be traced to the adamant stances that Simpson took—stances that were far too easily undermined by the introduction of other pieces of evidence. Petrocelli dramatically laid out the questioning regarding domestic violence:

Petrocelli: And how many times, Mr. Simpson, in the course of those physical altercations, did you hit Nicole?
Simpson: Never.
P: How many times did you shake Nicole?
S: Never.
P: How many times did you slap Nicole?
S: Never.
P: How many times did you kick her?
S: Never.
P: How many times did you beat her, sir?
S: Never. (TRL, 1996, November 22)

Later, such testimony was easily contradicted by pictures of Nicole Simpson's bruises and by the testimony of witnesses. Simpson responded similarly when questioned about the famous Bruno Magli shoes, arguing he would never own such shoes. Petrocelli explained his strategy to Dunne (1997), "I'm showing him 30 photographs of him wearing the Bruno Magli shoes, one of which was published six months before the murders, and he says they're not his. You know what that's like? That's like saying you're not standing here talking to me. He's denying the undeniable" (p. 138). As Christopher Darden (1997, February 14) noted,

> Ironic, isn't it, that both cases hinged on an n-word? Attorney Daniel Petrocelli asked Simpson how many times he had hit his wife. He answered "Never." Nobody believed him. When Simpson was asked if he had ever worn Bruno Magli shoes like those whose bloody prints were discovered at the crime scene, he replied, "I would have never owned those ugly-ass shoes." Those photographs proved otherwise and Simpson learned an invaluable lesson about the civil trial's n-word— never say never. The jurors had 31 reasons to disbelieve Simpson and find him liable in the deaths of Ron and Nicole. (p. 38).

The absoluteness of Simpson's answers put him in an untenable position when evidence surfaced to counter his claims of "never."

The beatings and the shoes were the most dramatic incidences of Simpson's testimony that backfired on him, but they were not the only times he was caught in a lie. Whether it was saying he had not received the messages from Paula Barbieri, despite telephone records to the contrary, or claims that his pants in the photos were fake, or his inconsistent statements about where he had cut his finger, Simpson's trustworthiness was constantly undermined when evidence was produced to counter it. As Simon (1997, February 11) reported, "The plaintiffs have picked apart Simpson's testimony by producing at least twenty witnesses who contradict his accounts, including some of his closest friends" (p. A19). Clearly, the weight of that counterevidence proved to be extraordinarily powerful.

In essence, the plaintiffs set forward a strong scenario. To believe Simpson, jurors would have to discount the testimony of many other individuals, individuals who generally were not perceived as having a vested interest in lying. The task for Simpson's attorneys was clear: "'The defense lawyers have to avoid the trap that [the plaintiffs] have so carefully set up, that you either believe O. J. or you believe every other witness in this case,' said civil litigator Steven G. Madison, who teaches trial advocacy at U.S.C. Law School" (Simon, 1996, December 9, p. A1). Reike and Stutman (1990) noted that "according to many practitioners, the more times you get the defendant to respond, 'I don't recall,' or 'I can't remember,' the closer you get to conviction" (p. 171). Ultimately, Simon (1997, February 11) said, "Simpson's contradictory statements, painstakingly laid out by the plaintiff's team, appeared to have sealed the verdicts against him" (p. A19).

The jury's judgment of Simpson's credibility may have been the most significant element in the outcome of the civil trial. Clearly, a unanimous verdict sent a clear message that the jury members accepted the plaintiffs' version of events and not that of the defense. However, it is not necessary to surmise that they totally rejected Simpson's credibility; a press conference held on the day the punitive phase of the trial was completed allowed the jurors to express their attitudes to the press.

Nine members of the jury panel met with the media shortly after the final verdict for a thirty-five-minute press conference. One juror left immediately after reading a statement, while the other eight, including three alternates, accepted questions from the press (*KNBC news*, 1997, February 10). The jurors were asked individually to offer their assessments of Simpson's credibility. These responses were revealing. An alternate male juror stated that he had "a lot of trouble believing what he was telling us. . . . I was sitting four to five feet away and he did not seem credible to me." Stephen Strati, foreman of the punitive phase, stated: "I did not believe in any credibility on Mr. Simpson's behalf. I did have problems with some of his testimony, in his denials of testimony, in his absolutes that I have never worn the shoes, I would never own those shoes, I have never hit Nicole. He was very definite in certain aspects and on other questions, he avoided the question." Only one individual on the panel, an alternate, who was an African American female, spoke out finding Simpson credible: "He was shaky on some points but for the most part he was pretty credible. The plaintiffs were more like bullies instead of professionals. They were very unprofessional as far as I was concerned." Interestingly, this was a juror who also suggested that she felt that the court itself had been complicit in some type of dishonesty and fraud by rigging the selections of those alternates who would ultimately be seated as jurors.

Another source also offered jurors' reactions. Zamichow, Malnic, and Gold (1997, February 11) report:

> [Orville] Bigelow said Simpson would have been more credible had he been more willing to admit some of the evidence and some of his own failures. "I would have respected him more if he had said, 'Yes, I own the shoes but it doesn't mean I'm a murderer.' Or the fact that he abused his wife and denied it. It would have been better if he had just said, 'Yes, I abused her, but that doesn't make me a murderer.'" (pp. A1, A20)

Bigelow went on to say, "I thought Kato Kaelin was more credible." Zamichow, Malnic, and Gold quote another juror, who identified a tug between the factors of goodwill and trustworthiness:

> Mr. Simpson, I feel, was a genuine hero to all of us. We found that we had a hero with feet of clay. The bottom line, as far as I was concerned, was the testimony regarding his beating his ex-wife. We had two witnesses who testified that they had seen it. Once he said that [he had never beaten her], I felt that he was lying. Once we felt he wasn't telling the truth, it went downhill from there. (1997, February 11, p. A20)

Juror Laura Fast Khazaee, speaking on *Larry King Live*, said she had an even more visceral reaction to Simpson. "O. J. insulted us on the stand," said the twenty-seven-year-old white Brentwood woman. "He insulted our intelligence. He looked us in the eye and said I did not kill Nicole. He said he never hit Nicole. It was sickening" (1997, February 5). Obviously, the jury did not find a significant degree of trustworthiness in Simpson's testimony. The impact of that lack of trustworthiness was the central factor in the trial. Jonathan T. Lovitt and Richard Price (1997, February 5) observed that

> most analysts agree the biggest weapon against him was the defendant's own words. The key in the overwhelming defeat handed Simpson Tuesday by the civil jury was the fact that he had to take the stand and face his accusers. And in two appearances, one before Thanksgiving and one early last month, he foundered in a sea of contradictions and inconsistencies. (p. 1A)

Echoing the refrain of Johnnie Cochran from the criminal trial, jury analyst Robert Hirschorn summed up the point: "If you can't trust the messenger, you can't trust the message. O. J. was the messenger; the jurors didn't buy his message" (p. 1A).

Image Restoration

In addition to the legal considerations, the O. J. Simpson testimony was important for the purpose of image restoration. William Benoit (1995) argues that

> human beings frequently must attempt to restore their reputations after alleged or suspected wrong-doing. . . . These attacks on our reputation are serious matters, for our image or reputation is extremely vital to us. Face, image, or reputation not only contributes to a healthy self-image, but it also can create important favorable impressions on others. Conversely, a bad reputation may interfere with our interactions with others. (pp. 1–2).

Such image rebuilding was one reason Cochran had urged the defense team to put Simpson on the stand during the criminal trial. Schiller and Willwerth (1996) reported the attorney's views: "If he walks out a free man, Cochran insisted, he also needs to walk out an innocent man, a decent man. He can't be stigmatized as a wife-beater forever" (p. 443). As mentioned earlier in this volume, Simpson did not take the stand in the criminal trial for other reasons, but the need for image restoration remained. It was more critical in the civil trial for two reasons. First, much of the public concluded that the jury had erred in the criminal trial, releasing a guilty man. Second, because Simpson's freedom was not at stake in the civil trial, even a "liable" verdict would leave him free to operate in society. Without image restoration, he could not move in the business and social circles in which he had traveled prior to the murders. The ability to do so was in Simpson's mind. Toobin (1996) indicates that following the criminal verdict, Simpson "tells [the sheriff's deputies who guarded him] he remains confident that, in time, he will be able to resume his former career of being O. J." (p. 442). Thus, image restoration was a significant concern for Simpson. Several potential ways of refurbishing his image were available.

Apologia

One such approach utilized in the civil trial can be traced to the work on apologia set forth by B. L. Ware Jr. and Wil Linkugel (1973). They suggest that several strategies are open to individuals rhetorically acting in self-defense. Three of those elements surfaced in Simpson's civil testimony.

The first approach of apology is denial, which "consists of the simple disavowal by the speaker of any participation in, relationship to, or positive sentiment toward whatever it is that repels the audience" (p. 276). Simpson repeatedly and forcefully denied upon questioning any involvement in the deaths of Nicole Simpson and Ron Goldman. An exchange with plaintiff's attorney John Q. Kelly, is indicative:

> *Kelly:* You murdered Nicole, didn't you Mr. Simpson?
> *Simpson:* That's absolutely false.
> *K:* And you murdered Ron Goldman.
> *S:* That's absolutely wrong. (TRL, 1996, November 26)

The defense was clearly using the strategy of denial. However, committing the murders was not the only thing Simpson strongly denied. The jury heard him deny beating Nicole Simpson and deny owning Bruno Magli shoes, two denials they found questionable. It should not have been a surprise these denials of the murders were not accepted by the members of the jury.

The second strategy of apology is bolstering. Here "a speaker attempts to identify himself with something viewed favorably by the audience" (Ware & Linkugel, 1973, p. 277). As Benoit (1995) explains,

> Bolstering is not aimed directly at the cause of the speaker's image problems. . . . Rather, it attempts to counterbalance or offset the audience's displeasure by associating the speaker with a different object or action, something for which the audience has positive affect. The hope here is that the new positive perceptions of the rhetor will outweigh the negative ones from the undesirable act. (p. 12)

In Simpson's case, the bolstering consisted not of introducing new positive perceptions but of reemphasizing the old perceptions. On January 10, Defense Attorney Robert Baker led Simpson through a recitation of both his career and his relationship with Nicole, painting them both in extremely favorable terms. It was a strategy that the plaintiffs anticipated. According to Lafferty (1997, February 17), Petrocelli told his associates, "What can Simpson say about anything? He can't talk about the evidence; he can't refute it. He's basically gonna say 'Listen, I won the Heisman Trophy, so I didn't do this. Period'" (p. 31). Lafferty concluded, "As it turned out, Petrocelli was right. Simpson's testimony during his lawyer's questioning was largely about his athletic career, his awards and achievements, and his idyllic life with Nicole" (p. 32).

Again, though, this strategy did not seem particularly persuasive to the jurors. Members of the jury did not regard Simpson's football career as a counterbalancing factor. As juror Bigelow observed, "He was a hero to us, and he betrayed us all. He's a charming man, a nice man, but charming men kill" (Simon, 1997, February 11, p. A19). There was too much evidence for the jury to accept that, while his relationship with Nicole was not perfect, it was a positive one that reflected well on Simpson's character. This strategy of bolstering was not effective with the jury.

Ware and Linkugel (1973) suggest that the third strategy of apology is differentiation, "separating some fact, sentiment, object or relationship from some larger context in which the audience presently views that attribute" (p. 278). Clearly, this was a major strategy for the defense: it was incumbent upon them to separate the issue of domestic violence from that of the murders. If the jury saw them as linked, it would provide a motive and, what is more important, it would provide an inference that his temper could get out of control with Nicole Brown Simpson. As a result, Baker led Simpson through testimony, stressing that he and Nicole "were very much in love. We traveled all over the world. Our house was always loaded with people" (TRL, 1997, January 10). He was given an opportunity to express his feelings in this exchange with his attorney:

Baker: Mr. Simpson, from 1977 to and including the present, did you love Nicole Brown Simpson?
Simpson: Yes, very much so.
B: And you told the jury that you never harmed her, never touched her physically, in any shape or form, after January 1, 1989?
S: That's absolutely correct. (TRL, 1997, January 10)

Simpson inferred that any cases of domestic abuse were exaggerated, were far in the past, and therefore should not be considered because he loved Nicole.

Petrocelli realized that he would have to take a different approach on domestic abuse than that taken by the prosecutors in the criminal trial. According to Lafferty (1997, February 17), Petrocelli stated,

> The least explored aspect of the case is Simpson's motive. You cannot just say this murder was a culmination of domestic vio-

lence incidents. You need to tell a jury a story. This was about a stormy relationship. I feel we really need to focus on the dynamics of that relationship and focus carefully on the last two months. That's why instead of talking with Nicole's friends, I want to focus on talking to O. J.'s friends. (pp. 32–33)

This approach was undoubtedly aided by rulings of Judge Hiroshi Fujisaki, allowing the introduction of evidence from Nicole Simpson's diary and from a worker at a battered women's shelter, evidence not allowed in the criminal case.

Oddly, none of the civil jurors commented on the role of domestic violence in relation to their decision-making process; on the surface, it appeared to have been a moot issue for them. However, that very lack of attention is *de facto* evidence, proving that the strategy of bolstering was not an effective one for the defense. Apparently, the jurors were not convinced by Simpson's protestations of a strong marital and even a strong postmarital relationship, which precluded him from murdering his ex-wife.

Most strategies of apologia were unsuccessful in the Simpson civil trial. Once the jurors found the strategy of denial ineffective, those of bolstering and differentiation had no effect. The murders were so heinous that none of the other approaches could overcome the revulsion to the acts themselves.

Impression Management
Another approach for image restoration is impression management. Individuals may find themselves in predicaments they need to overcome. B. R. Schlenker (1980) suggests that predicaments are "situations in which events have undesirable implications for the identity-relevant images actors have claimed or desire to claim in front of real or imagined audiences" (p. 137). Benoit (1995) adds that "the intensity of a predicament is directly related to its severity and the actor's apparent responsibility for it" (p. 37). In the civil trial, O. J. Simpson clearly found himself in a predicament, and the issue for him was how best to resolve it.

With respect to the charges of murder, the line of defense was clearly that of innocence. Benoit (1995) explains, "Defenses of innocence attempt to demonstrate that the actor had nothing to do with the supposed untoward event; either the event never happened, or, if it did, the actor was not responsible for it" (p. 37). From the time of the preliminary hearing, when he proclaimed himself absolutely, 100 percent not guilty, Simpson persisted in denying any role in the murder of Nicole Simpson and Ron Goldman. It was unthinkable that the strategy would change for the civil trial.

However, Simpson had to defend himself against accusations of both murder and domestic violence. As noted before, regardless of the verdict, Simpson would leave the courthouse a free man. For those who might believe in his innocence of murder, there was still the matter of spousal abuse. Thus, to restore his image, Simpson needed to address that concern. He utilized the innocence approach and another underlying strategy.

A second type of account identified by Schlenker (1980) is that of excuses, or attempts to minimize responsibility for the event. Benoit (1995) notes that "two variants of extenuating circumstances were mentioned by Schlenker: scapegoating, or arguing that others provoked the event, . . . and diffusion of responsibility, or suggesting that one or more others were involved, reducing the responsibility attributable to any individual" (p. 37). In describing the infamous January 1, 1989, incident, Simpson indicated that it was Nicole's fault that the argument had started: "[B]asically it was Nicole misinterpreting a conversation she had with Kathryn Allen." But not only was Nicole the instigator of the conflicts, Simpson claimed she was an equal participant in the violence. Under questioning by Baker, he stated "[W]e got physical with one another," and "I felt something was wrong if we had to get physical with one another" (TRL, 1997, January 13). In earlier questioning conducted by Michael Brewer, the following exchange took place:

Brewer: When you said you were a battered husband, you intended that someone battered you?
Simpson: I meant to convey that at times I felt battered. . . . We both came to the conclusion that at times we were abusive to each other. Sometimes it was more verbal than abusive.

The follow-up was revealing:

Brewer: Can you name a specific instance when you were a battered husband?
Simpson: No.
B: Mr. Simpson, in connection with the 1993 incident in which Nicole called 911, were you battered in that instance?
S: No. (TRL, 1996, November 26)

In his testimony, Simpson utilized both the scapegoating and the diffusion of responsibility strategies suggested by Schlenker.

Once again, the lack of direct comments by the jury members in the postverdict period relating to the shifting of responsibility indicates that the strategy was not effective. They had seen the photographs of a bruised Nicole Simpson, had heard excerpts from her diary, and had concluded either that abuse was an irrelevant issue or that Simpson was, in fact, responsible for battering and killing his former wife. The strategies did not serve to restore his image.

Schlenker's (quoted in Benoit, 1995) third type of account is justification, an approach that attempts to mitigate the objectionable nature of the event, specifically including an attempt to minimize the negative consequences of the predicament (p. 37). Obviously, Simpson could not attempt to minimize the murders themselves because to do so would horrify all receivers. Rather, his major attempt was to minimize the significance of any spousal abuse. As noted before, such efforts were not persuasive to the jury.

While they did not deny the importance of the murders, defense attorneys did utilize a strategy that seemed to mitigate the worth of the individuals. On January 10, 1997, Baker led Simpson through an extended discussion of Nicole Simpson's relationships with other men, out-of-wedlock pregnancy, alcohol abuse, friendships with prostitutes, and physical battery. Simpson was probably the one who decided to take such an approach. Dunne (1997) continues, "As for those few times during the trial when Baker hit below the belt—when he denigrated Nicole and said she hung out with prostitutes, or when he minimized what the future might have been for Ron Goldman—a person who knew Simpson very well told me, 'I bet O. J. insisted he say that'" (p. 138).

The jury's response to the strategy of justification can be assessed through the size of the compensatory and punitive damages awarded to the plaintiffs. The Goldmans were awarded $8.5 million in compensatory damages, and the Goldmans and Browns received $12.5 million each for punitive damages. Neither the nature of the crime nor the value of the victims had been mitigated by the defense strategy. Maria Sanoba of Jury Verdict Research said, "It appears the jury thought his conduct was very reprehensible" (Weinstein, 1997, February 11, p. A21). Clearly, none of the strategies suggested by Schlenker were effective in Simpson's civil trial.

Ebmos

While Schlenker does discuss the aspect of excuse making in his assessments, he does not give significant attention to it. Excuse making was a major approach that the defense took in the civil trial, specifically regarding the charges of spousal abuse. As a result, more attention needs to be given to this area.

Patricia Ganer, K. Jeanine Congalton, and Clark Olson (1991) offer insights in their discussion of ebmos, "the process of publicly explaining and/or justifying personal behavioral actions which society finds unacceptable" (p. 619). The contention is that "when a public figure encounters difficulties as a result of his personal behavior, it requires a response that offers some type of explanation or justification for the action which centers on the persona of the individual" (p. 619). They argue that ebmotic behavior

> is characterized by public figures who argue that some "universal," non-inherent force has affected their behavior and forced them to commit the deed under scrutiny. In this way, rhetors shift attention to some force outside of or greater than themselves and thereby place the blame for the behavior on a causal agent other than a "true" character defect. Once named as such, the agent, then, is said to have temporarily governed the person's behavior. (p. 619)

Several times, this was the specific tactic taken by Simpson to explain actions he took in his relationships with Nicole Simpson. One type of ebmotic excuse is that of "illness," including alcohol abuse (p. 622). Significantly, in responding to Baker's questions about the murders, Simpson relied on the outcome of the alcohol use to explain his behaviors. Baker asked: "O. J., had you had too much to drink that night?" Simpson replied: "Yeah, I, you know, if I would have been stopped by the police, I don't think I could have passed a test" (TRL, 1997, January 13). Thus, any potential wrongdoing that night could be excused by blaming the alcohol, rather than a character defect in Simpson.

A second excuse is relational concerns, where "the greater good of a family member is the motivating force behind the questionable behavior" (Ganer, Congalton & Olson, 1991, p. 623). In covering the issue of his alleged stalking of Nicole Simpson while she was in her home with Keith Zlomsowitch, Simpson portrayed his actions as having been done out of concern for his children. Thus, any behaviors that seemed untoward or overly possessive were a sign of love for his children and therefore should be excused.

Simpson engaged in ebmotic behaviors during civil trial. Again, though, the focus was largely on the issue of spousal abuse rather than the issues of wrongful death and battery, the actual charges pending in the trial.

Image Restoration Strategies

Drawing on the works of others, Benoit (1995) establishes a topology of different image restoration strategies. While several of the approaches have been discussed above, Benoit offers additional items to be considered in the development of arguments in the civil trial.

First, Benoit considers the strategy of denial, an approach discussed above. However, Benoit adds two items that pertain to the civil trial strategy. He contends that "it is possible to reinforce one's denial. . . . Denial may be supplemented with explanations of apparently damaging facts or lack of supporting evidence" (p. 75). This was the precise approach taken by the defense with respect to the photographs of the Bruno Magli shoes. When presented with the first photograph, Robert Groden was called to the stand to argue that they were fake. Even if Peter Gelblum's withering cross-examination of Groden had been insufficient to undermine his contention, the lack of any defense response to the other thirty photographs served to invalidate the approach.

Benoit also contends that one

> form of refusal is applying guilt to another person. This strategy can be considered a variant of denial, because the accused cannot have committed the repugnant act if someone else actually did it. This strategy may well be more effective than simple denial, for two reasons. First, it provides a target to any ill will the audience may feel, and this ill feeling may be shifted away from the accused. Second, it answers the question that may lead the audience to accept a simple denial: "Who did it?" (pp. 75–76)

The use of this strategy was precluded in the civil trial because Judge Fujisaki ruled that the defense could not offer arguments about possible perpetrators in the absence of specific evidence supporting those suggestions.

Second, Benoit describes evading responsibility. He notes that "those who are unable to deny performing the act in question may be able to evade or reduce their apparent responsibility for it" (p. 76). Renaming the concept of scapegoating and terming it "provocation," Benoit suggests that "the actor may claim that the act in question was performed in response to another wrongful act, which understandably provoked the offensive act in question" (p. 76). In this instance, Simpson's focus was once more on the issue of spousal abuse rather than the issue of the murders. As noted before, he largely argued that Nicole Simpson had been the instigator of their conflicts, thus evading sole responsibility for any of the actions. Although on January 10, 1997, he said that "no matter how they happened, I was responsible" for her injuries, the context of his remarks indicated that he did not know how Nicole sustained her injuries and that no part of his hand, arm, shoulder, or elbow had ever come in contact with her. He continued, "I was told that she fell outside, but I didn't see her fall outside" (TRL).

Third, Benoit (1995) defines the strategy of reducing offensiveness. He states that "it is possible for the accused to attempt to minimize the amount of negative affect associated with the offensive act. If the rhetor can convince the audience that the negative act isn't as bad as it might

first appear, the amount of ill feeling associated with that act is reduced"
(p. 77). Again, Simpson's approach focused on the issue of spousal abuse
rather than the murders themselves. He consistently tried to indicate that
the accounts of the abuse were overblown. For example, in discussing
an incident about his having allegedly bashed her car, Simpson spoke
about how he had "tapped the hubcaps" (TRL, 1997, January 13). This
attempt was obviously being made to portray Simpson as an individual
who was not given to outrageous behavior, much less the type of individual who could commit a double homicide.

Finally, Benoit discusses the strategy of corrective action as one form
of "promising to 'mend one's ways' and make changes to prevent the
recurrence of the undesirable act" (1995, p. 79). As before, Simpson
addressed only the spousal abuse. After discussing and minimizing one
of the incidents, Baker and Simpson engaged in the following exchange:

Baker: What did you do to change what would happen in the future, O. J.?
Simpson: Well, I was very disappointed in myself. . . . I felt that something was wrong if we had to get physical with one another. . . . I
immediately got started seeking counseling, to try to understand how
it happened. (TRL, 1997, January 13)

While never directly stated, the implication seemed to be that any individual who would seek therapy for fairly minor incidents would certainly
not, at a later date, commit murder.

Simpson attempted to employ several of the strategies that Benoit
discusses. However, with the exception of denial, all of the strategies
focused on attempts to explain domestic violence. The defense simply
isolated the incidents of abuse as if they were the sole issue in determining the homicides.

Conclusion

While some have argued that the outcomes of both the criminal and civil
trials were foreordained once the juries were empaneled, such a position
ignores the extraordinary dynamics that occur during trials. This belief
does not take into account the differences in the juries, the judges, the
attorneys, the witnesses, the evidence, and the effects of media coverage.
There were numerous distinctions, but one of the most important elements was the fact that O. J. Simpson had to take the witness stand and
undergo a rigorous cross-examination. While his freedom was not at risk,
what remained of his fortune and reputation were. If he could convince
the jury—and the public—that he "did not, could not, would not" have
committed two brutal murders, he would be able to resume the prominent place he had in society before June 12, 1994. If he could not, he

would remain free—but he would also be a pariah. Much was riding on O. J. Simpson's being able to establish himself as a credible individual on the stand.

Yet, on virtually all aspects involving credibility, Simpson was unable to establish a level of ethos that would allow the jurors to draw the conclusion that he was innocent of the charges against him. While the extrinsic factors of credibility worked to his advantage, he was unable to sustain the level when the jurors got access to the intrinsic characteristics. Trustworthiness was the most important factor, and, because of his adamant positions on so many points that were undermined by the testimony of others, Simpson's overall credibility was destroyed.

In addition, in their defense, Simpson and his attorneys focused more on issues of spousal abuse and domestic violence than they did on the wrongful death and battery charges. Most of the attempts to reconstruct Simpson's image before the jury and the public were made by justifying and explaining incidents that had occurred during his relationship with Nicole Brown Simpson; little was done to justify and explain his actions on the night of the double homicide. Even if the jury had been convinced of his fine character with respect to his treatment of Nicole, the issues of battery and wrongful death were not addressed. The defense approached the case as though refurbishing the dimension of Simpson's goodwill would be enough to absolve him of all charges. Their approach proved to be wrong.

The media that had elevated Simpson to celebrity status now reported his demise. The O. J. Simpson who once dashed to the sound of cheers from behind an offensive line as a famed running back at the University of Southern California, who then led a phalanx of police cars in a slow-speed chase across southern California, to fewer cheers, left a Santa Monica courthouse surrounded by family, attorneys, and a bodyguard to fewer cheers still. This time, the crowd reserved its greatest cheers for Daniel Petrocelli, his associates, and the families of Nicole Brown Simpson and Ronald Lyle Goldman.

6
Final Summation: Narratives in Contrast
Janice Schuetz

FINAL SUMMATIONS TAKE ON ADDED DRAMATIC IMPORTANCE in telelitigated trials because the public anticipates that the attorneys will offer conclusive proof about what the verdict should be. Not only does the public emphasize closing argument, but the media commentators also promote this part of the trial as crucial in the determination of the verdict. This media hype about final summations elevates public expectations about the potential persuasive impact of the arguments, the likelihood of intense adversarial feelings, and the necessity for attorneys to present dramatic performances. Many practitioners and legal scholars disagree on the importance that final summation has for the outcome of trials (Schuetz & Snedaker, 1988, p. 143). What many contemporary legal scholars and practitioners do agree about is the importance of the narrative content to the persuasiveness of final summations (see Brooks & Gewirtz, 1996). For this reason, this chapter focuses on the narrative similarities and differences in the final summations of the Simpson criminal and civil trials.

The narratives told in summation arguments are bound by the strictures of law. Gewirtz (1996b) emphasizes that legal narratives must conform to certain distinctive rules of storytelling contained in the law of evidence and procedures. Summation consists of two parts—closing arguments and rebuttal. The law typically defines the scope and content of summations as "an organized presentation of your case in its best possible light: a theory of what happened supported by evidence and common sense" (Tanford, 1983, p. 133). The goal of the attorneys is to organize and emphasize favorable evidence, present the position they want the jury to adopt, refute the allegations of the opposition, suggest ways the jury should resolve conflicting testimony, explain how the law applies to the issues, and demonstrate how the evidence mandates a verdict favorable to their own side of the case (Schuetz & Snedaker, 1988, p. 143). The content of summation is confined to the testimony and exhibits introduced in the preceding record of the trial as well as to fair inferences about that evidence. Normally, attorneys are not permitted to appeal directly to the jurors' sympathy or to play on their emotions or prejudices. In the rebuttal, attorneys are expected to emphasize the issues presented in their closing and are only permitted to introduce new lines of argument and demonstrative exhibits that pertain to the issues already presented (Schuetz & Snedaker, 1988, p. 143).

This chapter examines the summations presented during the criminal and civil trials of O. J. Simpson by (1) showing how the narratives are framed by legal requirements, (2) describing the narrative characteristics, (3) comparing and contrasting the rhetorical features of the summations in the criminal and civil cases, and (4) evaluating this segment of the trials according to narrative standards.

Legal Requirements

Although the content of summation features the attorneys presenting practical reasoning in a narrative form, legal requirements enter into summation to restrict and limit the narrative content. The court has discretion in deciding the order in which parties present the closing argument, but typically, the prosecution or plaintiff gives the first argument, the defense replies, and the prosecution and plaintiffs respond in rebuttal. Other procedures unique to a trial surface in the order of presentation and in the judge's instructions to the jury.

Order
Final summation in the Simpson trials followed the typical organizational pattern. In each case, the judge instructed the jury prior to the summation and again after summations were completed. The closing argument was presented first by the prosecution and plaintiffs and then by the defense. A rebuttal, given by the prosecution and plaintiffs in order to respond to the closing argument of the defense, ended the summation.

In the Simpson criminal case, Prosecutor Marcia Clark summarized the evidence, and Christopher Darden told the story of domestic violence that led Simpson to murder his victims. Defense Attorney Johnnie Cochran presented the defense story of a police frame-up, and Barry Scheck addressed the technical evidence. Both Clark and Darden shared the rebuttal. In the civil case, summation began with a long closing argument by Daniel Petrocelli, attorney for the Ronald Goldman family. His summation was followed by shorter presentations from John Kelly, representing the estate of Nicole Brown Simpson, and from Michael A.

Brewer, representing Goldman's mother, Sharon Rufo. The summations for the defense commenced with Robert C. Baker who refuted the evidence of the plaintiffs and suggested a story of police frame-up, and Robert D. Blaiser followed with refutation of the plaintiffs' case and jury instructions. Rebuttals were presented by Peter B. Gelblum, Thomas P. Lambert, and Daniel Petrocelli, attorneys for the Goldman family.

Content of Instruction

Both trial summations began and ended with instructions given by the respective judges in the trial. Since the criminal trial featured many witnesses testifying for long segments of time and many contentious exchanges between attorneys, the summations in the civil case were half as long as those in the criminal case. The different instructions given by Judge Lance Ito in the criminal trial and Judge Hiroshi Fujisaki in the civil trial point out the differences and similarities that jurors are expected to use in interpreting closing argument.

In the criminal trial, the prosecution and defense hotly debated the content of jury instructions, especially those that applied to Mark Fuhrman. The instructions given by Ito in the criminal case prior to summation consumed eight single-spaced pages. These instructions emphasized the law and how jurors should interpret the case in that frame. Ito began, "You must base your decision on the facts and the law. . . . You must accept and follow the law." He then emphasized that the jury "must not be influenced by pity for a defendant or by prejudice against him. You must not be biased against the defendant because he has been arrested for this offense, charged with a crime or brought to a trial"(TRC, 1995, September 29). The instruction about the credibility of witnesses was particularly salient given the testimony late in the trial involving Fuhrman and his racist behavior. Although a standard instruction, the content seemed clearly to refer to Fuhrman:

> You are the sole judges of the believability of a witness and the weight to be given the testimony of each witness. . . . A witness who is willfully false in one material part of his or her testimony is to be distrusted in other [areas]. You may reject the whole testimony of a witness who willfully has testified falsely as to the material point unless from all the evidence you believe the probability of truth favors his or her testimony in other particulars. (TRC, 1995, September 29)

Ito's instructions concluded by defining reasonable doubt as "not mere possible doubt, because everything relating to human affairs is open to some possible or imaginary doubt." Ito then reiterated the presumption:

"The prosecution has the burden of proving beyond a reasonable doubt each element of the crimes charged in the information and that the defendant was the perpetrator of any such charged crime. The defendant is not required to prove himself innocent or to prove that any other person committed the crimes charged" (TRC, 1995, September 29). At the conclusion of summations, Ito gave only a short instruction about jury responsibility and then outlined the process to be followed when filling out the verdict forms.

In the civil case, Judge Fujisaki began with a single page of instructions regarding the law. Since a civil case is based on the preponderance of evidence rather than on reasonable doubt, Fujisaki emphasized what constitutes evidence. He explained: "What the attorneys argue to you, what they state to you at this stage of the proceedings are not evidence. . . . Evidence is only that which you heard from the witness stand and the graphics and other types of evidence that we denote as evidence that we've received in the trial" (TRC, 1997, January 21).

After the summations were completed, Fujisaki gave detailed instructions on civil law and juror responsibility. He began with contrasts to the criminal case: "This is a civil case. You may know that the defendant Simpson was already tried in a criminal case for the murders of Nicole Brown Simpson and Ronald Goldman and that the defendant Simpson was acquitted in that criminal case. The acquittal in the criminal case has no effect on this case." He continued discussing why it was legal to have both a criminal and a civil case. He described the role of plaintiffs as "personal representatives" of the deceased. He then defined evidence as "testimony, writings, material objects, or any other thing presented to the senses and offered to prove the existence or non-existence of a fact." He distinguished evidence from inferences, that is, deductions from facts "established by the evidence." He told the jury that they should evaluate evidence not by "counting the number of witnesses" but by "the force of the evidence. . . . Preponderance of evidence means evidence that has more convincing force than that opposed to it." Then he made an elaborate explanation of the legal meaning of wrongful death and the concept of damages. He concluded by stating, "Everything you decide in this case is based upon the evidence that you received in the trial process, okay?" (TRL, 1997, January 28).

Both instructions emphasized the role of jurors in deciding the respective cases based on the evidence, their interpretations of evidence, and the charges. The instructions changed to reflect different obligations of proof—reasonable doubt versus preponderance of evidence. Whereas Ito emphasized what evidence to consider, Fujisaki emphasized how to interpret the evidence. Both the evidence and its interpretation are embedded in the narratives of summation.

Narrative Characteristics

The era of telelitigation has challenged the norms for final summation in several significant ways. Although the legal procedures and statutes dictate what can be said, summations have evolved into dramatically portrayed stories presented to the jury, the media, and public audiences. The stories emphasize the character and personality of defendants, plaintiffs, and witnesses, and they have a dramatic structure that embodies persuasive themes and language.

Storied Persuasion

Final summation no longer consists of meticulously demonstrated deductive logic and reiteration of facts. Instead, it consists of reconstructed narratives that condense and connect all of the stories told by the witnesses into a unified theme or theory. The refutation presented as part of summation presents counternarratives to challenge or question stories presented by opposing attorneys. In both the criminal and civil cases, similar stories were presented by the prosecution and plaintiffs. Their stories emphasized that the murders were "rage" killings motivated by a long history of domestic abuse and jealousy. The plaintiffs in the civil case, who had the benefit of Simpson's testimony, further emphasized that O. J. Simpson had lied repeatedly to cover up his crime. The defense in both cases emphasized the theory that a police conspiracy existed with the purpose of framing Simpson even though Fuhrman did not testify in the civil case. In the civil case, defense attorneys also suggested the possibility of two professional killers.

Audiences

The summation, although featuring prepared speeches by individuals to the jury and to the public, is a transactional process in which audiences participate in the creation of the meaning of the stories. Clearly, the televised criminal trial allowed more extensive participation by the public audience than the civil trial did. Nonetheless, the public followed the civil trial through constant television updates, dramatizations of the trial on CNBC, newspaper discussions and records of the testimony, and daily transcripts on the Internet. After the trials, some jury members justified their decisions in television news conferences and on television talk shows. The media compared the summations of the prosecution to those of the plaintiffs and the criminal defense to those of the civil defense.

Courtroom narratives are persuasive because audiences listen to the narrative with a "stock of stories in their minds," and they use these stock stories to decide whether the courtroom narratives ring true with the stories they know and understand (Gewirtz, 1996a, p. 8). These stories come from the social knowledge of the audiences. The social knowledge of audiences that applies to the Simpson cases includes stories about his football fame, domestic abuse, police corruption, and excessive monetary settlements in civil lawsuits. The stories about the criminal case and its verdict also entered into the interpretive frames of reference for the jurors and for the public during the civil trial.

Characterization
Summations emphasize the characters and personalities of the legal story and draw inferences about how their intentions, motives, and behaviors affected the outcome of the story. The main characters in the criminal trial were Simpson and Fuhrman, whereas the main characters in the civil trial were Simpson, the victims, and the representatives of the victims' estates.

The defendant, Simpson, was characterized in quite different ways in the criminal and civil trials. The prosecution seemed to acknowledge Simpson's stature. Darden noted:

> All along I have asked you to be open-minded, to be open-minded about this man and who he is, and . . . I think we have proven to you that he is not the person that you see on those TV commercials and at half-time in those football games. . . . We have a very, very important example of who this man is, of who he is at home, of who he is in his private life. (TRC, 1995, September 27)

Petrocelli's characterization of the defendant was direct and vicious. He began by asking a series of questions—

> What kind of man says cheating on your wife isn't a lie? What kind of man says that virtually every other person in this case who testified on the stand against him is either lying or mistaken? What kind of man would try to ruin the lives of innocent people?" [Petrocelli concludes:] A guilty man. A guilty man. A man with no remorse. A man with no conscience. This man is so obsessed with trying to salvage his image and protect himself that he'll come into this courtroom, knowing that the whole world is watching, and he will smear the name and reputation of the mother of his children while she rests in her grave. (TRL, 1997, January 21)

The character of the police was the centerpiece of criminal trial testimony. Defense attorneys demonized Mark Fuhrman and Philip Vannatter, making them the central actors in a story of a police frame-up. Cochran emphasized:

That is Mark Fuhrman. And he is paired in this case with Phil
Vannatter. They are both beacons that you look to as the
messengers that you must look through and pass. They are
both people who have shown that they lie, will lie, and did
lie on the stand under oath. . . . This is really a case about a
rush to judgment, an obsession to win, at all costs, a willing-
ness to distort, twist, theorize in any fashion to try to get you
to vote guilty. (TRC, 1995, September 28)

Because of the rulings by Judge Fujisaki excluding Fuhrman's testimony
and because of the brevity of testimony from other police investigators,
the defense in the civil case had less ammunition for demonizing the police
than the criminal defense did. Still the defense managed to get Fuhrman's
name before the jury several times. In one case, Blaiser explained, "There
is one man that wants to be, more than anybody else, the linchpin of that
case, and that's somebody who . . . has been [part of the plaintiffs'] effort to keep out of this trial: Mark Fuhrman" (TRL, 1997, January 27).
This content was overruled by the judge, but Blaiser nonetheless got it
heard by the jury. Blaiser's storied description of the investigation at the
crime scene used Fuhrman's name frequently. In the absence of a clear
defense theory, Baker blamed the media and plaintiffs' witnesses for their
role in the civil trial: "If, in fact, you find him not responsible, the gravy
train is over. The case is over. It's not in the news everyday. It is gone."
He also accused key witnesses, such as India Allen and Albert Aguillara,
who testified that they observed Simpson hit Nicole Brown Simpson, of
seeking media publicity (TRL, 1997, January 22).

Narrative Structure
Finally, the story is part of a text with a narrative structure, presented
through the medium of language. The text is rhetorical; it presents a structure and gives meaning to the story. Brooks (1996) explains that narrative structure has two parts: the *fabula* is the order of events as they take
place in a real context, and the *sjuzet* is the manner in which events are
reconstructed in the narrative discourse. The attorneys structured their
stories differently in the criminal and civil cases.

In the criminal case, Clark presented the chronology of events, or
the *fabula*, as pieced together by the witnesses and retold as the timeline, or the *sjuzet*. After she completed her part of the summation,
Darden presented the chronology of domestic abuse between the defendant and his ex-wife. This story was organized around a series of domestic abuse episodes relating chronologically in the *fabula*. They were
told in the metaphor (the *sjuzet*) of a burning fuse that grew shorter
through more and more incidents of domestic abuse and finally ex-

ploded like a bomb into the brutal murder of Nicole Brown Simpson and Ronald Goldman.

The *fabula* is similar for both cases, but the *sjuzet* changes in the civil case. Petrocelli emphasized Simpson's history of domestic abuse prior to and during the night of the crime as the *fabula*, which eventually led to the *sjuzet* of jealousy, a rage killing, and a cover-up. Kelly and Brewer repeated the *fabula* of Petrocelli's story, but they emphasized the suffering of the victims and the impact of the murders on their clients, a somewhat different *sjuzet* than offered by Petrocelli.

Thus, the form of the narrative changed to reflect the issues that needed to be proven to secure a favorable verdict. Darden, Cochran, and Petrocelli developed compelling stories with protagonists and antagonists, a theme, and a conflict. The rest of the attorneys delivering summation arguments presented less developed story forms and gave only parts of a story. For example, Scheck, Clark, and Lambert repeated scientific evidence and drew inferences from this evidence without incorporating it into a complete narrative.

Rhetorical Features

Several features of the narrative contribute to its persuasiveness. Issues provide the legal referents, but the narrative themes and the depictions of the character and credibility of the people in the alleged action provide the skeletal dramatic form for the summation narratives. Persuasive summations present the legal content through a dramatic form.

Issues

Issues arise out of the charges in the case. In the criminal case, the issues related to the crime of murder. According to the California Penal Code (Section 187, 1994), "Every person who unlawfully kills a human being with malice aforethought is guilty of the crime of murder." So the issues to be decided were the following: Was a human being killed? Was the killing unlawful? and Was the killing done with malice aforethought, that is, willful, deliberate, and premeditated? To accomplish this goal, Clark and Darden presented a three-part summation.

Clark began the summation by giving a chronological account of the timeline and showing that this timeline proved "malice of forethought." She emphasized that "with the nature and number of the wounds that were suffered by those victims, it's very obvious that the killer went to great lengths to disable and kill them with the throat slashing wounds" (TRC, 1995, September 26). Prosecutor Darden presented the second part of the closing argument in the form of a compelling story. This story was promoted by the police's release of the 911 call in 1993 of Brown Simpson to the police and the subsequent reprimand of Simpson after police officers came to the scene of the abuse. Darden argued, "This relationship between this man and Nicole, you know, it is like the bomb ticking away. Just a matter of time, just a matter of time before something really bad happened" (TRC, 1995, September 26). Although this theme connected with the social stories of abuse and murder, it did not seem to fit with the stock narratives of some of the criminal jurors. According to one of the jurors, many of the other African American jurors had trouble believing this theme because of the celebrity status of the defendant (Knox, 1995, p. 135).

The summation of the defense in the criminal case presented a clear competing narrative, one that fit with jurors' stock narratives. The defense story was about police racism. Defense Attorney Cochran argued that because Detective Fuhrman was a racist, as was shown in the testimony of several of their witnesses, it was likely that he and other police framed Simpson because he was a black man. Cochran promoted this theory in his summation:

> Why did they then all try to cover for this man, Fuhrman? Why would this man, who is not only Los Angeles' worst nightmare, but America's worst nightmare, why would they all turn their heads and try to cover for him? . . . There is something about corruption. There is something about a rotten apple that will ultimately infect the entire barrel. (TRC, 1995, September 29)

The issues of these narratives were embedded in themes that related to the theories for each side of the case.

Themes

The general narrative themes of the civil case paralleled those of the criminal case. However, because of the new evidence, new witnesses, and the testimony of Simpson, the story had a different angle. Petrocelli placed Simpson at the center of the story; he was the active agent perpetrating the crime. Petrocelli summarized:

> It is very clear that Nicole Brown Simpson was the target of this attack by someone who knew she would be home and someone who knew where she lived. It's not a gunshot killing. We're talking about a killing by a knife, up close, by a person . . . in a state of rage. All of these signs, ladies and gentlemen, point directly to a person who knew Nicole, knew where to find her, and had no reason to go to her house that

night except to confront her. . . . There's no such person other than O. J. Simpson. . . . The physical evidence all points to him. (TRL, 1997, January 21)

This preview is followed by a detailed presentation of the evidence—cuts on Simpson's left hand and the blood, fiber, shoe, socks evidence (TRL, 1997, January 21).

The defense need not present a competing story, although a compelling alternative story gives jurors optional categories for interpreting the evidence. Defense Attorneys Baker and Blaiser did not present complete or compelling stories. Rather, they emphasized that the issues were about various actions, including police misconduct, erratic and immoral behavior by Nicole Brown Simpson, greed on the part of the plaintiffs, and unknown assailants who may have committed the crime. Baker and Blaiser were unable to condense evidence into a story; instead, they presented a disorganized series of attacks on the evidence. Baker began by claiming that the plaintiffs failed to talk about problems with the investigation, but "it's here. It's in this case. And it's not going away because they don't want to talk about it. We'll ask you if that conduct is appropriate by LAPD." Even though this line of reasoning hinted that the defense story was about police misconduct, there was no compelling evidence of malfeasance. Rather than presenting a persuasive counterstory, the defense maligned the victims and impugned their motives. For example, Baker emphasized, "This isn't a fight for justice. It's a fight for money. . . . That is all it is about" (TRL, 1997, January 22).

It is not surprising that fragments of the themes and strategy of the criminal case enter into the summations of the civil case. Defense Attorney Blaiser was part of the defense team in the criminal case, and he appeared to borrow much from that case. For example, he claimed that Petrocelli's explanation of blood evidence was incorrect: "Now, this is the myth of this case that got started way back in the very beginning of the criminal case." Then he explained that the blood was not to the left in the photos as the plaintiffs had concluded (TRL, 1997, January 23). This was one of several references to the criminal trial about the improper procedures of Fuhrman and Vannatter, the incompetent work of the criminalists, and the testimony of witnesses who appeared in the criminal trial but not in the civil case.

The prime storytellers in the criminal case were Darden for the prosecution and Cochran for the defense. Both presented persuasive stories in a narrative form. The prime storytellers for the civil case were Petrocelli for the plaintiffs and Baker for the defense. Clark's prosecution story and Blaiser's defense story in the civil case lacked structure and precision. Both of these closing arguments suffered from digressions or examples not relevant to the case, a lack of internal transitions, and a failure to focus on characters, action, and planning.

Credibility

Theories of argument credibility help explain both the stories' contents and the reception of summation stories by the jury and the public at large. Credibility refers to "the judgments made by a perceiver concerning the believability of a communicator" (O'Keefe, 1990, pp. 130–31). In both the civil and criminal trials, jurors attributed credibility to the judge, the attorneys, the accused, and the witnesses. Since credibility is relational, audiences attribute credibility in different ways. In fact, one of the primary goals of the attorneys in any case is to establish their credibility with jurors, to build the credibility of their own witnesses, and to impeach the credibility of the witnesses who present the most damaging testimony against them. Defense attorneys are more likely to attack the credibility of the opposing attorneys as Cochran, Scheck, Baker, and Blaiser did in these cases. Typically, the arguments about credibility surface in cross-examination and then are summarized and packaged for persuasive effect in the narratives of summation.

Attempts to create and destroy credibility were the central focus of the refutation segment of summation in both the criminal and civil trials. This segment of the chapter first shows the uses of credibility in the criminal case, follows with a discussion of the civil case, and concludes with a summary of these strategies in both trials. The credibility refutation was directed at opposing attorneys, witnesses of opposing attorneys, and Simpson himself.

Several credibility factors surfaced in the telelitigated summations in the Simpson criminal case. One noticeable credibility argument present in defense summation and absent in that of the prosecution was a systematic attack on other attorneys. This kind of attack is common in defense summations because it is a way of drawing inferences about the competence of the attorneys by stating that their witnesses, arguments, and evidence are ill conceived, so therefore the attorneys are not competent representatives for their side of the case. Cochran began his assault on the prosecutors by claiming their case was "speculative and cynical," a subordinate theme that bolstered the defense's claim that the police framed Simpson because they were racist. He called the prosecution's case "contemptuously distrustful" and "gloomy," an approach he argued that prosecutors had taken because they "had an obsession to win." He justified this characterization by saying that defense witnesses were "entitled to dignity," but they were treated by the prosecution in a rough manner, using a "contorted version" of reality. Cochran constantly demeaned the prosecutors' credibility, claiming they were "in a rush to judgment" and "want[ed] to win at any cost"; their conclusions were "totally ridiculous" and "completely preposterous," inferring that they kept changing the case to "make it fit, but it doesn't fit so you must acquit." He ridiculed the prosecutors, saying they were "not medical doctors so they can't draw inferences from the evidence"; "they are wearing blinds, they have lost their objectivity, they don't understand what they are talking about"; and they "can't turn the Constitution on its head" (TRL, 1995, September 28).

The civil defense summations likewise called into question the credibility of opposing counsel, but they did so in a more cautious and indirect way than attorneys did in the criminal case. For example, Baker faulted the plaintiffs' attorneys because they had their picture taken with their clients and because they had law enforcement officers available to testify free for the case. He noted that "plaintiffs' attorneys have twisted, expanded the witnesses to fit within the story that they want to fit," engaged in "character assassination of O. J. Simpson, demonized my client, and misstated the evidence." The focus of the credibility arguments in the civil case was on the defendant. The defense was unable to deal with many of the inconsistencies presented in Simpson's testimony just as the prosecution was unable to deal with the problems of Fuhrman's testimony in the criminal case.

In both cases, a second strong credibility argument was the attack by the defense on many of the key witnesses of the prosecution. The attack in the criminal case began first with generalizations about the quality of the LAPD. Cochran stressed, they are "more concerned with images" than "with justice," are untrained, "delayed unconscionably procedures," "are vain," "never looked for anyone else," and "engaged in sloppy errors and coverups." He levied the worst character assassination at Detectives Mark Fuhrman and Philip Vannatter. Using a preachy style, he condemned the men in this way: "And the two of them need to be paired together because they are twins of deception. Fuhrman and Vannatter, twins of deception who bring you a message that you cannot trust. . . . Vannatter who carried the blood; Fuhrman, the man who carried the glove" (TRC, 1995, September 28). The attack by Cochran on the two investigating detectives was persistent, coded in invective language, and delivered in a tone of condemnation.

The impugning of credibility of the criminalists was left to Defense Attorney Scheck, who recast the prosecution's evidence in evaluative terms. One example of Scheck's attack on witness credibility centered on Dr. Dennis Fung. He summarized eight days of testimony, claiming that Fung contaminated the crime scene by his reckless behavior. Scheck concluded:

> We have the issue of the blanket. I mean, this, as Mr. Fung admitted, was colossal stupidity. To take a blanket that

people—Mr. Simpson and others—with Bronco fibers, hairs from all kinds of African Americans on that blanket and then throw it out over the crime scene, over the bodies, over the evidence items, everywhere is asking for trouble. . . . It's ludicrous. And nobody ever came clean and said who it was that moved those bodies through the envelope and the hat. And we all know that happened right. You have to admit it happened when they pulled Mr. Goldman's body through Lord knows what was going on [*sic*]. (TRC, 1995, September 29)

This sarcastic and feisty condemnation by Scheck of Fung emphasized the overall incompetence of the criminalists and impugned the facticity of all of the evidence collected by dozens of crime scene investigators. Clearly, the defense tried to impeach witnesses' competence by portraying their behavior in negative terms, by repeating their faults, and by using general innuendoes to challenge the competence of all the other witnesses.

The arguments in the civil case about character and personality centered on the credibility of the defendant versus that of the victims. Petrocelli began his closing argument by showing pictures of Nicole Brown Simpson and Ronald Goldman actively living their lives. He annotated these pictures by saying, "Ronald Goldman would have been 29 years old, and I think he would have had that restaurant that he wanted to open shaped in the design of tan ankh, the Egyptian symbol for eternal life, which Ron always wore around his neck." He then talked about the vibrant image of Nicole he had projected on the screen in front of the jury. Petrocelli said: "Nicole Brown Simpson would have been 37 years old. Not on a day unlike today, I think she would have, like she did every day, gotten up and taken care of her children, fed them; taken them to school, karate lessons, dance lessons; brought them home, fed them dinner, played with them, and put them to bed." Then before he projected pictures of their bodies on the screen in front of the jury, he said: "Ron Goldman will never get to open his restaurant. . . . And Nicole Brown Simpson will never see her children grow up." He continued with this transition, "Even though Ron's and Nicole's voices will not be heard in this courtroom, . . . their last struggling moments to stay alive . . . provided us the key evidence necessary to identify their killer. . . . The voices of Ron and Nicole [are] speaking to us from the grave telling all of you that there is a killer in this courtroom." After this compelling prologue to his summation story, Petrocelli pointed to the defendant (TRL, 1997, January 21). The message of the narrative was clear; it was a story about innocent victims and two vicious murders committed by O. J. Simpson.

Petrocelli then engaged in several minutes of attack on the testimony of Simpson, claiming that he either directly lied or made excuses. This attack was made by posing a rhetorical question previewed with "what kind of man?" and followed by an elaboration of what Simpson had said and pictures of what he allegedly did. One example of this storied version of Simpson's testimony contrasted him with his ex-wife. Petrocelli elaborated: "What kind of man, ladies and gentleman, confronted with this bruised and battered picture of Nicole, says, 'I take full responsibility for causing all those injuries; but I didn't hit her, I didn't strike her, I didn't do anything wrong. I was just defending myself'?" He continued his sarcastic challenges to the testimony of Simpson claiming, "What kind of a man, who has shared a bedroom with his wife for ten years, calls it *my* bedroom, *my* house, *my* property, *me?*" (TRL, 1997, January 21). The first hour of the closing argument emphasized that Simpson was an evil person who was unable to explain why he battered his wife or where the missing evidence from the case was.

Brown family attorney Kelly repeated this characterization in his closing argument, comparing the victim, Nicole, with the defendant. According to him, Nicole "was a great mother," "a great daughter," "a great sister." He emphasized: "She was beautiful. She was happy. And she was healthy. She was everything Mr. Simpson was not. She was private. She was caring. She was sensitive" (TRL, 1997, January 21).

The defense responded in its closing argument by minimizing the incidents of battering and by making disparaging comments about the victims. Baker explained that one domestic abuse incident that was reported to the police in 1989 was a mistake. Baker reflected that Simpson "was disappointed with himself. Did he minimize it on national television? You bet. . . . Did he take procedures to ensure it never happened again? Yeah, he did. He immediately went to counseling." At the same time that he attempted to redeem Simpson's behavior, Baker explained how forgiving Simpson had been even after the excessive transgressions of Nicole. He recalled that one night after they had separated Simpson just happened to be close to Nicole Brown Simpson's house. He walked by, and he noticed she was in the living room. He was shocked to find she was "in the living room with the draperies to the front room wide open, light on, performing oral sex on this man." But he implied that Simpson was so forgiving that he rang the doorbell and later Nicole apologized (TRL, 1997, January 21). Baker then related a series of incidents over the four years prior to her death to show how, even though Nicole was uncommitted in her relationship with Simpson and sometimes acted badly, Simpson still gave her money.

By extolling the weaknesses and ignoring virtues of witnesses, the defense in the criminal case cast doubt on the massive amounts of evidence against their client, and the verdict indicated that they succeeded. The defense's method of attacking credibility succeeded because the prosecution failed to either establish or rebuild the credibility of its own witnesses.

First, Darden and Clark made almost no effort to establish the credibility of key witnesses in summation even though they knew some of these witnesses were vulnerable. Instead, both admitted the weaknesses of Fuhrman. Clark noted: "Is he the worst LAPD has to offer? Yes. Do we wish that this person was never hired by LAPD? Yes. Should such a person be a police officer? No. In fact, do we wish there were no such person on the planet? Yes." And Darden acknowledged his embarrassment about Fuhrman, claiming "We're not hiding Fuhrman. He's too big, especially now, to hide. So hey, Fuhrman testified" (TRC, 1995, September 26).

The attorneys in the civil case asked jurors to balance the credibility of the defendant, called by Petrocelli and Kelly "a compulsive liar," with the credibility of others testifying in the case. Unlike the criminal case, in which the prosecution failed to rehabilitate Fuhrman, in the civil case the defense tried to rehabilitate Simpson by minimizing his actions and by showing the weaknesses of those who testified against him. But given the standard of preponderance of evidence, jurors likely observed too many inconsistencies in Simpson's testimony to find him believable. The defense team was never able to explain why Simpson claimed he never owned Bruno Magli shoes even after over thirty photographs surfaced of him wearing those shoes, nor were they able to explain why he told several different stories about the source of the cuts and abrasions on his hands even though jurors saw many pictures of these cuts.

Both sides attempted to diminish the credibility of each other's witnesses. One standard strategy of impeachment is to claim that the expert witnesses have an economic motive. For example, Marcia Clark called attention to the money that Simpson's doctor, Baden, had been paid to testify about the cuts on Simpson's hand. Clark noted, Dr. Baden "came here and told you gravity doesn't work, paid over $100 thousand in this case. He is very charming, he is very affable, I enjoyed seeing him in court, but hearing him was something else. Over $100 thousand he got paid in this case" (TRC, 1995, September 29).

Another typical strategy in a high-profile media case is for opposing counsel to claim witnesses testify for publicity. For example, Defense Attorney Baker made this argument when he tried to impeach India Allen, a veterinarian's assistant who claimed she saw Simpson slap Brown Simpson. Baker said Allen wanted to be on television. He concluded, "If you want your 15 minutes of fame, . . . be a witness in this case. You can get photographed going out of the hotel with these guys [plaintiffs and their attorney], and you'll be photographed going back in. You'll be on national television" (TRL, 1997, January 21).

A unique feature of the use of credibility in closing arguments in the civil case was the attack on the motives of the parents of Ronald Goldman, who were seeking liability for the wrongful death of their son. Baker first demeaned the victim's father, saying, "Fred Goldman, . . . didn't help his son go through bankruptcy, and he had to go through bankruptcy. Ron Goldman wouldn't have a restaurant now. He'd be lucky to have a credit card." In rebuttal, Petrocelli responded,

> And Mr. Baker got up here—In one of the lowest moments of the trial, he mocked this young man who lies in his grave. . . . If O. J. Simpson were innocent, truly innocent, would he let his lawyer mock this young man? . . . Only a guilty man has his lawyers stand up there and disparage this person and disparage his loss and cheapen his loss. (TRL, 1997, July 28)

Credibility was a major issue for the jurors in the posttrial interviews for both cases. The credibility of Fuhrman appeared to be central to the verdict of the criminal trial just as the credibility of Simpson was in the civil trial. For example, criminal trial juror Carrie Bess recalled her reaction to Fuhrman in this way: "When I heard those things about the n-word, it was like a hot flash hit me. It just made me realize how badly I hate that word. For him to sit up here and pretend that he never used it, it made me feel like just jumping up and slapping him down right then and there (Cooley, Bess, & Rubin-Jackson, 1995, p. 105). In the civil case, Laura Fast Khazaee (*Burden of Proof*, 1997, February 11) said that Simpson "was a very poor witness; he danced around important evidence. He wouldn't face up to the abuse of his wife."

Telelitigation encourages summations focused on character, personality, and feelings to get the jurors to identify their own stories with those told in the courtroom. Summations in popularized trials call attention to social conflicts and emphasize the contentious issues of the trial. Moreover, arguments about character divert attention from the evidence and enhance both the jurors' and the public's interest in the characters who participated or observed the disputed actions of the crime. Arguments about credibility also allow public and juror audiences to compare the likability and perceived similarity of witnesses and attorneys to themselves since audiences are persuaded more easily by people they like and whom they perceive as similar to themselves (Rieke & Stutman, 1990).

Evidence and Patterns of Inference

Much of the summation narrative appealed to feelings using the means allowed under the rules of summation. Attorneys are not permitted to appeal directly to jurors' sympathy or to play on the emotions and prejudices of the jurors (Stein, 1985, secs. 21 and 22, pp. 54–57); and they are forbidden from putting themselves in the client's position, asking jurors to base their decisions on broad social issues, or addressing a single juror by name (Tanford, 1983, pp. 146–47).

In the summations in the Simpson criminal and civil cases, attorneys circumvented some of the procedural norms by developing complex modes of inferences leading to complicated forms of justification. Inferences are the movement from some evidence or facts that are known to some conclusion or claim that is in doubt. Jasinski (1990) identifies several inferential forms that help to explain the complexity of summation arguments. In the Simpson case, analogies, metaphors, images, and parallel cases were the key inferences.

Analogies and metaphors. Arguments have general forms that are "abstract patterns of reasoning," such as analogy, parallel case, and generalization. The persuasive force of inferences based on analogy "depends on securing audience participation in the unfolding form" by engaging the audience and then by demonstrating that the form is legitimate (Jasinski, 1990, p. 60).

A contrast between the analogies in the prosecution and defense summations in the criminal trial explains why the defense persuaded the jury better than did the prosecution. Clark used a few general and undeveloped analogies. She began her closing argument by telling the jurors that they had to act like sculptors—to take the evidence as if it were a whole piece of marble and then, like a sculptor, weed out what was not relevant, so they could get an accurate portrait of the crime. This analogy failed to identify substantive parallels between the sculptor and the process of jury decision making and, thus, lacked a direct fit with the experiences of this jury. Early in her closing argument, Clark also presented the analogy that the defense was headed up false roads: "There were false roads. They are false roads because they lead to a dead-end. The false roads were paved with inflammatory distractions" (TRC, 1995, September 26). But this analogy also lacked sufficient detail and parallel language to create persuasive imagery for the jury.

Whereas Clark used a few analogies ineffectively, Cochran used many linguistic techniques with mixed persuasive effect. For example, Cochran used a general analogy that wove a theme for the case, "the journey toward justice." He did not develop this analogy by relating the incidents of the trial to a journey but merely repeated the words throughout his closing argument. What he did do effectively was refute prosecutors' analogies by adding contrasting metaphorical language of his own. For example, he claimed the prosecutors said that "a fuse was burning," but "the fuse kept going out" because there was "no triggering mechanism." He noted that the prosecutors had given the jury "oceans of evidence," but they really had only "little streams" (TRC, 1995, September 27). These refutative metaphors demonstrated clever use of language that contributed to his aggressive rhetorical style.

Blaiser tried to develop several analogies as he refuted plaintiffs' expert testimony about the blood evidence. He used a paint-by-number analogy to explain what was missing from the plaintiffs' evidence. Blaiser noted:

> The picture that we have, that's our defense, is that we have a picture of corruption, of contamination, of planting, of tampering. And we don't have all the paint. We're not going to be able to paint you a complete picture of that. We're going to paint some of it, from which you're going to have to infer that we can't trust the evidence. (TRL, 1997, January 27)

He used this analogy as a preview to his argument and as an instruction about how the jury should respond to the evidence. After introducing the analogy, he never followed through with it during the rest of the closing argument by telling the jurors how each doubtful piece of testimony was filling in the picture of the corrupt investigation of the crime scene. Because the metaphor was not complete, it failed to produce a persuasive narrative.

Images and parallel cases. Another type of inferential form is based on social knowledge, that is, references to "statements about important values and beliefs adhered to by members of a society" (Jasinski, 1990, p. 60). To be persuasive, this type of inference connects with the audience members' sense of what they value and what they know usually happens in their social world with the arguments they are hearing in the courtroom. One common type of inference about social knowledge is the "imaginative" social inference, which links together what happens in a case with what audiences expect will happen in a similar set of circumstances (Jasinski, 1990, pp. 60–61). This kind of inference is created through imagery and parallel case.

Darden based his entire summation argument on the image of a fuse burning through a long history of domestic violence, a reference to the social knowledge of jurors about this contemporary problem. He used this image both to establish Simpson's motive of domestic abuse and to malign the character of the defendant. The inference was developed in a chronological sequence with this time bomb imagery:

> This relationship between this man and Nicole. . . . It is like the time bomb. . . . You see that the fuse is lit in 1989. . . . It is burning October 25 of 1993, and Nicole doesn't know it at the time, [but] she knows [later] he is going kill her. . . . There are certain things that can set him off, that can set that fuse to burning. . . . The fuse is becoming shorter. . . . It is the day of the recital . . . and the fuse got shorter. . . . After the

recital, the fuse is getting shorter and there is going to be an explosion. (TRC, 1995, September 26–27)

Darden's image was well developed because it pointed to a case theory and focused the evidence on the social theme of domestic abuse using a dramatic narrative that fit with images jurors likely would recall. The problem with the image was that it lacked the underlying evidence needed to make the theory compelling legal persuasion, only the 911 call and the testimony of Brown Simpson's sister. Moreover, some jurors had experienced domestic violence and did not feel it inevitably culminated in murder.

In the civil case, Petrocelli used imagery to describe the quick and violent killing of Brown Simpson. He explained:

> O. J. Simpson was a man in a state of total rage, armed with a 6-inch knife. He's a powerful man, over six feet, 200 pounds, played one of the most violent sports in American sports; and not only played it, but played it well, excelled at it. . . . This is a man of extraordinary strength and power. And here he is with a knife, enraged beyond belief, out of control. Think how much control a person has to have to be able to do this. He's up against a woman, 5' 5", 5' 6", 120 pounds. . . . Nicole died in about 15 seconds. All those wounds were delivered in rapid fire succession. And she died immediately from a gaping wound to her throat, and she bled profusely out on the ground. (TRL, 1997, January 21)

The defense should refute images by suggesting contrary images. However, Baker tried to show that the violence was so extensive that it must have been caused by "two assailants" (TRL, 1997, January 23), but he was unable to provide images or parallel cases that would show the likelihood of other assailants, nor was he able to deny the size and power differences between Simpson and his ex-wife Nicole. Further, if there were two assailants, he did not eliminate the possibility that one could have been Simpson.

Imagery should paint vivid pictures of what the crime scene looked like and thereby reveal a realistic context for jurors to use when interpreting the entire crime story. Even though there were no eye witnesses to the crime, Petrocelli, through his imagery, tried to make jurors see the crime as it happened. Images call forth audience members' knowledge about violence, showing them that this was an extremely bloody crime scene with a helpless female struggling against a strong and violent perpetrator. Imagery is effective because it aids memory and assists recall. For jurors, imagery likely assists them to "imagine an event in a particular way" and leads them "to think that event is more likely" than the ones portrayed in a competing story (Rieke & Stutman, 1990, p. 209).

Implications

The texts of the summations give some tentative answers to questions of interest to rhetorical and legal scholars. How are these summations affected by telelitigation? Which narrative is stronger and why? To what extent are summation narratives limited by the laws of evidence? What narratives fit with the stock stories of jurors and public audiences?

Telelitigation affected summations by increasing public attention about this segment of the trial, often by exaggerating the significance of this persuasive discourse. Attention to the final summations of both cases was high. More of the public watched the criminal summations than they did any other part of the trial besides the verdict. The media also gave extensive attention to the closing arguments in the civil case, reporting large segments of the content of the discourse and interpreting the feelings that observers in the courtroom had toward the summations. Additionally, the media coverage created expectations for the public that the attorneys would be dramatic, adversarial, and contentious, fighting for their clients in an effort to reach justice. This chapter shows that Cochran and Petrocelli, in fact, met these expectations through their passionate style and their argumentative content.

The answer to the second question seems clear. In the criminal case, the summations of Darden and Cochran fit standards for strong narratives because of their emphasis on character, conflict, and feeling. In the civil case, the summation of Petrocelli was the only complete narrative with a beginning, middle, and end. Clark and Scheck in the criminal trial and Blaiser in the civil trial presented evidence and gave jury instructions in ways that disconnected the chronology of the crime from the dramatic presentation of the narrative.

The answer to the third question is that the law of evidence had a major effect on the summations. In the criminal trial, prosecutors were hampered because they were unable to introduce all of the incidents of abuse or to use the diaries of Brown Simpson. This made their stories of domestic abuse more fragmented than Petrocelli's civil arguments because he was permitted to use this evidence. The evidence of over thirty pictures of Simpson wearing Bruno Magli shoes in the civil trial was compelling visual evidence not available to the criminal prosecutors. The defense attorneys in the civil case were severely limited in arguing their case about the malfeasance of police because they were not permitted to introduce evidence about Mark Fuhrman's perjury and his racism. The plaintiffs and the defense in the civil case had the advantage of Judge

Fujisaki's gag and silence orders and of having no live television coverage in the courtroom. Nonetheless, the frequent news conferences and commentaries extended and challenged the courtroom narratives and made it possible for media reports to seep into the jurors' perceptions. In the civil case, the plaintiffs had the advantage of observing what was wrong with the prosecution's case and of making repairs. Clearly, too, the standard of proof was weaker; the prosecutors in the criminal case had to prove their case beyond a reasonable doubt, and the plaintiffs only had to show preponderance of evidence.

The answer to the fourth question is that the verdicts indicate that the stock stories of the jurors differed significantly because of the location of the trial and the subsequent demographics of the jury. Moreover, the ethnically diverse jurors from Los Angeles in the criminal trial were more likely to accept Cochran's story of racism and conspiracy to frame Simpson than were the predominantly white jurors in Santa Monica. The verdicts in both cases, if they represented adherence to the stories presented in summation, may continue to reflect racial differences among the public, may demonstrate the way the jury system works, or may show that racial differences are exploited by the media to add an angle of social conflict to their stories about the trial. Civil juror alternate Dragolub Djurkovic said, "Americans witness the drama of this giant sports figure being accused and proved guilty, now we are further trying to complicate it and make it appear black and white. The jury, I am convinced, was color blind" (1997, February 11).

This chapter has identified the functions, characteristics, and uses of narrative in the summation of the criminal and civil trials of O. J. Simpson. These summation narratives supply an important set of texts for understanding the trials as a whole because they show connections for all of the testimony in their story form of the summation. Summation narratives provide an important focal point for telelitigation because they center on conflict, character, drama, and feeling. But these narratives must be understood in the context of the judges' instructions and the charges. The summations of the prosecution in the criminal trial were expected to prove beyond a reasonable doubt that Simpson was guilty. The counternarratives presented by Cochran and Scheck promoted reasonable doubt by emphasizing the character faults in Fuhrman, the deceit of Vannatter, and the ineptitude of the criminalist.

However, in the civil case, plaintiffs' summation established a preponderance of evidence, showing that the defendant committed battery with malicious intent against Nicole Brown Simpson and Ronald Goldman; and therefore, he was liable for their deaths. To do this, the plaintiffs established a persuasive narrative by juxtaposing the positive character traits of the victims against the negative traits of Simpson. Plaintiffs cast the defendant's mental and physical character traits in vivid negative imagery, showing that Simpson was a jealous, arrogant, and angry man who killed the victims quickly and violently in a fit of rage. They repeatedly portrayed Simpson as a liar who was covering up his mistakes.

The civil case allotted $12.5 million each to the estate of Nicole Brown Simpson and to the Goldman family for punitive damages and $8.5 million for compensatory damages. As of March 1999, Simpson has not paid any of this money to the plaintiffs. So the case goes on in the form of motions and challenges to the monetary verdict in the civil trial. New and emerging legal and media narratives will likely contribute to the ongoing conversation about the most telemediated trials of this century.

7

Jury Decision-Making Processes in the O. J. Simpson Criminal and Civil Trials

Ann Burnett

THE CELEBRITY STATUS OF THE DEFENDANT, the extensive media attention to the crime and Simpson's arrest, and the live television coverage of the preliminary hearing complicated the role of the criminal jury. On the one hand, the excessive media coverage led to the sequestration of the jurors, which, in turn, created psychological and social hardships for them. On the other hand, service on the criminal jury made them into temporary celebrities during and after the trial. Many jurors dismissed during the trial appeared on television and participated in media interviews. Some members of the jury that decided the criminal verdict appeared on television, wrote books, and were guests at a party at Simpson's estate to celebrate the "not guilty" verdict.

These jurors made large personal sacrifices to serve on the sequestered jury but received extensive criticism after they rendered the verdict. Profiles of the criminal jurors appear in appendix B.

As a result of the extensive problems with the criminal trial, the civil jurors were treated in a different manner. They were not sequestered, and the publicity about the trial was reduced by Judge Fujisaki's silence and gag orders. Nonetheless, they were conscious of the media because they were aware of the criticism of the criminal jurors' speedy verdict; had knowledge of key witnesses, such as Mark Fuhrman, who did not testify in the civil case; and recognized that key evidence missing from the criminal trial, such as O. J. Simpson's testimony and the pictures of him wearing the Bruno Magli shoes, was crucial to their deliberations. Although they did not seek media attention to the extent that the criminal jurors did, many appeared on television or agreed to interviews with major newspapers. Profiles of the civil jurors appear in appendix B.

When Johnnie Cochran labeled the Los Angeles Police Department's (LAPD) tactic of going after O. J. Simpson as a prime suspect in the murders of Nicole Brown Simpson and Ronald Goldman as a "rush to judgment," he was referring to the early investigations of the crime. However, the media attached a new meaning to the label when the jury in the criminal trial rendered its decision only four hours after beginning deliberations. In a trial lasting over nine months, the public was astonished that the decision was made so quickly. Critics argued that the verdict came at "breakneck speed" (*CNN*, 1995, October 4a) and that the jury was "bamboozled" (*MacNeil/Lehrer News Hour*, 1995, October 4). There also was an outcry for reform of the jury system.

In contrast, on February 11, 1997, the jury for the O. J. Simpson civil trial awarded punitive and compensatory damages. Even though the decision on punitive damages was not unanimous, the jury in the civil trial was not criticized as harshly as the criminal jury. While some individuals accused the predominately white panel of making a racist decision, one of the jurors responded that "people who say that 'are being racist themselves.'" In fact, to most individuals, the results of the civil trial "evened up the books" (*National Public Radio*, 1997, February 14).

Now that time has passed, and the jurors in both trials have had time to reflect upon and to report their decisions and reactions to the trials, it is time to step back from the criticisms to praise and to evaluate the juries' decision-making processes. The purpose of this chapter is to examine (1) the factors the jurors considered as part of their decisions, (2) the moment of personal decision and the amount of time spent in deliberation, and (3) the procedures by which the jurors made their decisions—the decision-making process itself.

A few cautions ought to be observed concerning my analysis. First, this investigation of the juries' decision-making processes relies on the jurors' reports from their books and from their interviews with the media. Self-report data can be skewed, especially when, as the criminal jurors found shortly after leaving sequestration, the media was sharply critical of their decision, causing the jurors quickly to defend themselves (*National Public Radio*, 1997, February 14). In addition, the jurors were paid for their interviews, and they were not questioned systematically. In fact, after the civil trial, eight of the jurors and one alternate juror did participate in a press conference, but they did not appear on morning news programs or talk shows. To date, no civil juror has written a book about the experience. Therefore, some of the analysis of the civil trial is dependent on others' observations. However, self-report data, posttrial interviews, and observations are the only way we can learn about these jurors' important decisions, and we must make use of the information they have provided. I collected all available juror comments, so my description will be as well rounded and accurate as possible.

Second, this chapter is rhetorical in nature. I was more concerned with the gist of the jurors' comments than with the number of comments made in a particular "category." Since I wanted jurors to tell their own stories of the decision-making process, I have included numerous quotations, allowing the reader to gain the best possible "feel" for the process. Yet, because of this rhetorical approach, not all jury decision-making theory is covered here.

Factors Influencing the Jurors' Decisions

Several factors influenced the jurors in these two cases, including the evidence, the attorneys, the defendant, and the charges. These factors were mentioned specifically by jurors in their posttrial responses.

Evidence

In general, studies of jury decision making have indicated that jurors assess the evidence in relation to the law. For example, Reskin and Visher (1986) discovered that jurors appropriately use evidence when assessing a defendant's guilt or innocence, although they are likely to select which evidence they use, preferring "hard evidence" over eyewitness testimony (pp. 437–38). Burnett Pettus (1990) found that jurors seriously consider all evidence, but they are particularly influenced by ineffective evidence.

Overwhelmingly, the O. J. Simpson criminal jurors noted that evidence played an important role in their decisions. The day of the verdict in the criminal trial, juror Brenda Moran noted on the *MacNeil/Lehrer News Hour* (1995, October 4): "We [weighed] the evidence. We were fair. It was a matter of evidence." A later CNN interview (1995, October 29) reveals the same kind of reliance on evidence. Reporter Jim Hill asked both Moran and Gina Rosborough, "Was there any piece of prosecution evidence, any compelling piece of prosecution evidence, that you believed?" Moran responded, "Well, not really." Hill then asked, "Can't think of anything right now?" and Rosborough replied, "No, not right off hand."

Evidence played a key role in the civil trial as well. In fact, several news articles reported the jurors as saying that Simpson was guilty "beyond a reasonable doubt, even though the burden in a civil trial is proof by a preponderance of evidence" (Perlman, 1997, February 11, p. A03; "Jury Socks O. J. with Huge Tab," 1997, February 11). On *ABC World News Tonight* (1997, February 10), reporter Cynthia McFadden said that jurors indicated "it wasn't a very difficult decision" since the plaintiffs could prove their case even using the higher burden of proof standard required in a criminal matter.

Jurors in the civil case focused on Simpson's testimony regarding the evidence presented against him. In their press conference (*KNBC News*, 1997, February 10), one female juror couldn't believe how Simpson dealt with the evidence. She said, "He would change his mind. First, he said he cut his finger, which were obviously fingernail gouges from the attack. He said he received those from roughhousing with his young son and then later . . . he changed his mind and said he cut his hand when he was in Chicago in a hotel room." This same evidence bothered a male juror who concluded, "I find it hard to believe that someone the day after cannot remember a scar-producing cut." One of the female jurors observed differences between Simpson's interview with police and what he later said in the trial. She noted, "For me, the inconsistency between the interview that he had with the officers the day after the incident happened to the pretrial testimony, to the criminal trial testimony, and to how the plaintiffs brought it all together. . . [these factors] showed the inconsistency throughout. He really should have gotten his stories straight before he got up there." Not only did the civil trial jurors hear different evidence than the criminal trial jurors, they heard Simpson's version of what this evidence meant, and in most cases, they were unimpressed with his explanations.

In fact, upon comparing the evidence in both trials, attorney Robert Gottlieb (1997, February 6) concluded that, regardless of race, if the criminal jury had heard the same evidence as the civil jury—if it were presented in the same manner, by the same attorneys, with the same judge—"there is little doubt that the verdict would have been 'guilty'" (p. A49).

Demeanor consists of attributes and performance, and this quality affects jurors' decisions. For example, Burnett Pettus (1990) found that when jurors discuss evidence, they are likely to talk about the witnesses in terms both of their attributes and their performances. In line with research, some of the jurors' comments in the criminal trial focused on witness credibility. For example, Brenda Moran recalled that detective "Vannatter's statement that Simpson wasn't a suspect when the police went to his house wasn't believable, and that harmed his credibility" (Perlman, 1995, October 5, p. A01). Armanda Cooley (1995) claimed that L.A. county chief medical examiner Lakshamanan "was one of my favorite witnesses. He was protective of his department, but he still verified all the errors that were made by his department" (Cooley, Bess, & Rubin-Jackson, 1995, p. 115 [all subsequent citations from Cooley, Bess, and Rubin-Jackson will be from this same source and designated only with the date and page number]). During this long criminal trial, some witness testimony was recalled simply because it stood out either as especially strong or as flawed.

In the civil trial, jurors indicated that Simpson's testimony lacked credibility. Most jurors felt that Simpson's credibility diminished when he denied ever hitting his ex-wife—a denial he made despite his plea of no contest to spousal battery in 1989 and despite the bruises jurors saw in pictures of Nicole Brown taken shortly after the attack ("Jury Socks O. J. with Huge Tab," 1997, February 11, p. A1). A male alternate juror recalled, "O. J. ruined his credibility so fast on the stand that later on when he might [have been able to] answer something truthfully . . . we really didn't know what to believe and what not to believe. Some obvious things that he was saying that are not so. The guy was lying on the stand" (*KNBC News*, 1997, February 10). However, an alternate juror expressed a different view: "He was shaky in some parts, but I felt he was pretty credible" (Perlman, 1997, February 11, p. A03).

Other comments in the criminal trial reflected evaluations of witness behavior. For example, Bess (1995) recalled, "You're looking at all these people. You're waiting. You can watch their mannerisms, their expressions. You got eye-to-eye contact. You're waiting for them to tell you and look at you" (p. 106). Of Kato Kaelin, Cooley (1995) remarked, "I must admit the first thing I thought when he came to the witness stand is he must be a drug dealer because he looked like he was high . . ." (p. 108). When talking about the primary DNA witness for the prosecution, Rubin-Jackson (1995) said, "She talked down to us like we were illiterates. I didn't like that, but the woman knew what she was talking about" (p. 114). Sheila Woods noted that police witnesses made a negative impression on her. She concluded, "Philip Vannatter and Mark Fuhrman were poor witnesses; neither one ever made eye contact with the jurors" (Woods, 1995, October 7).

Civil jurors emphasized their impression of Simpson as a witness. One juror concluded that Simpson did not help his own case because his reactions seemed so rehearsed. Zamichow, Malnic, and Gold (1997, February 11) reported that "[a]mong the most damaging evidence against Simpson, many of the jurors agreed, was his own vague and inconsistent performance on the stand" (pp. A1, A20).

In the process of evaluating evidence, researchers have found that jurors tend to construct "stories" or narratives of what occurred. Pennington and Hastie (1990) argue that jurors go through a three-step process. First, they try to make sense of all the evidence together to determine what is "true." Next, they attempt to apply the instructions. Finally, they attempt to match the "story" with the possible verdicts to find the "best fit" (Pennington & Hastie, 1981a; Pennington & Hastie, 1981b; Pennington & Hastie, 1986; Pennington & Hastie, 1990, p. 95). Holstein (1985) and Burnett Pettus (1990, p. 93) also found that jurors attempt to determine "what really happened," filling in gaps in order for the story to make sense. In addition, Davis and colleagues (1977) discovered that jurors deliberate longer when the consequences to the victim do not fit with the potential sentence, an issue that seemed to be inapplicable in both Simpson trials.

When jurors in the O. J. Simpson criminal trial discussed the reasons for their decision, it appears that they attempted to construct a coherent story, as suggested by the research. They were determined to figure out what really happened, and they did so by relying on hunches or guesses to fill in the gaps created by incomplete evidence. Their main areas of concern were the bloody glove, the DNA tests on the blood, and the method by which the LAPD investigated the crime scene.

When the prosecution asked Simpson to try on the glove—the one discovered at the crime scene that purportedly belonged to him—in the presence of the jury, he strained and pulled, and apparently it did not fit. In his closing argument, Cochran argued that "if it doesn't fit, you must acquit." Brenda Moran, in constructing her view of the story, said, "The gloves on O. J. appeared short on O. J.'s hand. They seemed too tight to even clench or make a fist, to even hold the knife" (*CNN*, 1995, October 29). In response to this same evidence, Cooley (1995) remarked, "Now, when I saw that demonstration [using the glove], I thought, 'why in the hell didn't the prosecution try that glove on somebody else that had the same hands as O. J. before they allowed him to get out here and do this?' I was sick when I saw they didn't fit because I just thought for sure that they were going to fit" (p. 125).

The jurors also were stymied regarding the lack of Simpson's blood at the scene, the way the LAPD handled the blood, and the DNA tests. For example, Rubin-Jackson (1995) explained, "I had problems understanding how they found the blood smears on the console of the Bronco. Why were they seen after they had torn the inside of this car completely up?" (p. 122). Moran remembered, "It was a long pathway, and where the glove was found, it was covered with blood, but the pathway had no blood, no blood on the leaves, on the ground, nowhere down that pathway. So why was there so much blood on that glove and not a drip of blood on the ground anywhere around in that back way?" (*MacNeil/Lehrer News Hour*, 1995, October, 4). Bess (1995) recalled jurors' concerns that Simpson's blood may have been planted when she noted, "The fact that it had not degraded and it had more DNA in it than most of the evidence they had collected, that was the problem we had" (p. 119).

Due to the actions of Mark Fuhrman and the LAPD, the jurors generally had a difficult time constructing a story in favor of the prosecution. First, Fuhrman, one of the primary detectives at the crime scene, lied about calling African American people "niggers." The jurors, in turn, thought he was a liar and discounted his testimony entirely. Cooley (1995) said she believed his early testimony, but when Fuhrman was questioned about using the term *nigger*, she concluded, "The one lie that he should have just never said was when they were asking him, 'Have you ever used the n-word?' He would have been a lot better off" (p. 105).

Jurors also had a tough time believing testimony of other LAPD officers. For example, Rubin-Jackson (1995) recalled, "They weren't straight with us about why they chose to do what they did, and that made us suspect everything else we heard from them. . . . So, from jump street, I'm very, very concerned why you would neglect what you're supposed to do to try to solve a crime, which is gather and protect the evidence" (pp. 100–101). Moran (*CNN*, 1995, October 29) was particularly troubled that the lead detective, Philip Vannatter, walked "around with [Simpson's] blood in his pocket for a couple of hours." Rosborough (*CNN*, 1995, October 29) remembered, "Vannatter and Fuhrman may have planted the evidence. Given this fact they may have perjured themselves; therefore, I couldn't believe their testimony." Rubin-Jackson (1995) focused on the same testimony and concluded, "They just botched up, messed up, and when they tried to cover up for themselves, it just got out of control" (p. 103).

The story that criminal jurors constructed was one of reasonable doubt. They questioned the amount of blood on the glove and on Simpson's belongings, given the nature of the killings. The gloves that were supposed to place Simpson at the scene of the crime did not fit him. The primary detectives who seemed determined to pin the crime on Simpson were, at best, careless and, at worst, ruthless. The presumed carelessness was evident to jurors when one detective carried around a vial of blood for hours, and jurors perceived ruthlessness through their alleged conspiracy to frame Simpson by planting evidence. In addition, when one of the primary investigators was caught perjuring himself, the jurors found they could not render a guilty verdict. Interestingly, some jurors felt that Simpson was involved, but they could not create the story they needed to convict. Cooley (1995) remarked, "I felt that there was a lot of evidence that pointed to Mr. Simpson's guilt—for example, the blood. There was no question in my mind that it was Mr. Simpson's" (pp. 193–94). Michael Knox, an excused juror, argued that Simpson was at the crime scene. "That was indisputable. Without a doubt he was definitely there. The shoe print; the gloves I do believe were definitely his. The fiber in the Bronco and all the other evidence definitely put him at the crime scene" (Cooley, Bess & Rubin-Jackson, 1995, p. 195).

In the civil trial, the jurors placed O. J. Simpson at the scene of the crime because of his Bruno Magli shoes. They found that the "distinctive shoes [were] similar to those worn by the killer" ("Jury Socks O. J. with Huge Tab," 1997, February 11, p. A1). The more than thirty-one photographs presented "concrete proof that Simpson was a liar" (Gottlieb, 1997, February 6, p. A49), and similar to the manner in which jurors in the criminal case viewed Fuhrman, they could not believe a liar in this case. Only the alternate juror felt that the photographs were inconclusive and that the blood and other evidence was planted (Perlman, 1997, February 11, p. A03). In addition, jurors stated that Simpson was not able to explain the cuts found on his hand after the killings ("Jury Socks O. J. with Huge Tab," 1997, February 11, p. A1). They also found Simpson's denials of physically assaulting his ex-wife difficult to believe because of the contradictory evidence presented in court (Perlman, 1997, February 11, p. A03). The civil jurors, as the criminal jurors had done before them, constructed a coherent story. Only this time, evidence about the shoes, the cuts on Simpson's hand, and Simpson's abuse of his ex-wife wove a narrative of liability.

By contrast, the jurors in the criminal trial had difficulty constructing a story of Simpson's domestic violence. The defense strategy was to characterize evidence of domestic violence as merely being "domestic discord." In this context, it is interesting to note that five of the twelve jurors who decided the verdict in the criminal trial indicated in their jury questionnaires that using physical force against a family member was sometimes justified (Toobin, 1996, pp. 66–67). Given the jury's disregard for this evidence, it appears that Cochran's portrayal succeeded. He made all the domestic violence evidence sound just like a family matter that did not need to be aired in court. Goldberg (1996) reports that at least one female juror in the criminal trial questioned the severity of the abuse since Brown Simpson returned home the day after Simpson threw her and her sister Denise out of the house (p. 348). Jurors often question how women can return to abusive situations if the behavior is truly abusive, and it is not surprising that at least one juror accepted this classic defense argument.

Attorneys

Although there is little research suggesting that jurors make their decisions based on their reactions to the attorneys in the cases, Burnett Pettus (1990) found that attorneys influence the jurors and are evaluated like the witnesses in terms of attributes and performance (p. 93). In her study, the attorneys who were evaluated most favorably ultimately "won" their cases.

In the Simpson criminal trial, the jurors commented on the attorneys' attributes. For example, Rubin-Jackson (1995) remembered, "[Darden] . . . was very moody. He never could look you in the eye, either" (pp.

88–89). Bess (1995) observed that "on the prosecution side, Marcia would just get too frustrated. I'm . . . watching all her sighs and that to me was a sign of weakness" (p. 97). Moran (*MacNeil/Lehrer News Hour*, 1995, October 4) offered a different assessment. She concluded, "Actually, I liked the prosecution. I really did, but they just didn't convince me."

Jurors also remarked about the performances of the attorneys. Michael Knox (1995) saw the courtroom presentations as high drama when he said, "Man, what a show! Talk about power and charisma. You don't nod off when Johnnie Cochran, F. Lee Bailey, or Carl Douglas take the floor . . . Johnnie and F. Lee have different styles, but they're both great orators" (pp. 261–62, 264). Cooley (1995) reacted to Marcia Clark's closing argument: "Jesus Christ. Please. Somebody help me. Get these people to understand that I am not totally illiterate here. That we don't need this" (p. 137). She also observed the defense as engaging in one respect but insulting in another: "When Johnnie Cochran put that hat on his head, everybody wanted to die. You could see stomachs literally moving. He's looking like a damn fool standing there. . . . The only thing he could have done for me was sit his ass down. There's no need for you to get out here for me and do seal acts" (p. 139).

While the jurors in the civil trial did not report their reactions to the attorneys, the media pointed out that Daniel Petrocelli, attorney for the plaintiffs, made a positive impression in the courtroom. Calling him "Mr. Simpson's courtroom nemesis" (Cornwell, 1997, February 7, p. 12), observers found that he was in control, that he tried the case in "streamline fashion," and that he was "properly outraged" (Gottlieb, 1997, February 6, p. A49). If jurors respond to attorneys as they did in Burnett Pettus' study (1990), predictably, they would side with the attorney who had more positive attributes and a more positive performance. In this case it was Petrocelli.

Defendant

There is no consensus about the defendant's role in the trial. In a landmark study, Landy and Aronson (1969) found that the attractiveness of the defendant made a difference in the severity of the sentence imposed. Miller and colleagues (1986) argued that defendants received more lenient treatment when they had higher status and when jurors perceived this status. While Burnett Pettus (1990) found that although jurors noticed the behavior of the defendant in the trial, this was not a significant factor in their decisions. However, Simpson's celebrity status may have altered these findings.

Jurors in the Simpson criminal trial offered few comments about Simpson. They said they tried not to establish any eye contact with him (Cooley, Bess & Rubin-Jackson, 1995, p. 131), but they did not comment about his status or prestige. Jurors report in their books and interviews that they considered Simpson a "typical" defendant on trial and that his prestige and attractiveness had little to do with the verdict. As Rubin-Jackson (1995) stated, "If they had proven to me that he had done it, I would have found him guilty" (p. 185).

However, in the criminal trial some indication exists that Simpson's celebrity status was difficult for some jurors to get past. Goldberg (1996) recalls that in one of the postverdict interviews, one male juror asked, "How could a man with everything commit murder?" (p. 352).

Jurors in the civil trial had the opportunity to observe Simpson's testimony. According to the media, Simpson appeared nervous at times and arrogant at other times during cross-examination (Gottlieb, 1997, February 6). The posttrial interviews revealed that several jurors in fact thought Simpson was nervous and rehearsed (Zamichow, Malnic, & Gold, 1997, February 11, pp. Al, A20). They claimed this behavior raised questions about the truth of his testimony and made them discount some of what he said.

Seriousness of the Charge

Some scholars have investigated the relationship between the seriousness of the charge and the final verdict. For example, Freedman and others (1994) concluded that there is no relationship between the charge and the verdict. It appears that the jurors did not consider the outcome when making their decisions. There were no comments suggesting that Simpson was acquitted because of the severity of the penalty or charge in the criminal trial, nor is there any indication that the complaint filed in civil court had any effect on the final verdict in that trial.

Moment of Personal Decision and Length of Deliberations

A great deal of evidence exists that suggests jurors make their decisions prior to deliberation. Some scholars have discovered that jurors make up their minds as early as opening statements (Bridgeman & Marlowe, 1979; Leigh, 1984; Burnett Pettus, 1990). Others (Sonaike, 1978; R. J. Simon, 1980) have found that jurors rarely change their minds in deliberation. In a recent study, Sandys and Dillehay (1995) concluded that deliberations serve a useful purpose as jurors can be influenced prior to taking the first straw vote. Therefore, the juror's initial inclination might not match his or her vote in the initial straw ballot.

There is no indication in the civil trial showing when jurors made their decisions. The foreperson said that the jurors examined every bit of evidence, because they wanted to have clear consciences and they knew that their findings would be scrutinized by the media. Deliberations were longer in the civil trial than in the criminal trial partly because jurors had to determine monetary figures. In the punitive phase of deliberations, they did not achieve consensus, which also prolonged deliberations.

By contrast, it appears that many jurors in the criminal trial had made their decisions before deliberation. For example, Cooley (1995) recounted her decision making in this way: "Actually, I felt that Mr. Simpson was guilty when the prosecutors were putting on their case. [But] one of the crucial moments where I changed my thinking was when I heard evidence about the glove" (p. 195). However, Bess and Rubin-Jackson do not acknowledge making up their minds prior to deliberation. Bess (1995) recalled, "I had ups and downs quite a few times . . ." (p. 196), and Rubin-Jackson (1995) indicated, "I had never really formed an opinion during the case" (p. 196).

The length of the deliberation also suggests that many of the jurors in the criminal case already knew how they were going to vote. In this case, the Simpson jurors took a straw vote but did not deliberate beforehand. Comments after the trial by Beatrice Wilson suggest that they already had their decisions made: "We had almost a year. We was in there nine months. All the whole time we was there we had plenty of time to think" (Howlett, 1995, October 5, p. 5A). Moran (*MacNeil/Lehrer News Hour*, 1995, October 4) sarcastically remarked, "We've taken this case serious for nine months. We didn't take it serious for four hours."

While studies have not been done correlating the length of deliberations with predeliberation decisions, it is possible that the actual deliberation time was relatively short because most jurors already knew how they were going to vote. An investigation of the actual decision-making process will provide additional insight.

The Group Decision-Making Process

Most research on jury decision making has focused on the individual juror. Many of the studies deal with how the juror processes information. For example, Kaplan (1977), utilizing group polarization theory, found that after group discussions, judgments of a defendant's guilt become more pronounced. With regard to information integration, jurors average new information, as opposed to adding information (Moore & Gump, 1995); jurors adjust their opinions toward the new message they hear (Boster, Hunter & Hale, 1991); and jurors weigh the evidence in comparison to the decision criteria (Thomas & Hogue, 1976).

Another prominent area of focus for the study of jury decision making is that of majority influence. While Foss (1976) discovered that jurors are allowed equal participation in the process, Tanford and Penrod (1986) concluded that the majority tends to prevail. MacCoun (1990) found that jurors are influenced by pressures to conform and by the number and persuasiveness of arguments presented, and Boyll (1991) suggested that "the more cohesive the group is or the more attracted the person is to the group, the greater the conformity" (p. 180). It would be difficult to apply these research findings to either Simpson jury since, at this point, we know only some of what occurred in the criminal deliberations, and we know even less about the civil ones. However, a summary of what jurors reported about the criminal deliberations might serve as a beginning point to draw some conclusions about their decision making.

The jury began deliberations at approximately 9:20 A.M. During the first forty minutes, jurors elected Armanda Cooley as foreperson, and they attempted to establish a procedure. At 10:00 A.M., the foreperson called for a straw vote in which jurors wrote "guilty" or "not guilty" on small slips of paper, similar to what occurred in *Twelve Angry Men*. The jurors placed their ballots in a candy jar; Carrie Bess tallied the votes on the blackboard, and the vote was double-checked: 10–2.

After the straw vote was taken, David Aldana (1995, October 10) said that some of the panel still had unresolved questions. After some prodding, one minority juror, Anise Aschenbach, admitted that she was one of the two; the other minority juror never identified him/herself. While some of the jurors wanted the two minority jurors to explain their positions, they declined. Instead, Sheila Woods said minority jurors "listened to the other 10 explain why there was reasonable doubt" (Woods, 1995, October 7). In doing so, however, Bess (1995) indicated that no one spoke out. She said, "I feel he is guilty because of such and such a thing" (p. 154). The clerk had wheeled in a cart of notebooks and charts; each juror took a notebook and looked through it. If a question was asked, Bess (1995) said that the person with the appropriate notebook answered it— "it was like brainstorming" (p. 154). Aldana (1995, October 10) said, "There was constant, nonstop discussion" (p. 3A).

The jury was confused about the testimony of Allan Park (the limousine driver). Jurors checked their notes, which according to Heuer and Penrod (1994), do not overemphasize or distort evidence and become a useful, accurate record of the trial. Although Cooley (1995) indicated that their "notes were basically all consistent" (p. 160), there was still some confusion concerning the time element, so jurors requested that Park's trial testimony be read back. However, before the court had a chance to reconvene for the transcript reading, one juror observed that the jury had some reasonable doubt (p. 163). The jury took another secret vote, and this time it was unanimous. Cooley (1995) polled each juror to make sure that he or she was satisfied. She asked, "Are you going to be able to sleep tonight? Is there something on your mind that we need to stop and discuss that will help you know that you have made the right decision?" (p. 168). She concluded, "You know, you've got to live with yourself. But everyone was sure" (p. 163). When asked how they changed the minority's opinions, Moran (*MacNeil/Lehrer News Hour*, 1995, October 4) argued that "they turned themselves around. We talked about it inside the court. They had a perfect opportunity to stick with what they thought, but we discussed it.... And they changed their vote." After they notified the bailiff, the jurors thought they would go back to the courtroom to reveal their decision, but instead, they were sent back to the hotel. The verdict was announced the following day.

Was the decision-making process effective, or was the minority pressured by the majority? An examination of the jurors' accounts suggests that the process was healthy and nonintimidating. Cooley seemed to be an excellent leader/foreperson. However, this question is difficult to answer since we must rely only on the jurors' recollections.

What other factors may have contributed to their relatively quick decision? The cohesiveness of the jurors, as discussed by Boyll (1991), might have been a factor because they had become well-acquainted during the trial; pressure might have been placed on some to come to agreement. The jurors might have wanted to avoid a hung jury after having spent nine months in trial. In addition, the fact that the jurors were about to go home might have brought about a quicker verdict. However, in the books and interviews, there is no indication that group cohesiveness or excitement about going home made the decision-making process any quicker. Unlike jurors in Sandys and Dillehay's study (1995), the jurors in the criminal case did not discuss the evidence prior to the straw vote. It is possible that the distribution of votes would have been different if it had been taken after some discussion. Because the jurors voted without discussion, it appears that they made up their minds before deliberation, and the deliberation merely reinforced their individual opinions.

Conclusions

Telelitigation affected the jurors in both trials in the following ways: their different treatment, especially sequestration versus nonsequestration, by the respective judges; the presence of courtroom cameras in the criminal trial in contrast to their absence in the civil case; the speed of the second trial in comparison to the first; and the length of deliberation in the second trial compared to the first. Although the media spectacle continued throughout both trials, the impact on jurors differed, perhaps because the civil trial judge benefited from the mistakes of the judge in the criminal trial. And the jurors in the civil trial learned from the public criticism of the criminal jury that jurors in telemediated trials need to show the public that they spend time deliberating and weighing the evidence. Regardless of the differences, both panels of jurors seemed to take their responsibilities seriously by valuing the opinions of other jurors.

By examining the books, interviews, and observations provided on the Simpson jurors, readers can gain an understanding of the decision-making processes that occurred in both trials. In general, the jurors' behaviors were consistent with a majority of social scientific research. They appear to have based their decisions on the evidence, particularly the ineffective or nonexistent evidence. In the criminal trial, jurors constructed a story about the murders in which they had a reasonable doubt. In the civil trial, jurors decided that a preponderance of evidence showed that Simpson committed the murders.

Most of the criminal trial jurors made their decisions during the trial, even though they were instructed to wait until deliberations to decide. Ironically, despite the cautions, they defended their short deliberation time by pointing out that they had been thinking about the case and making their decisions for the previous nine months. Their decision-making process was characteristic of a typical jury deliberation, with votes taken and the first-ballot decision becoming the final verdict.

However, it is important to note that in my attempt to examine the Simpson juries' decision making, I have, like them, constructed my own "story"—a narrative of their experiences based on bits and pieces of their reflections. One of the limitations, yet also one of the beauties, of a rhetorical study is that the rhetor is able to construct her own reality, utilizing the materials she needs to create the clearest picture. Perhaps others who study the books and interviews will derive different conclusions.

Two additional observations about the criminal jury are consistent with other findings about juries (Myers, 1979; Burnett Pettus, 1990). First, I do not believe that the jurors discussed this case with anyone, particularly with each other, prior to deliberation. Knox (1995) remarked, "Judge Ito had warned over and over that we must NEVER discuss the trial. No one ever broke that rule, to my knowledge" (p. 185). Cooley (1995) said, "The only other things [other than jokes] we would comment on would be whether that day in court was a good day or a bad day. This was the extent of discussing the trial. Certainly we did not discuss anything concerning guilt or innocence" (p. 84). All jurors who were questioned about this issue were adamant that they did not discuss the trial, including during conjugal visits, in which they suspected their rooms were bugged. Their ability to abide by the admonition is admirable, considering that they were sequestered from their families and friends for nine months, and the only thing they had in common was this highly stressful case.

The criminal jurors were sincere and took their jobs seriously. For example, Moran (*MacNeil/Lehrer News Hour*, 1995, October 4) concluded, "My heart went out for the Goldman family. My heart went out for the Brown family. My heart went out for the Simpson family. I felt bad for everyone, but I wasn't brought here on feelings. I was brought here to find out who murdered these victims, and that's exactly what we did as a jury." Knox (1995) stated, "I remember how, after the initial thrill of being chosen for the O. J. Simpson jury had worn off, I started to think of the tremendous responsibility we all had" (p. 40). And Bess (1995) recalled, "I tried extremely hard to keep all the evidence in mind and tried to weigh it appropriately" (p. 130).

Was the first Simpson verdict a "rush to judgment?" Admittedly, the jury reached its decision quickly, given the length of the trial and the fact that many of the jurors basically admitted that they made their decisions early. Many of us would have taken some comfort if they had poured over the trial notebooks and more thoroughly discussed every bit of testimony. Perhaps that is why many people were more comfortable with the decision in the civil case. However, in terms of both juries, their memories and personal notes, in conjunction with their perception of careful reasoning and their apparent reliance on the evidence, must lead one to a deeper appreciation and understanding, not only of the work they did, but also of the jury system in general.

Editors' Note

As Burnett explained, one of the limitations and yet one of the advantages of rhetorical studies is the ability to derive differing interpretations from the same data. We differ from Burnett's interpretation in a significant way. We question whether the reasoning of jurors in the criminal case was indeed as well thought out as Burnett suggests. In particular, we are concerned that the jurors may not have understood the exceedingly imprecise standard of proof instruction. Several jury researchers have addressed the ambiguity of the beyond-reasonable-doubt standard (for example, B. J. Shapiro, 1986, and Simon & Mahan, 1971) and recognized how jurors well may have differing decision thresholds for determining how much reasonable doubt is enough to vote "not guilty."

Some posttrial interviews point to jurors' having begun the deliberation process by reviewing their doubts and then agreeing on a verdict when they felt they had amassed enough doubt to have reasonable doubt. Aldana and Crawford (Goldberg, 1996, quotes their *Larry King Live* interviews) explained that it was not necessary to review all the evidence because the jurors all agreed there was reasonable doubt. This jury apparently began by formulating its own question and then attempting to answer it, "Do we have any doubts?" Once jurors reached a threshold of doubt that they considered to be reasonable doubt, they promptly voted "not guilty." As Burnett reports, jurors reached a decision on doubt so fast that, even though they had requested the Allan Park testimony be re-read to them, they chose not to wait for the testimony to be read back.

By approaching deliberations in this fashion, the focus was drawn away from all the proof of guilt that the prosecution had amassed. Simulated trial research shows that some juries choose a reverse approach that seems to focus on all the evidence of guilt rather than on doubt. Such juries formulate their working questions as follows: "What proof do we have that the defendant committed the crime? What proof do we have that the defendant did not commit the crime? Do we have reasonable doubt?" By first enumerating the bases of guilt, juries keep the focus on the weight of the evidence calling for a guilty vote. The discussion usually stays centered longer around "You think he's guilty because . . ." than around "I think he's not guilty because . . ."

This type of deliberation takes longer and thereby emphasizes the elements of guilt. However, if jurors start from the basis of trying to ascertain doubts, there is substantially less discussion of guilt factors.

Defense lawyers, of course, subtly encourage jurors to search for doubt rather than to review all the ways their clients might be guilty. Defense attorneys begin the process in *voir dire* when they talk with jurors about the standard of proof. One favorite tactic is to ask jurors how they would vote if they just had a suspicion the defendant was guilty. Obviously, the attorney is hoping for a "not guilty" response, and if she does not receive it, she proceeds to coach the prospective juror on presumption of innocence, that the defendant is presumed to be not guilty unless and until the prosecution can prove its case beyond a reasonable doubt. The second-level *voir dire* question talks about possibility: "How would you vote if you thought it is possible that my client committed the crime? Is possibility enough?" Once again, if the juror fails to reply "not guilty," the defense attorney focuses on presumption of innocence. Finally, the defense attorney asks, "How would you vote if you thought my client probably did it?" and then lectures any jurors who say "probability is enough" that proof beyond a reasonable doubt requires more than probably believing the defendant committed the crime.

Although we have no indication that the defense in the Simpson criminal trial used such a tactic in *voir dire*, it is clear that the defense concentrated on enumerating doubts. But the defense went even further and argued for jury nullification (discussed in chapter 8). When Cochran urged jurors to "police the police. You police them through your verdict. You are the ones to send a message. Nobody else is going to do it in this society" (TRC, 1995, September 28), he empowered jurors to follow the law of community rather than the law provided by Judge Ito. In criminal trials, on the one hand, juries indeed have the power to nullify or give leniency. In civil trials, on the other hand, the court can set aside a jury's verdict by ordering a new trial or by reducing or increasing the amount of damages determined by jurors. Wallace D. Loh (1985) describes jury nullification in this way:

> This power implies the right to set aside the judge's instructions on the applicable law as well as upon the evidence presented in order to reach an acquittal verdict based upon the popular sense of fairness and wisdom of the common man. The jury can ameliorate the harshness of the criminal law by interjecting communal morality into its secret deliberations. (p. 17)

Ito erred in allowing Cochran to make an overt nullification argument, but the jury may well have moved toward nullification even without the explicit argument. After all, Simpson was a sympathetic defendant and a celebrity. Further, it is difficult to separate the decision-making process where jurors focus on doubt rather than on evidence of guilt in cases where jurors look to nullify. In both instances, jurors give less weight to the prosecution's evidence.

The jury may have chosen to nullify based on the racial arguments Cochran provided. All we have are hints that racial aspects were significant. For example, Goldberg (1996) reports that shortly after the verdict was read, "One of the male African-American jurors gave a black power salute to Simpson" (p. 354). Burnett is correct when she discusses the limitations of self-reports. We may never know whether this jury chose to nullify. Criminal juries do not have to explain the reasons for their decisions. Nor can their acquittals ever be reversed.

8

Race and Money Matter:
Justice on Trial
Ann M. Gill

THE SPECTACLES OF THE TWO SIMPSON TRIALS allowed the media to
set the agenda by establishing the issues about which the public thought
and spoke. This chapter explains how the issues surfaced in the trials,
what the media contributed to the discussion of these issues, and how
these issues contributed to commonsense understandings of the trial process and verdicts. The media commentary in the trials' wakes, which has
been almost as overwhelming as the media coverage of the trials, includes
both "reaction and meta-reaction" (Wesson, 1996, p. 949). Commentators typically form two conclusions about the trials: (1) the rich and famous can get away with murder (Keeva, 1995, p. 78; Anastaplo, 1995);
and (2) race, which affects the functioning of the criminal justice system
in many ways, once again was a deciding factor in trial outcome ("Unreasonable Doubt," 1995, October 23). The defendant's wealth was particularly apparent in the criminal trial because of the depth of the legal
and investigatory teams assembled in Simpson's defense. Race, an underlying tension in nearly every aspect of society, surfaced in media coverage of the criminal trial.

Analysis of the roles of wealth and race should go beyond the carapace of law, which makes trials appear to be neutral and color-blind
searches for truth conducted with objectively applied procedural rules.
Close analysis of the Simpson trials cracks that carapace. No longer can
Americans interpret the law only in terms of rationality. The Simpson
cases supplant the traditional legal notion of rationality with a form of
commonsense justice that is actually objective, universal, and quite un-
impeachable. This chapter (1) identifies the celebrity quality of Simpson's

trials, (2) describes the role of wealth and race, and (3) explains the connections between rationality and commonsense justice.

Tale of Two Celebrity Trials

People v. Simpson was extraordinary in every aspect—the famous defendant; the "dream team" defense; the huge amount of money spent by both sides; the delayed and carefully orchestrated announcement of the verdict; the fascination the trial held for the public, both in the United States and in other countries; and the effects of the trial on public perception and discourse. In many respects, though, these were rather unremarkable murders. It was the defendant's celebrity status that turned this into the trial of the century—catapulting it into popular media, consciousness, and culture. Although other trials have been televised, none attracted the media and audience equal to that of *People v. Simpson* (see chapter 1). For example, on October 3, 1995, an estimated 150 million viewers in the United States watched the announcement of the criminal trial verdict (Alexander, 1996, p. 169).

As the previous chapters have indicated, the defendant's celebrity status had a major influence on the criminal trial. The trial started later than any other activity in the Los Angeles courthouse because, as Judge Lance Ito noted, "When O. J. comes into the building, everything stops" (TRC, 1995, March 27). Simpson's celebrity status also had profound effects on other trial procedures. In many criminal trials, defense attorneys must devise ways either to humanize the defendant or to focus attention away from the defendant, such as targeting the character of the victim. In this trial, however, the members of the defense tried to draw as much attention as possible to the defendant. Their apparent goal was to get him in front of the jury without testifying, thus avoiding cross-examination. Defense attorneys petitioned the court to allow Simpson to make an opening statement. They argued that Clarence Darrow had been allowed to do this during his trial on jury bribery charges. Prosecutor Marcia Clark argued against allowing this tactic, saying it was "simply an attempt to capitalize" on the defendant's "star appeal" (TRC, 1995, January 24).

The defense tried other ways of getting the jury to focus on Simpson, the star of the litigated drama. In an unusual request, Defense Attorney Johnnie Cochran said Simpson might have to leave during the coroner's testimony, as it would be "very, very difficult" for him to listen to the details of his ex-wife's murder. The defense asked for an admonition to be read to the jury if he did leave, explaining that "they're not to infer anything from his leaving the courtroom and that it's a normal human reaction for anyone that you love and that this is consistent entirely with the presumption of innocence." The prosecution argued that Simpson could leave the courtroom, but the proposed jury instruction was "totally inappropriate . . . [and] one might argue whether this is a performance by Mr. Simpson the actor or truly a reflection of Mr. Simpson's alleged grief" (TRC, 1995, June 5). In addition, when he waived his right to testify, Simpson got a chance to make a brief speech, albeit in the absence of the jury, without opening himself to cross-examination:

> Good morning, your Honor. As much as I would like to address some of the misrepresentations made about myself and my—and Nicole concerning our life together, I am mindful of the mood and the stamina of this jury. I have confidence, a lot more it seems than Miss Clark has, of their integrity, and that they will find, as the record stands now, that I did not, could not and would not have committed this crime. I have four kids, two kids I haven't seen in a year. They ask me every week, "Dad, how much longer?" I want this trial over. Thank you. (TRC, 1995, September 22)

The defendant's celebrity status, most significantly, led to an amazing amount of media attention and gavel-to-gavel live coverage. Not only did this lengthen the trial, but it often became the central issue. Many mornings, the trial began with a side-bar conference or other on-record proceeding—out of the presence of the jury—discussing something an attorney had heard on television the night before. In addition, one witness felt compelled to put into context his nationally aired statements, which countered his in-court testimony. He explained the media encounter as follows: "I was coming to work that morning. I parked my car, and as I opened my door of my car, I found several cameras and saw Sam Donaldson coming[,] approaching me suddenly and [he] started asking questions on the current cases which I'm testifying . . . on." He attempted to explain his responses to Donaldson in that context, saying that "it was not an intelligent conversation which took place at that time because he suddenly surprised me" (TRC, 1995, June 13).

This widespread coverage brought forward witnesses and people with knowledge about other witnesses. For example, the tapes ultimately used to impeach Mark Fuhrman surfaced after a television audience saw Fuhrman testify that he had never used the so-called n-word. As discussed later in this chapter, the tapes—whose existence apparently was unknown to any of the attorneys when the trial began—became a major feature by the time of closing arguments.

Cameras both outside and inside the courtroom caused unusual situations. The trial was halted a number of times so Judge Ito could deal with problems relating to what the viewing audience was allowed to see. For instance, during Clark's opening statement, Ito was uneasy about the court camera focusing on a small photograph of the victims. The judge chastised Clark for not giving him ample notice so that he could cut the video feed. Of even more concern to Ito on the first day of opening statements was the photographing of alternate jurors (TRC, 1995, January 24) since under Rule 980 of the California Rules of Court, closeup photography of jurors is prohibited (Cal. Ann. Code, R. of Ct., 980, 1994). The judge was so upset about the latter incident that he threatened to terminate televised coverage. The defense vehemently argued against this termination, and the prosecution joined in its protest.

Previous chapters explain the effect of live television coverage on both the prosecution and the defense. The examples here show how the coverage affected the judge and witnesses. Toward the end of the trial, Ito threatened, "I'm concerned that attorneys from both sides have referred to what other people around this country may think. That causes me to believe that the lawyers are pandering to the cameras" (TRC, 1995, August 22). In addition to using the in-court camera to their advantage, attorneys attempted to use the media in a direct fashion to influence the verdict. The defense called as a witness the author of a *Penthouse* article who had quoted a member of the Los Angeles Police Department (LAPD), "'There has been enough leaking out there to sink [C]amp O. J. if it were on a barge by the defense and the prosecution alike. But both are pikers compared to the Los Angeles Police Department.'" This person went on to detail some of the leaked information, which included "the LAPD passing out 911 tapes to journalists as if they were courtesy trinkets welcoming them to town" (TRC, 1995, August 1).

Pretrial television coverage also had a significant impact on the trial. Never before had the investigation of a crime scene been so thoroughly committed to videotape. These tapes, then, were available to both sides to impeach witnesses' testimony during the trial. For example, in cross-examining LAPD officers and investigators as well as members of the coroner's staff, the defense had access to videotape taken by television station and network employees standing just outside the Bundy property where the murders occurred. Perhaps no witness was more challenged by videotape impeachment than Dennis Fung, a criminalist for the LAPD who was in charge of gathering evidence. On a significant number of occasions, Fung either was forced to recant his testimony or his testimony was put in doubt by various videotape segments. At one point in the trial, Judge Ito noted the unusual nature of this "testimonial evidence": "Always interesting to hear these arguments. And I don't mean that facetiously, because I mean it is fascinating, since it is a videotape, which ostensibly is as accurate a depiction as we will ever get, it is not someone's recollection or interpretation, it is the events as they unfolded" (TRC, 1995, February 21).

Although Simpson's celebrity status affected the civil trial, the effects were different. He now was famous not only as a sports icon and actor but as someone who, according to many in the media and public, got away with murder. The spectacle of the criminal trial then became a significant part of his celebrity persona. So, while the defense attorneys tried to rely on his former celebrity identity ("he was a sports hero . . . [who never] tried to renegotiate a contract . . . [or] spit in the face of an umpire. He never, ever told a fan he didn't have time for an autograph" [TRL, 1996, October 24]), attorneys for the plaintiffs focused on his more recent notoriety. The plaintiffs used this explanation in closing argument: "This was his chance to tell us what the answers were. Confronted with all this evidence, highly incriminating, conclusively incriminating evidence, pointing right at him, and what did he choose to say, what did he choose to tell you, ladies and gentlemen of the jury? Well, he talked about his accomplishments as a football player" (TRL, 1997, January 21).

Just as the media coverage brought evidence and witnesses to the criminal trial, so did it at the civil trial. As chapter 5 demonstrates, some of the most significant evidence that emerged because of the media coverage were pictures of Simpson in what appeared to be Bruno Magli shoes, the type of shoe that left a print at the murder scene, a type Simpson claimed never to have owned (TRL, 1996, November 20).

The trial procedures affected the outcome. Criminal and civil trial procedures are fundamentally different, as the consequences of a criminal verdict of guilty, which can include incarceration or death, are so much greater than a civil verdict, which can result in loss of property or money but not liberty or life. To begin with, the differences in consequences are reflected in the different burdens of proof for criminal and civil trials. The prosecution's burden of proof in the criminal trial was "beyond a reasonable doubt." In the civil trial, the plaintiffs' burden of proof was "a preponderance of the evidence" for most issues they had to decide. The civil trial jurors were instructed that meant "evidence that has more convincing force than that opposed to it" (TRL, 1997, January 22). The jurors at the civil trial thus could be much less certain about their conclusions to render a verdict against Simpson than jurors in the criminal trial.

Another procedural difference is the Fifth Amendment privilege against self-incrimination, which applies only to criminal charges. Without this privilege in civil proceedings, the plaintiffs were able to depose Simpson and to call him to the stand during the civil trial. The plaintiffs in the civil trial also had the significant benefit of the previous criminal trial over the same issues. They knew the evidence available to Simpson and the flaws in the prosecution's case that they had to overcome. As just one example, the plaintiffs did not ask Simpson to try on the gloves, one of which was found at the scene of the murders. One of the prosecutors' worst mistakes at the criminal trial was asking Simpson to try on the gloves in open court—only to find that they appeared to be too small for him.

Simpson's criminal and civil trials certainly can be categorized as "popular trials." Communication scholar Janice Schuetz (1994) identifies four characteristics of such trials. Popular trials (1) "involve persons, issues, or crimes of social interest," (2) "attract extensive public interest and involvement," (3) "make a contribution to the ongoing historical conversations about the meaning of justice and the legal system," and (4) "reflect the values of the context in which they take place" (p. 2). The defendant's celebrity status guaranteed the first two. The second also are present. The next two sections of this chapter demonstrate how the media coverage emphasized the defendant's personal wealth, the role played by race, and the controversies about the justice system.

Wealth

Telelitigated trials call public attention to the role of money in the justice system. Although the financial resources of a criminal defendant always affect the nature of a defense and the trial itself, no other case has ever been quite like *People v. Simpson*. No previous defendant has ever assembled the sheer numbers of attorneys with the combined reputations of the Simpson defense team. This affected the criminal trial from its earliest stages. Less noted, but in some ways no less significant than the defendant's "dream team," was the large number of prosecuting attorneys, which some estimate at nearly fifty, working on the trial in the Los Angeles District Attorney's Office (Dershowitz, 1996, p. 150). In the course of the trial, nearly a dozen prosecutors appeared in court. One or two attorneys per side could not possibly have had the combined legal experience and expertise nor have devoted as much time to researching issues, preparing witnesses, or planning trial strategy as did the teams of attorneys working for each side in this case. The large numbers of attorneys on both sides naturally led to more hearings over evidence and procedure.

As significant as the number of attorneys was in the criminal trial, of equal importance was the ability of the Simpson team to secure the assistance of top forensics experts, as the evidence was circumstantial and depended heavily upon forensic analysis. To challenge or even refute such evidence requires piercing the aura of validity that often accompanies testimony by a "scientific expert." The Los Angeles prosecutor's office has at its disposal the investigative personnel of its own office and of federal and even international law enforcement. Few criminal defendants can afford a level playing field, and Simpson was highly unusual in this regard. In his posttrial book, Defense Attorney Alan Dershowitz (1996) argues that "the outcome of the Simpson case was largely determined *outside* the courtroom in the first few weeks following the murders." The defense secured the "world's leading forensic experts, Dr. Henry Lee and Dr. Michael Baden, who immediately flew out to Los Angeles and inspected and photographed the crime scene, the forensic evidence, the autopsy results, the crime lab, and everything else to which they were able to secure access." He further contends that scrutinizing the work of police and state investigators during the early stages of their work "would prove to be pivotal during the trial" (p. 27).

A direct effect of the number of attorneys, investigators, and experts was the length of the criminal trial. Although not the lengthiest in U.S. history, this trial certainly was among the longest. The record of the trial is contained in approximately 45,000 pages of transcripts. Opening statements began in January 1995. The judge instructed the jury on September 29, 1995; jurors began deliberations on October 2 and, four hours later, announced they had reached a verdict. The jurors were sequestered for 266 days. On August 25, 1995, Ito announced, "I don't know quite how to tell you this. You have a rather unusual distinction as a sequestered jury. As you know, you've been sequestered since mid-January, and as of yesterday, you have surpassed the amount of time that the Manson jury, if you recollect from 20 years ago, was in sequestration. So some kind of dubious record I'm sure" (TRC).

The civil trial found the defendant with less wealth, as a result of his legal fees for the criminal trial and cancellation of endorsement contracts, and without many of his dream team lawyers, although both he and the plaintiffs were ably represented in court. Similarly, few additional experts were hired. As a result of there being fewer attorneys and less money and the trial management of Judge Fujisaki, the civil trial was significantly shorter. Opening statements began on October 24, 1996, and the jury's award of punitive damages was announced on February 10, 1997. Judge Fujisaki was determined to restrict media interference, and he threatened to shorten the trial even more if witnesses consorted with the media. At one point, Fujisaki announced that "any witness who prejudices this trial by making public comment in the media with regards to the matters that are directly involved in this case, will be precluded from testifying" (TRL, 1996, November 11).

At the criminal trial, Simpson's wealth allowed him the finest legal representation and scientific analysis available. It also cracked the color-blind veneer of the system and exposed, to varying interpretations, the role of race in the administration of justice.

Race

The media coverage of these trials focused public attention on issues of race. Race is, as Cornel West (1996) notes, "America's most explosive issue" and "rawest nerve" (p. xi). Disparate treatment by race has been a problem in the criminal justice system for centuries. Nevertheless, for a significant portion of white Americans, it was not the disparate treatment of the racial issue that the Simpson trials brought to the fore. Instead, they saw the verdict as "racially biased," with a predominantly African American jury refusing to convict an "African-American icon" (Taff, 1996, p. 552).

Whether acknowledged or not, race is a significant issue in U.S. criminal trials. The American Bar Association (ABA) cites "longstanding patterns of racial discrimination" in "courts across the country" (American Bar Association, 1997, p. 13). Although this affects all aspects of the criminal justice system, one significant example relates to death penalty cases. White defendants convicted of capital crimes against blacks are far less likely to be sentenced to death than blacks convicted of similar crimes against whites (Dershowitz, 1996, p. 110). According to the American Civil Liberties Union ("Double Justice," 1997), of the 232 executions carried out in the United States since 1977, only one white person has been put to death for the murder of a black person. This 1997 report by the ABA (Recommendation No. 7) indicates:

> Numerous studies have demonstrated that defendants are more likely to be sentenced to death if their victims were white rather than black. Other studies have shown that in some jurisdictions African Americans tend to receive the death penalty more often than do white defendants. And in countless cases, the poor legal services that capital clients receive are rendered worse still by racist attitudes of defense counsel. This disparity and unfairness is startling in a system that purports to be color blind and evenhanded. (p. 13)

Although blacks always have been defendants in criminal trials, for many years they could not serve on juries. The Supreme Court outlawed this practice in 1880 (*Strauder v. West Virginia*, 100 U.S. 303, 1880), but it continued in another form until very recently, as many prosecutors would use peremptory challenges to eliminate blacks from juries when the defendant was black. It was not until 1986 that the Supreme Court specifically ruled discriminatory use of peremptory challenges invalid (*Batson v. Kentucky*, 476 U.S. 79, 1986). Despite this ruling, discriminatory use of peremptory challenges still occurs since proving the reason for exercise of a peremptory challenge is often difficult. Indeed, the prosecution in *Simpson* used eight of its ten peremptory challenges to excuse black jurors (Dershowitz, 1996, p. 101). Thus, race, as it relates to jury composition, always has been an issue, whether in the exercise of peremptory challenges or in a court's decision to change the venue of a trial. When it comes to the effect of race and venue, the Rodney King case, moved from central Los Angeles to the predominantly white suburb of Simi Valley, resulting in a jury of ten whites, one Filipino, and one Hispanic, is a classic case of race making a difference.

Many Americans, most of them white, believe that the law is color blind. For them, racial issues in the criminal justice system are hidden. Race moved from tacit to explicit, however, in the Simpson criminal trial when the prosecution called Detective Mark Fuhrman to the stand, and he became not only the biggest issue in the trial but also a household name. The issues surrounding his testimony and impeachment by the defense were the most unusual procedural aspects of the criminal trial. As Judge Ito said, "This is a unique factual and legal situation, something I've never seen before, never contemplated before, never had to contemplate before. Of course, that's nothing unusual in this particular case" (TRC, 1995, September 7).

Despite the prosecution's protestations to the opposite, Fuhrman was a key witness, whose testimony established the chain of custody of the evidence and the history of how it was discovered. He was one of the first LAPD detectives on the scene; he scaled the fence at Simpson's home, which resulted in a warrantless search; and he was the one who discovered the second glove behind Simpson's home. Defense attorneys contended that Fuhrman planted the glove, and, as evidence of his motive, they were anxious to present his attitudes about race to the jury. Fuhrman played into their strategy by lying. In a now-famous exchange early in the trial, Fuhrman responded to Defense Attorney F. Lee Bailey's cross-examination (see chapter 4) by claiming he had not used a particularly offensive term to refer, in a derogatory fashion, to African Americans (TRC, 1995, March 13).

The most explosive part of the trial came with the surfacing of tapes made by Laura Hart McKinny, a writer who had interviewed Fuhrman extensively. In arguing that the tapes should be admissible to impeach Fuhrman, Cochran stated: "Now, this is a bombshell. This is a critical bit of evidence for a critical witness in this case. It goes even beyond this case. It talks about a culture. It talks about so many of things[,] things we've talked about. It talks about framing people, setting up people, falsifying reports" (TRC, 1995, July 31). The question of the tapes' relevancy and admissibility was argued at length. The prosecution tried hard to keep them out of the trial and to downplay the importance of this impeachment testimony, knowing the effect it would have if admitted. Cheri Lewis argued for the prosecution:

> I'm asking the Court to look purely at the probative value of extensive evidence to impeach Detective Fuhrman, given the lack of any evidence in this case linking him to actually do-

ing anything wrong. That makes the probative value of him being a racist almost nil, because even if the Defense were to successfully convince the Court or anyone else that Detective Fuhrman made these racial slurs and is a racist, that does not prove, that does not show any kind of link to him actually planting the Rockingham glove. . . . On the other hand because of the inflammatory nature of the remarks at issue, especially in front of this predominantly African American jury[,] it does have a substantially undue prejudicial impact on the People. (TRC, 1995, July 27)

Another opinion regarding the tapes' admissibility was delivered by an "unidentified woman," who announced in open court: "Judge Ito, I have a message to you from God. God wants you to play the tapes." She was escorted from the courtroom (TRC, 1995, September 15). But perhaps the most bizarre request of the trial came at the end of arguments about admissibility of the taped evidence when Cochran argued:

We hereby would ask this court to modify the sequestration of the jury. . . . You can still have the ramifications of sequestration. And you'll recall that when picking the jury, you told these jurors not to watch television, not to do certain things, and by and large, they complied with the order. These people have been here almost nine months and I think they would do this. I think they would welcome it and it would take a lot of pressure off them. . . . It will be a lot fairer for these people if the court will consider doing it.(TRC, 1995, September 12)

Marcia Clark responded: "I think this takes the cake for the most transparent motion ever made by the defense. Now that this man has been all over the community, all over Los Angeles . . . I wonder why the defense wants the jurors to be unsequestered. I wonder if I can figure this one out." Ito denied the motion (TRC, 1995, September 12). After several days of deliberation, Ito allowed only a small number of the numerous references on the tapes to be admitted into evidence. Chapter 4 explains the strong reaction of the prosecutors to this revelation. Before the tapes surfaced, Marcia Clark argued the defense was trying to "slur Mark Fuhrman again unfairly in the eyes of this jury" (TRC, 1995, March 14). After the tapes came out, her posture shifted rather dramatically, when she concluded:

And as a citizen, I am deeply offended and I'm shocked and I'm disgusted with what I have heard. . . . I stand before you today, your Honor, not in [d]efense of Mark Fuhrman, but in [d]efense of a case, a case of such overwhelming magnitude in terms of the strength of proof of the defendant's guilt that it would be a travesty to allow such a case to be derailed with a very serious and important, but very inflammatory social issue. (TRC, 1995, August 29)

Yet, the furor following the trial was not so much outrage at Fuhrman as at the verdict. Some have cited the Simpson verdict as an example of the practice of jury nullification—in which a jury, despite its instructions, simply refuses to follow the law. As Mark Taff notes, "Jury nullification, in the hands of those who feel disenfranchised because of race, gender, class, religion, etc., can be used as a political weapon to undermine the current criminal justice system" (Taff, 1996, p. 552). Harvard law professor Randall Kennedy (1994) cites a black juror who voted to acquit in a Washington, D.C., case in which Kennedy claims there was "overwhelming" evidence of guilt, as saying the jury acquitted because they "'didn't want to send any more Young Black Men to jail'" (p. 61). Holden and others (1985, October 4) claim that, although in 1993 the national acquittal rate of criminal defendants was 17 percent in areas where juries were predominantly black, acquittal rates were much higher when jurors were predominantly white. As criminal defendants are predominantly black, these statistics cause some to conclude that "racial bias now seems manifest in the acquittal of defendants of color" (Morgan, 1996, p. 984). The claims of jury nullification in *Simpson* similarly are couched in racial terms. So it was the jury, not Fuhrman, that caused race to become an explicit concern for many.

"Outrage at Simpson's acquittal is understandable," admits Dershowitz (1996), "in those who firmly believe that he did it. No one wants to see a guilty murderer go free, or an innocent defendant go to prison" (p. 45). No system of justice is perfect, however. The question that must be faced is in what direction a criminal justice system should err. Some systems regularly convict innocent parties, but, in the process, fewer guilty parties escape justice. In the American criminal justice system, the old adage is that it is better for ten guilty people to go free than for one innocent person be put in prison. Dershowitz explains, "Our system is judged not only by the accuracy of its results, but also by *the fairness of the process*" (p. 45). Knowledge that the process is not fair is a major issue underlying the racial divide in reactions to the Simpson criminal trial and verdict. "The drawn-out spectacle of the O. J. Simpson trial," says Kennedy (1994, November 14), "touches on deep resentments and grievances that African Americans have long harbored toward the criminal justice system" (p. 61). For them, race has always been an explicit issue.

The issue of race at the civil trial was, for many, at most a tacit concern. In that trial, Fuhrman did not testify, and the defense was not allowed to make any reference to these issues, as Judge Fujisaki ruled them irrelevant.

The Santa Monica jury, which did not include an African American, found Simpson to have committed the murders and awarded compensatory and punitive damages. However, rather than accusing the jury of some sort of racial motivation, as the majority-black jury in the criminal trial had been accused, much of white America seemed to feel that justice finally had been done in the Simpson case. For that segment of society, the issue of race and justice had become, once again, silent and suppressed.

Rationality Versus Commonsense Justice

Arguments that race was responsible for the derailment of rational decision making took a nearly hysterical form after the criminal trial. The lead editorial in the *New Republic* for October 23, 1995, for example, was titled "Unreasonable Doubt." The editors who wrote it claimed that announcement of the jury's rapid verdict raised hopes that jurors "had voted for facts over emotions, color-blind objectivity over racial contingency, reasoned deliberation over group loyalties and ethnic fears." Once the verdict was announced, they wrote, such thinking seems "naive." What is striking is not the editors' self-proclaimed naivete but the degree to which they unconsciously equated reason with their own point of view. In hyperbole that clearly matches his, they argue that Johnnie Cochran represents "the eclipse of civil reason." They go on to claim that democracy may not survive if such reason, along with civility, is not restored (pp. 7–8). Criticism in this vein involves rhetorical practices that rely on as well as reinforce an ostensibly objective legal world view, one that law professor Patricia Williams (1991) calls "essentialized." She warns against such a world view because of its "worrisome tendency to disparage anything that is nontranscendent (temporal, historical), or contextual (socially constructed), or nonuniversal (specific) as "emotional . . . or just Not True" (p. 9). It also is blind to its own tendency to vacillate between immediate and long-term justice as the most important or highly valued goal of the system, while labeling the same vacillation in others as unreasonable or worse.

Jurors' Reliance on Commonsense Justice

An important but frequently ignored part of the law is notions about what is just, notions that jurors rely on when deciding cases. This commonsense justice is defined by Norman Finkel (1995) as "what ordinary people think the law ought to be," including legal, moral, and psychological conceptions. Commonsense justice may be "at odds with" the more formal law in many instances (p. 2). Reliance on this commonsense understanding of the law is not reserved to jurors, however, as legislative bodies and others bring to bear on their work a sense of what is reasonable.

Judges also must rely on commonsense justice, as laws are written "abstractly, tersely, or even cryptically," requiring "construction rather than deduction" (p. 89). Finkel cites Oliver Wendell Holmes's analysis that judges do not 'sacrifice good sense to syllogism'"; instead, they refer to the 'felt necessities of the time, the prevalent moral and political theories, intuitions of public policy . . . , even prejudices'" (p. 3).

In attempting to understand how jurors use their notions of commonsense justice, and what these notions involve, Finkel refers to W. Lance Bennett and Martha S. Feldman's book, *Reconstructing Reality in the Courtroom* (1981), in which they argue that jurors transform evidence into stories. Competing stories or versions of stories must be evaluated. Communication scholar Walter Fisher (1987) says such judgments are made in terms of "narrative coherence," the internal probability of a story or whether it "hangs together," and "narrative fidelity," the ways in which a story conforms to accepted truths and values (pp. 47, 105–13). This view of narrative logic is consistent with Nancy Pennington and Reid Hastie's (1992) claim that jurors' stories about a case are constructed of three elements: (1) "case-specific information acquired during the trial," (2) "knowledge about events similar in content to those that are the topic of dispute," and (3) "generic expectations about what makes a complete story" (pp. 189–206). Thus, jurors rely on their socially constructed understandings and experiences as a filter for making sense of the contradictory case-specific information presented by opposing counsel during a trial.

Although all these scholars discuss to some degree issues of context, common values, and intersubjectivity, none of them focus on the important distinction between acknowledging the existence of different values and understandings and the loaded categories of "reason" and "prejudice" whereby those differences are labeled. The tendency of dominant society is to label their own understandings as reasonable. The editors of the *New Republic* display that tendency clearly, as did Prosecutor Lewis in the argument she made during the criminal trial to exclude the Fuhrman tapes, cited earlier in this chapter. She stated that the "probative value" of Fuhrman's racism was "almost nil" and would be too "inflammatory . . . especially in front of this predominantly African-American jury." The tapes, she argued, should not be admitted because they were "prejudicial" (TRC, 1995, July 27).

Yet commonsense justice is always filtered through community values and intersubjectively constructed understandings; it means something different for various groups and individuals because their experiences and socialization are different. Race is one major factor in those differences. There are deep divides among various communities within this society, and, increasingly, communities in the United States are segregated by race.

Cornel West (1991) notes that 86 percent of white suburban Americans live in neighborhoods that are less than 1 percent black (p. 4). In a book about the Rodney King and O. J. Simpson trials, Jewelle Taylor Gibbs (1996) notes some of the effects of this segregation by race on attitudes about police: "Living in the encapsulated but often exposed world of the inner cities, blacks and Latinos experience a daily reality very different from that of more advantaged whites who live in gated urban neighborhoods and suburbs. And one of these more pervasive and painful realities is the persistent presence of police harassment and brutality." After explaining the differences among people of different ethnic backgrounds, Gibbs speculates about how the jurors in the Rodney King trial differed from those in Simpson's criminal trial. She explains:

> Whereas Simi Valley jurors perceived the police as their familiar neighbors and friends, the majority of the Simpson jury might well have perceived the police as an occupying force of strangers and enemies. Whereas the Simi Valley jurors believed that the primary mission of the police was to protect and to serve their community, the majority of the Simpson jury probably believed that the police force's major goal was to repress and control their community. Whereas the Simi Valley jurors were usually treated with courtesy and respect by the police, the majority of the Simpson jurors were more likely to have encountered discourtesy and disrespect from police officers. Whereas the Simi Valley jurors probably had few relatives or acquaintances who had experienced physical or verbal abuse from the police, 42 percent of the Simpson jurors reported that they themselves or a family member had a negative experience with law enforcement. (pp. 225–26)

To illustrate the role of race in conceptions of commonsense justice, there is no better example than that presented by Fuhrman's testimony at the criminal trial, which is part of a larger issue in this trial and in the criminal justice system as a whole. Chapter 4 presents an extensive discussion of Detective Fuhrman and racial issues.

"Testilying"

Perjured testimony by law enforcement officials was, until the Simpson trials, a well-kept secret of the criminal justice system. Any knowledgeable observer of the trials or reader of the *Simpson* transcripts cannot fail to be surprised by some of the claims made by members of the LAPD. The most well-known perjured testimony in the case is Fuhrman's claim never to have used the particular racial epithet he is heard using on the tapes. However, other clear instances occur. For example, the defense team makes much of the claim by Fuhrman and Vannatter that they and two other detectives left the crime scene and went to Simpson's house on Rockingham to notify him in person of the murders.

If the police wanted to search Simpson's home, they needed a search warrant. However, when the four detectives went to Rockingham to "notify Simpson," Fuhrman, with Vannatter's approval, jumped over the fence. Fuhrman testified that he found the matching glove behind Simpson's house while walking around. Since they did not have a search warrant, the only way the police officers could use the glove as evidence was if they were on the grounds for reasons other than to search for evidence, which would require a warrant. The detectives, who claimed they originally went to his house to notify Simpson of the murders, then testified that, because of blood they allegedly saw on the white Bronco, they became worried that more victims might be inside Simpson's home. This, they claimed, resulted in Detective Fuhrman's going over the fence. Fuhrman testified that he told Detective Vannatter, "In my view, this is an emergency and we need to act now" (TRC, 1995, March 14).

The defense attorneys attempted to ridicule what they deemed unbelievable testimony. They elicited an admission that no LAPD detective, much less four, went to the home of Nicole's parents; they were phoned rather than notified in person (TRC, 1995, February 22). The defense attorneys also ridiculed the suggestion that Simpson was not immediately a suspect, and, on cross–examination, they got Fuhrman to admit that, once inside Simpson's property, he did not do a thorough search for victims—despite his claim that worry about more victims was the reason he had jumped over the fence rather than going to get a search warrant (TRC, 1995, March 14). However, no matter how hard they were pushed by defense counsel, the detectives would not admit that Simpson was a suspect when they went to his house—indeed they could not—as such an admission would be counter to testimony the officers gave earlier at the suppression hearing. As courtroom novelist Scott Turow argued in an op-ed piece in the *New York Times* (1995, October 4):

> The detectives' explanation as to why they were at the house is hard to believe. . . . Four police detectives were not needed to carry a message about Nicole Simpson's death. These officers undoubtedly knew what Justice Department statistics indicate: that half of the women murdered in the United States are killed by their husbands or boyfriends. Simple probabilities made Mr. Simpson a suspect. . . . Also, Mark Fuhrman had been called to the Simpson residence years earlier when Mr. Simpson was abusing his wife. . . . The fact that the dis-

trict attorney's office put these officers on the witness stand to tell this story and that the court accepted it is scandalous. It is also routine. (p. A21)

The detectives' testimony is by no means an isolated instance of aberrant behavior. Judge Alex Kozinski of the United States Court of Appeals for the Ninth Circuit stated: "It is an open secret long shared by prosecutors, defense lawyers and judges that perjury is widespread among law enforcement officers." The reason is that "the exclusionary rule . . . sets up a great incentive for . . . police to lie to avoid letting someone they think is guilty, or they know is guilty, go free" (Taylor, 1995, p. 72). The Mollen Commission, established to look into police corruption in New York City, reported: "The practice of police falsification in connection with such arrests is so common in certain precincts that it has spawned its own word: 'testilying.' . . . Officers also commit falsification to serve what they perceive to be 'legitimate' law enforcement ends" (Commission to Investigate, 1994, July 7, p. 36). One survey indicates that defense attorneys, judges, and prosecutors estimate that police perjury occurs in 20 to 50 percent of Fourth Amendment suppression hearings (Orfield, 1992, p. 107).

Sections of the Fuhrman tapes allude to this culture in the LAPD. In one instance, Fuhrman discussed turning a scab on a drug-user's arm into something that appears to be a fresh needle mark: "'[I]f . . . you find a mark that looks like three days ago, pick the scab. Squeeze it. Looks like serum's coming out, as if it were hours old. . . . That's not falsifying a report. That's putting a criminal in jail. That's being a policeman.'" When Dershowitz (1996) went public with his claim about police perjury on *Good Morning America*, the reaction was, in his words, "swift, vociferous, and well orchestrated" denial and outrage that he would make such a claim (pp. 61–62). That reaction comes from one particular version of commonsense justice, conceptions of which often are affected by race. For example, the white community sees police officers as friends, neighbors, and protectors, and finds it difficult to believe that police personnel would lie under oath, at least about anything significant. As a result, they may find the contents of the Fuhrman tapes more fact than fiction.

Race and Commonsense Justice

UCLA law professor Peter Arenella provides a classic example of how one member of the community judges such a story. He said on *The MacNeil/Lehrer News Hour* (1995, October 4), "I watched this trial every day, and there were detectives that lied to this jury." However, he went on to argue that those lies must be interpreted as attempts to avoid a Fourth Amendment warrantless search problem; thus, a juror should see them as such and believe that the rest of the police officer's testimony is true, even though he tells such blatant lies. Indeed, Arenella criticized the criminal jury's verdict, explaining it as a failure to make this distinction; since the jury did not understand that the lies were merely a reaction to constitutional interpretation they do not care for, "they read into it greater significance than was really there."

However, many in the black community have more direct experiences with the criminal justice system, experiences that cause them to see police officials as harassing, racist, or unfair. That community also knows firsthand about "testilying" and believes it is just the tip of the iceberg in terms of what police will do to convict a criminal defendant, particularly one who is African American. For many members of this community, the details of the Fuhrman tapes ring all too true:

> Many black jurors did not need to hear the Fuhrman tapes
> in order to accept the possibility that the police would lie and
> tamper with evidence in order to set up a black man. Many
> blacks, in Los Angeles and elsewhere, experience racist police
> harassment regularly. They also encounter more subtle dis-
> crimination from white-dominated authorities on a daily ba-
> sis. (Dershowitz, 1996, pp. 113–14)

Tanya Coke (1994) confirms this: "Rare is the African American who cannot relate a tale of having been stopped by police in an affluent neighborhood or followed closely at the heels around a clothing store." She goes on to cite black Harvard Law School professor Charles Ogletree, "'If I'm dressed in a knit cap and hooded jacket, I'm probable cause.' One consequence of such action," says Coke, "is that the attitudes of blacks and whites toward police diverge markedly" (pp. 354–55).

This is the crux of the racial divide in the Simpson trials and in feelings about the criminal justice system in the United States. These are the very different contexts of groups of individuals for whom commonsense justice is not the same thing. The jury verdict in the criminal case was no more an example of nullification[1] or racial bias than was the verdict in the civil case. Instead, as Gibbs (1996) argues convincingly, the criminal verdict was a classic case of cognitive dissonance (pp. 227–28); so was the civil verdict, at which most evidence of police misconduct or racial animus was excluded. Judge Fujisaki ruled that "whatever probative value they may have is far outweighed by the prejudicial fact" (TRL, 1997, January 10). In both instances, given the evidence presented at trial, the burden of proof, and, what is most important, the jurors' conceptions of commonsense justice and their experiences, whereby they evaluated the coherence and fidelity of competing stories of the murders and investigation, the verdicts make sense. One is no more racially biased than is the other.

The lesson of the Simpson trials is not a new one. Much of what humans deem "logical" and "rational" is instead contextual—it is logical and rational when viewed with a particular set of experiences and understandings shared by many individuals in what has been termed "dominant society." In the United States, that society is mostly white. When the focus is on O. J., it is easy for the majority to see how race affects rationality. When the focus is on Bernard Goetz or the police beating Rodney King, context takes on a different hue. Williams vividly demonstrates this with the following example:

> A lone black man was riding in an elevator in a busy downtown department store. The elevator stopped on the third floor, and a crowd of noisy white high school students got on. The black man took out a gun, shot as many of them as he could, before the doors opened on the first floor and the rest fled for their lives. The black man later explained to the police that he could tell from the "body language" of the students, from their "shiny eyes and big smiles," that they wanted to "play with him, like a cat plays with a mouse." Furthermore, the black man explained, one of the youths had tried to panhandle money from him and another asked him, "how are you?" "That's a meaningless thing," he said in his confession, but "in certain circumstances, that can be a real threat." He added that a similar greeting had preceded the vicious beating of his father, a black civil rights lawyer in Mississippi, some time before. His intention, he confessed, was to murder the high school students. (1991, p. 11)

This example, with minor changes to account for race, was excerpted from the videotaped confession of Bernard Goetz, who shot four black teenagers on a New York subway. Williams's point is that the significant number of people in the white community who felt Goetz had acted "reasonably" likely would not feel the same about her black murderer in the hypothetical example. Individuals with competing versions of commonsense justice respond very differently to the two cases. For members of dominant society, one is likely to be deemed reasonable, as it involves understandings and experiences more common to whites; the other is unreasonable. That two such similar cases would end in different results, which is quite likely, is also extremely unfair. Yet the criminal justice system and much of dominant society elevate one version of the competing stories about justice, authenticating it as "color-blind reason." The other version is "prejudicial," and trial results are more "rational" when any discussion of such issues is suppressed. However, the irrationality lies not in the competing versions of commonsense justice, but, as demonstrated by Williams' story, in the labels attached thereto.

Acknowledging this irrationality seems nearly impossible to many for whom the world view of the law is both comforting and very real. To challenge that world view requires asking hard questions about two thousand-plus years of Western rationality. Some of those questions already are being asked. For example, in recent years the metaphor has gone from being a stylistic device that did little but "insinuate wrong ideas, move the passions, and thereby mislead judgment" (Locke, *An Essay Concerning Human Understanding*, 2.10.34) to being the fundamental form of human conception, that is, a powerful rhetorical figure for redescribing and reconceptualizing experience (Lakoff & Turner, 1989, p. 214). Reconceptualization of rationality is exactly what is needed. Also open to question are some of the rules of evidence that allow, as a question of law, rulings about what "facts," although relevant, are too inflammatory to have probative value. If the judgment of inflammatory means that juries do not get full information about whether or not police personnel, or others, may lie while under oath, then one must question whether it is reasonable to allow a judge but not a jury to make such a determination.

The criminal justice system has twin goals—accuracy of the results and fairness of the system. Sacrificing the first to assure the second is nothing new. The exclusionary rule, presumption of innocence, and the high standard of proof (beyond a reasonable doubt) all are designed with that particular balance in mind. Yet race, our rawest nerve, confuses this, like it confuses so many other concerns. There was little stir when attorney Gerry Spence, during closing argument in the murder trial of white separatist Randy Weaver, urged the jury to send a message to government officials who set up surveillance at Ruby Ridge: "Doesn't this terror and this horror have to end sometime? Shouldn't it end with you and shouldn't it end without having to compromise? Shouldn't this jury have the courage to stand up and say no, they over exercised their power?" (1993, June 15). Yet Cochran is held to represent the eclipse of civil reasoning when he makes a nearly identical argument:

> They believed he was guilty. They wanted to win. They didn't want to lose another big case. That is why. They believed that he was guilty. These actions rose from what their belief was, but they can't make that—the prosecutors can't make that judgment. Nobody but you can make that judgment. So when they take the law into their own hands, they become worse than the people who break the law, because they are the protectors of the law. Who then polices the police? You police the police. You police them by your verdict. You are the ones to

send the message. Nobody else is going to do it in this society. (TRC, 1995, September 28)

Who is policing our attitudes, and who is labeling some as prejudiced or biased and others as reasonable?

These trials suggest that the law ought to recognize various commonsense conceptions of justice, that nothing in the law ought to be considered above challenge, and certainly that nothing should be considered purely objective, universal, and transcendent. We can do this by remembering that "much of what is spoken in so-called objective, unmediated voices is in fact mired in hidden subjectives and unexamined claims" (Williams, 1991, p. 11).

However, in challenging the world view of legal rationality, care must be taken. Understanding that race and racism have caused much of this division is not carte blanche to use race to create new divisions, merely reversing the labels applied to particular points of view. Instead, we need to acknowledge context and multiplicity in our moral reasoning. If we fall into the trap of racial reasoning, we merely rewrite the mistakes of the past. "Racial reasoning," says Cornel West (1991), involves a "deceptive cloak of racial consensus," and it can discourage moral reasoning (p. 26). It also can lead to an essentialism that is simply racism in another form. The result is as universalized and objectified as the thing it opposes. Legal reasoning instead should consider context and weigh such factors as the fairness of the system, the appropriateness of the actions of all parties, including the police, and the likelihood that the evidence is tainted when determining the guilt of the defendant. Justice is a larger concept than individual culpability.

Conclusion

In the cacophony following the trials, some conclusions in the commentary deserve serious consideration. One is the relationship of the quality of criminal justice to the wealth of the defendant. Although many argue that Simpson bought a not-guilty verdict, that claim blurs far more serious concerns about the possibility of justice for indigent persons charged with a crime. As Robert Cottrol (1996), professor of law and history at George Washington University argues, the not-guilty verdict in *People v. Simpson* may indicate "to what extent the Los Angeles District Attorney's Office was simply unused to fighting against . . . opponents capable of exposing significant flaws in the prosecution's case, flaws that are usually never exposed to the light of day by most defendants with limited resources and limited counsel" (pp. 916–17). This is a very serious issue, as *Simpson* was not a case in which the defendant significantly outspent the prosecution. One early estimate was that the district attorney's office had spent $8.1 million, while Simpson had spent less than $4 million (Holland, 1995, October 23). Problems ranging from the serious flaws in investigation and evidence custody to testilying and perjured testimony are not exposed in most criminal cases. When these flaws exist in a system that increasingly puts convicted defendants to death (Cottrol, 1996, p. 917), we should be moved to examine the system rather than bemoan the possibility that one criminal defendant escaped justice. If we do not, we no longer even can claim to have a system based on fairness.

Further, the role of race in the criminal justice system must not be reburied after this trial. Ironies about race abound. Despite race having little or no objective basis as a concept, it has more influence on daily life in this society than nearly any other concept. Therefore, we must face the ways in which race affects the criminal justice system. Those who see testilying as a reasonable response to the exclusionary rule also likely see law enforcement officers as the good guys and criminal defendants as the bad guys. However, the world is not always so neatly organized. Furthermore, when considered carefully, the implications of tolerating perjured testimony by law enforcement officials are frightening. Toleration authorizes the police to violate the law in the name of upholding the law. It gives them license to take whatever steps they deem necessary to convict those they wish to incarcerate. It is a logical leap to conclude that perjured testimony leads to the manufacture of evidence if one is certain a defendant is guilty. It is also a logical leap to conclude from the chilling images of law enforcement officers created by the Fuhrman tapes that police likely frame and harass African Americans and Hispanics with impunity. Further, I believe that racism permeates the criminal justice system in ways that are neither noticed nor experienced by many whites. In 1997, the ABA passed a resolution calling upon all jurisdictions not to carry out the death penalty until it is administered fairly, particularly with respect to race (p. 1). These and many other related issues are an indictment of the criminal justice system. The possibility that one defendant gets away with a crime pales by comparison.

Finally, these trials should persuade us to review our rigid conceptions of reason and justice as these issues surface in the media commentaries. After all, that is the role of public trials, according to Schuetz (1994); they bring such issues forward for public discussion (p. 2). Scholars must rethink legal standards for relevant, probative, and "inflammatory" evidence. "[I]f we are willing to ask uncomfortable questions," says Cottrol (1996), we may learn why blacks and whites have very different perceptions of the criminal justice system (p. 918). Although it will require similar levels of discomfort for communication and legal scholars, society would benefit from reexamination of centuries-old theories about logic and rationality in relation to the law.

Finally, Williams reminds us:

> That life is complicated is a fact of great analytic importance.
> Law too often seeks to avoid this truth by making up its own
> breed of narrower, simpler, but hypnotically powerful rhetori-
> cal truths. Acknowledging, challenging, playing with these *as*
> rhetorical gestures is, it seems to me, necessary for any con-
> ception of justice. Such acknowledgment complicates the sup-
> posed purity of gender, race, voice, boundary; it allows us to
> acknowledge the utility of such categorizations for certain
> purposes and the necessity of their breakdown on other oc-
> casions. . . . [O]ne of the most important results of reconcep-
> tualizing from "objective truth" to rhetorical event will be a
> more nuanced sense of legal and social responsibility. (1991,
> pp. 10–11)

This chapter continues the discussion of telelitigation in the Simpson
trials. The chapter emphasizes how the media coverage of these trials focused public attention on the defendant's celebrity and wealth and the
issue of race in the administration of justice. Both the media coverage and
the trials themselves illuminate the commonsense understanding of justice.

Note

1. W. William Hodes (1996) identifies three types of jury nullification.
The first, which is historically exemplified in the John Peter Zenger case,
occurs when the jury agrees that the defendant committed all the elements
of the crime but does not believe it should be a crime, so they acquit the
defendant, as they did Zenger for publishing material critical of government officials in the State of New York. In the second form of nullification Hodes identifies, the jury agrees with the law, such as that prohibit-
ing destruction of government property, but does not agree with its ap-
plication to the particular defendant, for instance, a war protester who
poured blood on Selective Service property. The final form of nullification occurs when jurors feel the need to send a message to someone. All-
white juries in the South who acquitted individuals who murdered or
assaulted those who were protesting for civil rights were attempting to
send just such a message, according to Hodes, who sees the Simi Valley
verdict as another example. Hodes argues that the Simpson criminal
verdict *was* this third type of nullification (pp. 1097–1100).

9

The Trial of the Century in Retrospect

Lin S. Lilley

THE 1935 HAUPTMANN TRIAL WAS ONCE LABELED "the trial of the century." For the first time, trial proceedings were shown audiovisually outside the courtroom, and millions of moviegoers watched newsreel footage of the trial of the alleged kidnapper of the Lindbergh baby. When the judge realized how the live shots were being used, he promptly put an end to the carnivallike atmosphere. In the aftermath of the Hauptmann trial, the American Bar Association House of Delegates recommended a ban on all photographs during court sessions and on the broadcast of actual trial proceedings. The ban stayed in place until the late 1950s and early 1960s when a few western states started experimenting with television cameras in the courtroom (Lassiter, 1996, pp. 936–37).

Now, sixty years later, the trial for the murders of Nicole Brown and Ronald Goldman has become the true trial of the twentieth century because of the amount of publicity generated. After the Simpson criminal trial, there was a plea, once again, to ban cameras from the courtroom. This plea worked. Judges have prohibited cameras in several recent high-profile cases, including Susan Smith's trial for the death of her young sons, Yolanda Saldivar's for the murder of the singer Selena, Richard Allen Davis's for the abduction and murder of Polly Klaas, rap star Snoop Doggy Dogg's for the murder of a rival, and the retrial of Erik and Lyle Menendez for the deaths of their parents. Most notably, though, Judge Fujisaki prohibited broadcast of the Simpson civil trial proceedings. Even so, the media "feeding frenzy" continued. Hollywood hired actors to reenact the civil courtroom saga, and the legal commentators continued to comment each night. Once again, ratings were high, and Americans just could not get enough of the O. J. story.

But it was not just Americans affected by the Simpson story. The media coverage of the Simpson trials created what Marshall McLuhan has called the "global village," in which people, though physically separated, experience an important event together. Spectators from South America to western Europe to Russia learned about the O. J. Simpson trials.

Nature and Extent of the Coverage

Just what made the Simpson trials heard around the world? First, there were changes in technology itself. Thanks to satellite relays, "live" television broadcasts were aired throughout the world. The Internet opened even more worldwide access. In the Simpson criminal trial, for the first time, citizens of the world could access the actual, though unofficial, transcripts of the trial proceedings simultaneously with the goings-on in court. In addition, the Internet allowed international spectators to participate in "O. J. chat rooms" and to compare their perceptions of the trials with those of Americans. Some turned to Web sites just for O. J. Simpson jokes or to one of some three thousand other sites for up-to-date information on the Simpson trials. These new forms of technolitigation no doubt came into being because of telelitigation and the seemingly insatiable curiosity its drama seemed to stimulate.

Second, the Simpson trials were followed throughout the world simply because of the mass of information available. Apart from the interactive technology discussed above, thousands of newspaper and magazine articles and more than 125 books have been published to date. It was difficult for average citizens not to be affected by the Simpson trials. For instance, of 485 New Mexico citizens called for jury duty on a federal death penalty case in late 1996, 72 percent reported in a questionnaire that they had followed the Simpson criminal trial. Almost 20 percent of the jurors who followed the trial indicated that they could not help but follow the trial since it was such an extensively publicized case.[1]

Finally, these trials were heard around the world in part because the media was invited into the process from the very beginning. Simpson's defense team intended to pitch its case to the media from the start. The talented attorneys assembled for the defense had significant experience in using the media for the advantage of their clients. Robert Shapiro has published articles, noting that a key to a successful defense is to develop a media strategy before the case even goes to trial. F. Lee Bailey has a long and distinguished history of understanding the media and using it for his clients, starting with his groundbreaking appeal to the Supreme Court in *Sheppard v. Maxwell*. Johnnie Cochran used the media for his successful defense of music star Michael Jackson; and Alan Dershowitz appeared frequently on television and wrote his own newspaper column.

The "dream team" was not alone in its desire to shape the media portrayal of Simpson. Early on, there were proprosecution leaks, particularly about Simpson's domestic abuse of his wife. Whether the media actually was fed the domestic abuse material or whether the media ferreted out the additional domestic abuse incidents on its own, the effect was pronounced. The viewing public would hear much more about alleged episodes of abuse than the criminal jury ever did. Thus, the media's role in the criminal trial set the stage for two significantly different trials: the one in front of the actual criminal jury, and a second before the court of public opinion. In the civil trial, most Americans relied on the descriptions of reporters instead of the day-after reenactments. Further, since many observers felt justice finally had been done, the civil trial jury's verdict received less scrutiny. Those who could not justify the verdict could at least explain it as the result of a predominantly white jury in an upper-class suburb.

Effects of the Coverage on the Media Itself

The very potential of television trial coverage to transform the courtroom into a global village has caused journalists themselves to question whether television should have the same First Amendment rights to be in the courtroom as the written press. For example, Max Frankel (1994), editor of the *New York Times*, questions the effect of televised trial coverage:

> I am certain now that the camera is not just another incarnation of "press," entitled to the unabridged freedom thereof. It's a different beast that should enter a court by a different door, under different rules. . . . Though there is no proof that television coverage alters the conduct of a case, the suspicion that it does inevitably grows as the camera magnifies the din and compounds the stakes, in fame and fortune, for every participant. Justice may not often be compromised, but society's sense of it can certainly be demeaned. (p. 28)

Frankel wrote in the early days of the Simpson story, after the grand jury was dismissed and as the preliminary hearing got underway. After the trials, one would expect his sentiments against television cameras in the courtroom to be even stronger.

The media's role was scrutinized from the beginning. Why did the low-speed Bronco chase deserve such full coverage? But, perhaps even more significantly, why did the media abet the prosecution and ultimately contribute to the dismissal of the grand jury? In an unprecedented move, California Superior Court supervising judge Cecil Mills agreed with a defense motion to discharge the grand jury hearing the Simpson evidence "on the ground that the deliberate prosecutorial and police leaks had improperly exposed the grand jurors to prejudicial information and misinformation" (Dershowitz, 1996, p. 26).

At times, though, the media's work seemed particularly helpful. The tremendous publicity surrounding Detective Fuhrman and his possible racism caused key witnesses Kathleen Bell and Laura Hart McKinny to come forward with testimony about Fuhrman's use of the so-called n-word. At other times, it seemed as if the media, in their eagerness to come up with new stories, put ratings above justice. When trials are televised, journalists no longer find it enough to review what happens in the court-room each day. Instead, reporters look for fresh trial-related stories and spin-offs. But has the pursuit of the investigative reporters now jeopar-dized the trial process itself? For example, when the defense announced that it would bring in an African American former marine, Maximo Cordoba, to strengthen Kathleen Bell's story of Detective Fuhrman's rac-ism, *Dateline NBC* rushed to interview Cordoba. Their first interview made it seem as if Cordoba had not talked with Defense Attorney F. Lee Bailey, even though Bailey already had told Judge Ito that they had talked "Marine to Marine" (TRC, 1995, March 15). In their second interview, Cordoba remembered having a phone conversation with Bailey, but in the process came across as an unreliable witness. These "tabloid TV" interviews, which occurred long before Cordoba was ever to testify and certainly long before the defense had prepared him for his testimony, impeached his potential testimony and caused the defense to drop him as a witness.

But the out-of-courtroom cameras hurt the prosecution as well. Two ready examples of technological witness tampering come to mind. First, during the grand jury proceedings, Marcia Clark denounced the testimony of her own potentially key witness, Jill Shively, who claimed to have seen a person resembling Simpson fleeing from the crime scene, after Shively admitted that she had accepted money for telling her story to *Hard Copy*. During the preliminary hearing, witness José Camacho, who testified that Simpson had bought a twelve-inch knife, which he wanted sharpened, was impeached by Shapiro's inquiry about selling his story to the high-est television bidder.

The use of "pundits" or "talking heads" or legal commentators added a media dimension to the Simpson trial discourse. During these trials, attorneys, trial consultants, and journalists offered their interpretations at the end of each court day. Often, it was difficult for the spectators to separate comment from the facts of the trial. Several of the authors of chapters in this book had the opportunity to become commentators, and all of them declined. My experience was typical of these requests to serve as a commentator. When I was recruited for the *Geraldo* and the *Rolanda* shows, I declined to participate because I was not able to spend my days watching the trial coverage. I was told that all I needed to do was read summaries of the goings-on because they only wanted to know in general how I felt about the criminal trial. Putting fresh faces on camera apparently came before in-depth analysis, as much of the commentary indeed revealed.

Although some have argued that the media circus occurred only outside the courtroom, the authors of this volume point to how cameras in the courtroom encouraged the criminal attorneys to engage in long and rancor-filled discussions outside the hearing of the jury and more extensive examinations in front of jurors. The overall effect was to heighten the conflict and add to the intrigue.

In the wake of the Simpson trials, a number of questions relating to the media's participation must be asked and ultimately answered. Should the media's role be restricted? In particular, should actual trial proceedings be televised? How can defendants' rights be protected if there initially is a hung jury and a retrial? If proceedings are televised simultaneously, should the viewing public see only what the jurors see and hear? Can we thereby eliminate the problem manifest in the Simpson trial where public judgment was rendered by intermittent viewers who saw all sorts of inadmissible evidence and who discussed the case long before the real jury ever received the official instructions of the court?

These trials also raised additional questions about the media's role in conjunction with the roles of attorneys, witnesses, and defendants. Should attorneys be restricted from talking outside court, as with the gag orders imposed by Judge Fujisaki in the civil trial? Should the media be allowed to interview any witnesses before they have given testimony? Finally, should there be tighter strictures on information attorneys, victims' families, police agencies, and defendants can distribute independent of the pretrial or trial proceedings?

Effects on Social Issues of the Day

The trials provided for public discussion of issues that divide the public and, as result, have forced the public to reflect on otherwise hidden issues involving race, domestic abuse, the power of money, and improper investigations.

Race. The primary divisive issue revealed by the Simpson cases was the racial divide in America. Frank Rich, columnist for the *New York Times*, wrote that "for two-and-a-half years, the O. J. case has been a grotesque but nonetheless piercing alarm telling us that there is a racial gap so wide in this country that most white and black Americans view the exact same events, not to mention our civic institutions, in exactly opposite ways" (1997, February 12, p. A8). Extensive comments about racial issues surfaced because of the testimony by and about Mark Fuhrman, as chapters 4 and 8 demonstrate. The public continued to react to the trials along racial lines even after the civil trial. By a strong majority, African Americans supported the criminal verdict and faulted the civil verdict, whereas whites, by a strong majority, faulted the criminal verdict and supported the civil verdict.

Despite this fact, the media showed a "virtual rainbow of color, gender, ethnicity, and class" among the courtroom participants (Dyson, 1996a, p. 55). In both trials, the judges were Asian, the attorneys were a mixture of white and African American, the juries included Hispanics. The reporters and commentators for the trials likewise featured persons of a variety of ethnic backgrounds. Women participated in various ways in both trials. These pictures conveyed images that the legal process was no longer the exclusive territory of white males.

Domestic abuse. Another key issue raised by the trials is the issue of domestic abuse. Many attorneys and social workers for domestic abuse victims saw the accusations of domestic abuse against Simpson as a rallying point for their cause. The cases raised the issue of domestic abuse as a legal issue and a social problem. After the verdict in the criminal trial, many domestic abuse centers reported huge increases in the number of calls they received from victims of abuse. The trials sparked conversations about abuse. In her reflections about the criminal trial, Elizabeth Schneider (1996), a well-known feminist attorney, concluded that the trials focused too little on the issue. She reported that "more that 1,500 women are murdered by their husbands or boyfriends each year, and nearly 33 percent of all women murdered are killed by husbands or boyfriends" (p. 77). She argued that even more information should have been reported about the domestic abuse issue. Because Judge Ito had to limit the evidence that could be introduced about incidents of domestic abuse in the criminal trial, advocates now have called for legal reform so that prosecutors can use expert witnesses on this issue. Even given current limitations on the admissibility of domestic violence evidence, chapters 3 and 6 show that extensive evidence was presented in the civil trial about domestic abuse and that this content entered into the themes of the narratives about both cases presented in opening statements and summations of both trials.

The academic press took up the issue in ways not covered by the popular press. For example, one entire edition of the *Hastings Law Review* featured a discussion of domestic abuse and the Simpson criminal case. An issue of *Trial*, the journal of the Association of Trial Lawyers of America, focused on victims and violence and included articles relating specifically to domestic violence. Several television programs and magazine articles used the Simpson trials as a focal point for more superficial discussions of the issue. Both Denise Brown, sister of victim Nicole Brown Simpson, and Kim Goldman, sister of victim Ronald Goldman, have become spokespersons for domestic abuse organizations. As a result of all of these efforts, reports of domestic abuse have increased since the trials.

Money. The trials also raised issues about the use of money in the legal system and hinted at the way the legal system works differently for the rich than it does for the poor. Many sources believe that the criminal trial was one of the most expensive in history both for the State of California and for the defendant, O. J. Simpson. Although the exact costs have not yet been published, the state spent at least $9 million for the prosecution, and Simpson attorneys purportedly earned more than $100,000 per month. One expert witness for the defense was paid over $100,000 to testify in the criminal trial. The jury consultant for the defense, Jo-Ellan Dimitrius, purportedly earned over $1 million from the case. In the punitive phase of the civil trial, the defense argued that defendant Simpson was broke and could not pay the millions in punitive damages because he had spent his fortune of nearly $10 million on legal fees. Although the defendant did not testify in the criminal case, he wrote a book published prior to the criminal trial that told his side of the story and earned $2.8 million. The costs of the criminal trial were only one feature of the money and justice debate. Several witnesses were not called to testify at the trials because they were paid by tabloid newspapers and television programs to give their stories prior to the trial. Even if they did not accept money, the jurors and the public may have believed that witnesses hoped their moment in the spotlight would result in fame and money in the future.

Money was the focus of the verdict in the civil trial. Plaintiffs' attorneys, as they presented evidence, emphasized the financial angle. The gloves, the shoes, the cars owned by O. J. Simpson were items owned by a wealthy person. Simpson associated, the plaintiffs said, primarily with the rich and famous and ate at their restaurants and attended their golf tournaments. After hearing extensive information about the assets and lifestyle of Simpson, this jury awarded a total of $33.5 million in compensatory and punitive damages to the plaintiffs. Even though the plaintiffs argued to the contrary, this case was about money as most civil trials are.

The issue of money and its uses in the trials remains a salient issue for those who believe that justice should not be for sale and that civil verdicts should not force bankruptcy on defendants. In the O. J. Simpson criminal trial, money helped O. J. Simpson buy justice. In the civil trial, it brought him to bankruptcy.

Faulty investigations. The theories of the defense in both trials emphasized the sloppy and improper investigative practices of many of the key witnesses for the prosecution and plaintiffs. For example, the defense criticized important witnesses, such as Mark Fuhrman, Philip Vannatter, and Tom Lange, for unauthorized search procedures, faulty search warrants, and negligence in securing the crime scene. In both cases, the investigatory practices of criminalists Dennis Fung and Andrea Mazzola were impugned by the defense. The defense in both cases also claimed that the technologically sophisticated DNA labs contaminated blood evidence and that the Los Angeles coroners provided faulty autopsy reports. Hardly one investigative procedure or expert witness survived the severe scrutiny of the attorneys under the processes of cross-examination. All of this negative information about the criminal investigation raised issues for jurors and left the public with negative impressions about how crimes are investigated.

Even more serious allegations, a police frame-up and planting of evidence, seemed to be the decisive factor in the criminal verdict. Many jurors doubted that the evidence presented was found or handled in a legitimate manner, as defense attorneys argued in both cases. The media raised issues about the honesty and integrity of police in general. Dershowitz (1996) claims that abuse of police power and the mishandling of evidence are common practices in most jurisdictions. Some local stations produced investigative programs about police procedures as a way of countering or supporting the challenges made in the Simpson case against the crime scene procedures.

Trials of the century have consequences beyond the verdict, especially if there is telelitigation that creates public conversations about social issues. In these cases, Simpson's trials sparked discussions about social issues of race, domestic violence, money, and improper investigations.

Effects on Legal Issues

The Simpson trials have affected more than just O. J. Simpson's fate. They also have affected attitudes about lawyers and the justice system. In particular, Americans are questioning whether, in the criminal trial, the justice system worked or whether the adversary system as we know it is fatally flawed.

How do we know that citizens are concerned about the criminal justice system in the aftermath of the Simpson criminal trial? In my own personal experience observing jury selections, I have found that jurors are expressing increasingly critical opinions about the criminal justice system. For example, when I analyzed juror responses to a supplemental juror questionnaire given in a death penalty case in federal court in Albuquerque, New Mexico, I found that 350 of 485 jurors who completed the questionnaire acknowledged following the Simpson case (see note 1 for the questions asked). Of these 350 jurors, 81 percent offered negative comments about the criminal justice system, 15 percent offered neutral comments about the system, and only 4 percent offered positive comments. Some of the negative comments were broad-based and simply reflected that "the system is messed up." Most of the negative comments, though, fell into one of five categories: money can buy good lawyers a verdict; the media turned the trial into "a dog and pony show," "a mockery," etc.; attorneys distort the truth; the judge was too lenient; or the prosecution was bad. Four percent of the potential jurors offering negative comments blamed the criminal jury for the verdict. For example, people who blamed the jury in the criminal trial wrote: "The system fails when it relies on juries of immoral or ignorant citizens"; "O. J. was a crock—jurors didn't use their heads—anti-scientism has made people stupid, as has racism in all its permutations"; and "[t]hought it a *complete* travesty. How any juror could disregard the . . . evidence to come back with their finding is incredulous!"

Juror education. While media advocates argue for the value of televising trial proceedings, we have to wonder what lessons the jurors actually are learning from a telelitigated trial. In postverdict interviews with jurors in three unrelated civil cases, I have heard more than a dozen jurors admit that the jurors had made their minds up on the first vote or within the first hour but continued to talk so that everyone would take their verdict seriously. When I served as a trial juror in an assault case in the spring of 1997, several of the other members acknowledged slowing deliberations and taking an entire day, after a trial of only two days, so that our jury would not be accused of rushing its decision like the Simpson criminal jury had done. In addition, two of the jurors talked about the need for such deliberativeness in the context of the jury's reaching a potentially unpopular verdict of only finding for the prosecution on two counts, acquitting on two counts, and hanging on the remaining count. Is the lesson being taught that jurors will be criticized if they acquit or if the jury hangs? Or have jurors merely been schooled in the importance of appearing to take their jobs as jurors seriously?

The Simpson trials also have offered lessons in how to get out of jury duty. Several jurors in the venire during my own personal jury service bragged about learning this lesson from the criminal trial. One juror used her newfound knowledge and told a judge in a robbery case that, based on what she had read in the paper, she had formed an opinion. Unfortunately for the juror, the case had received no publicity, and the judge saw through the ploy.

In cases where the trial and verdict are likely to be publicized, jurors are expressing concerns about the media learning their names. Some jurors in the recent New Mexico death-penalty case discussed above even asked if the jury could be anonymous. These jurors wanted the same rights they believed Simpson jurors had been accorded—to speak out after the verdict or to remain anonymous.

The public learned about trial consulting, and since the Simpson trials, jurors routinely have begun to ask trial consultants conducting postverdict interviews about their roles in the trials. In my own research, I am finding that half of the mock jurors in focus groups report having read or heard about trial consultants or seen them as television commentators. Before the Simpson cases, approximately 10 percent understood the role of trial consultants.

Two beneficial lessons emerged from the Simpson trials. First, jurors seem to have a much clearer understanding of the different burdens of proof for criminal and civil trials, and now they often refer to "proof beyond a reasonable doubt" and "preponderance of the evidence" without first being prompted by attorneys. Second, in criminal trials more jurors today are willing to consider that police officers could be lying, especially about the circumstances leading to warrantless searches and the planting of evidence or in cases involving nonwhite defendants.

Jury reform. In the wake of the Simpson trials, critics of the American legal system focused on four major jury reforms. None of the arguments were novel. With the exception of the sequestration issue, all of the suggested reforms were discussed after the Rodney King beating trials. For example, Abramson (1994) and Adler (1994) emerged in this earlier call for reform.

First, critics reconsidered jury sequestration. In calling for reforms related to jury sequestration, critics have been more concerned with an attempt to protect jurors from the media than with easing the burden sequestration has on them. In high-profile criminal cases, some legal scholars now favor the use of an anonymous jury, similar to the one in the Simpson civil trial. The assumption is that anonymity and explicit instructions will keep the media at bay and that the juror will do the rest by staying away from any media reports. Unfortunately, postverdict interviews reveal that jurors often indicate to other members of their panel that they learned something during the course of the trial from outside sources. However, no indication has come from the Simpson civil trial that such a breach occurred, perhaps because jurors knew they faced public ridicule if they broke the mandate against avoiding media reports related to the case. Yet, in everyday trials there is reason to question jurors' ability to adhere to the rule against potential media contamination. The problem is so perplexing that some judges have assigned attorneys the task of exploring alternatives to sequestration. One proposed alternative is to send a bailiff home with each juror, but to my knowledge this proposal is yet to be tested.

A second reform tries to ease the time burden on jurors. The large number of jurors dismissed for hardship in the Simpson criminal trial and the resulting drain of educated, professional jurors has renewed the call for reforms such as one day, one trial. Under this proposal, jurors report for jury selection for only one day, and if they are not chosen, they are dismissed from service. This system is far less burdensome than some that now require jurors to return for multiple jury selections over a two-week, three-month, or six-month period.

Although it made no difference in the Simpson criminal trial, jury reformers are advocating a third reform, nonunanimous verdicts in noncapital murder cases. Oregon and Louisiana already allow 10-to-2 decisions in felony cases, and Oklahoma uses 9-to-3 for misdemeanor cases. Supporters for nonunanimous verdicts argue that they are needed to put an end to so many hung juries. Pete Wilson, governor of California during the Simpson trials, began pushing for nonunanimous juries and speaks often about this concept and emphasizes California's need to reform its jury system in the aftermath of the Simpson trials.

Finally, the Simpson trials sparked renewed discussion about abolishing or severely limiting the use of peremptory challenges, which attorneys exercise to strike jurors whom they suspect of bias. According to reformers, limiting or abolishing peremptory challenges would deprive attorneys of strategically using their challenges to shape the makeup of the jury. By doing away with the peremptory system, critics argue that there would be less need for employing trial consultants, many of whom spend considerable time advising attorneys on which jurors to challenge peremptorily.

Although it is not yet clear how much momentum jury reform has gained because of the Simpson trials, judges and attorneys are concerned about the public's increasingly negative perception of the legal system. Telelitigation, as it evolved in the Simpson trial, may yet prove to be the proverbial straw that broke the camel's back.

Trial reform. But, if jury service is to be manageable for the average citizen, reformers insist that there also must be better trial management. The Simpson trials, for instance, stimulated discussion about whether judges should be setting time limits for trials as a whole and for various components, such as opening statements. Finally, lawyers were asked to hold the mirror to their profession and examine issues of professional conduct. For example, should there be stricter enforcement or more severe penalties for discovery abuses or for talking about likely inadmissible evidence in opening statements or for introducing blatantly prejudicial factors, such as race, if they are not reflected in the evidence? Lawyers are debating such issues and looking at ways to police themselves before politicians attempt to do the policing instead.

The Simpson murder trial has become the criminal justice system's equivalent of the civil trial known as the McDonald's coffee cup case. In both cases, a lot of Americans wondered what happened to result in such seemingly aberrant verdicts. Indeed, after the Simpson trials, the average citizen's concern about the criminal justice system was so profound that lawyers and judges no longer turn their backs on zealous advocacy that runs counter to the rules of fair play. Nor, as this volume illustrates, can the media dodge similar ethical scrutiny. The media must evaluate whether providing entertainment with a capital "E" is truly in the best interest of justice.

Implications of Telelitigation

Telelitigation is defined not just by a camera in the courtroom. Rather, as the authors in this volume show, telelitigation is defined by the drama itself. Telelitigation is drama so real that it seems "made for television." With telelitigation, the story is so compelling that journalists can no longer just report what happened in court on a particular day. Instead, as Furno-Lamude suggests in chapter 2, journalists must react to what the public already has seen and must spin an even more captivating story to secure broadcast time or press space.

In the chapters of this volume, the authors extend the definition of telelitigation beyond the parameters that Schuetz outlines in chapter 1. In particular, the contributors point to the following determinants of telelitigation:

- Several of the authors suggest that telelitigation is defined, in part, by who the rhetor is and what he or she brings to the situation (e.g., wealth or celebrity). But telelitigation also can be understood in terms of the roles rhetors adopt or their attorneys adopt for them and the constraints that accompany a particular role. In chapter 5, Ganer points to this fact when she explains how Simpson had to reframe the evidence once his attorneys redefined his relationship with Brown Simpson as one of marital discord. Given the amount of domestic violence evidence presented in the civil trial, the constraints left little room for l and his attorneys to manipulate the evidence. Their attempts to handle the constraints intensified the existing drama.

- Telelitigation demands public involvement. It encourages the public to take an active role in the trial and even offers the public the opportunity to draw its own conclusions on guilt or innocence. According to Simpson attorney Alan Dershowitz (1996), people who watched the criminal trial were more pro-Simpson than those who depended on journalists' reports (p. 147).

- Telelitigation educates as well as entertains. Unfortunately, as most contributors see it, telelitigation arouses skepticism, not reassurance. Hence it has a radicalizing effect rather than a stabilizing one. The aspects of the Simpson trial that made it compelling drama now have the public saying that the criminal justice system is broken and calling for its reformation.

- Finally, telelitigation is meant to be controversial and meant to challenge. In the Simpson trials, when the defense attorney played the race card, neither journalists nor the public could turn away from the controversy and the dissension.

The consensus among the authors of this volume is that telelitigation shaped the public's perceptions of the Simpson trials in a fashion never previously experienced. Television and press coverage alone were not the reason. Other trials have been televised and received considerable public attention. For example, the first trial of the Menendez brothers and the trial of William Kennedy Smith presaged the explosive potential of telelitigation, but they failed in their attempts to engage and empower the public. The very strength of telelitigation as we saw it in the Simpson trials and all its effects cause us to question whether such a media spectacle should ever again be allowed. We have yet to formulate an answer. That is the subject for yet another book focusing on the trials of O. J. Simpson.

Note

1. Jurors were asked: What criminal cases, either national or local, have you followed in the media? (a) What interested you about these cases? (b) How did the case(s) affect your impression of our system of criminal justice?

Appendixes

References

Contributors

Index

Appendix A: Key Dates in the O. J. Simpson Cases

The material below is adapted from the following sources:

The Associated Press. (1995, October 3). Key days in O. J. case. The Albuquerque Tribune, p. C2.

Key dates in the O. J. Simpson case. (1997, February 5). CNN Interactive [On-line]. Available: http://cnn.com/US/9702/05/oj.timeline/index.html.

1994

June 12	Nicole Brown Simpson and Ronald Goldman are stabbed to death outside of Nicole's condominium.
June 13	O. J. Simpson, Nicole's ex-husband, arrives in Chicago. Detectives go to Simpson's estate and conduct a warrantless search. Simpson is told of the slayings and flies back to Los Angeles. He undergoes questioning at police headquarters.
June 16	Simpson accompanies his youngest children, Sydney and Justin, to his ex-wife's funeral; friends and family attend Goldman's funeral.
June 17	Simpson is charged with murder. Upon failing to surrender as promised, Simpson is declared a fugitive. He is later spotted in a white Ford Bronco with friend Al Cowlings driving. Police follow for sixty miles, ending at Simpson's home where he is arrested.
July 8	After a six-day preliminary hearing, Judge Kathleen Kennedy-Powell finds "ample evidence" for a trial.
July 2	Simpson pleads "absolutely, 100 percent not guilty"; the case is assigned to Judge Lance Ito.
July 2	Goldman's mother files a wrongful-death lawsuit against Simpson, alleging he "willfully, wantonly and maliciously" killed her son.

July 30	Grand jury transcripts depict Simpson as a jealous man who stalked his ex–wife.
Aug. 18	The defense files a motion, which is later denied, seeking Detective Mark Fuhrman's personnel and military records. Defense sources earlier said they might portray Fuhrman as a racist cop who moved a bloody glove to Simpson's estate.
Aug. 22	Court papers disclose that some DNA tests show Simpson's blood has the same genetic makeup as samples leading from the homicide scene.
Sept. 2	Prosecutors file a motion for jury sequestration.
Sept. 9	Prosecutors announce they will seek a sentence of life without parole rather than the death penalty.
Sept. 19	Judge Lance Ito rejects defense claims of sloppy detective work, saying police acted properly when they searched Simpson's house without a warrant.
Sept. 26	Jury selection begins.
Nov. 3	A jury of eight women and four men is selected—a panel composed of eight African Americans, one Anglo, one Hispanic, and two people of mixed race. [See appendix B for jury list.]
Dec. 8	An alternate jury of nine women and three men is selected—seven African Americans, four Anglos, and one Hispanic.
1995
Jan. 4	The defense abandons this challenge to the DNA evidence.
Jan. 11	Jurors are sequestered; the court releases explosive prosecution documents accusing Simpson of beating, degrading, and stalking Nicole throughout their seventeen–year relationship. These documents are released as the hearing on admissibility of evidence relating to domestic violence begins. Defense attempts to bar this evidence and accuses the prosecution of character assassination.
Jan. 12	Prosecutors withdraw eighteen of the sixty-two abuse allegations.
Jan. 13	At the hearing to determine whether defense will be permitted to question Fuhrman about alleged racial slurs, Prosecutor Christopher Darden and Defense Attorney Johnnie Cochran Jr. engage in an emotional ex-

change over the role of race in the trial, and Cochran offers an apology to African Americans.

Jan. 17   Prosecution documents allege Simpson hit his first wife, Marguerite Thomas Simpson. The officer who responded to a domestic call twenty years earlier says that Simpson's then–wife said Simpson hit her, and she was taken to a hotel for the night. In a June police interview, Thomas denied that Simpson ever abused her.

Jan. 18   Ito rules that the jurors can hear the evidence of domestic violence, and he dismisses two jurors. After highly publicized bickering between Simpson attorneys Robert Shapiro and F. Lee Bailey, Cochran takes the lead on the defense team.

Jan. 20   Ito allows the possibility of Fuhrman's racism to be introduced if the defense can prove it is relevant.

Jan. 24   Ito rejects Simpson's request to speak to jurors before defense's opening statements, but he does allow him to show the scars on his knees. Darden and Clark begin opening statements.

Jan. 27   Simpson's book, *I Want to Tell You*, is released in response to more than 300,000 pieces of mail sent to him.

Jan. 31   The first prosecution witness testifies. Sharyn Gilbert, a 911 operator and dispatcher, testifies that she answered the call from Simpson's home on New Year's Day, 1989.

Feb. 3   Denise Brown sobs on the witness stand as she testifies how Simpson humiliated her sister Nicole in public and once threw her against a wall.

Feb. 7   Another juror is dismissed.

Feb. 12   Jurors take a daytime tour of the Simpson estate and the slaying scene.

Mar. 1   Another juror is dismissed.

Mar. 15   Fuhrman denies under cross–examination that he has used a racial slur in the past ten years.

Mar. 17   Another juror is dismissed.

Apr. 5   Another juror is dismissed.

Apr. 11   Criminalist Dennis Fung testifies and concedes that he did not detect blood on the socks at Simpson's home or on the back gate of the slaying scene until weeks later.

Apr. 21	Jurors wear black to court and refuse to hear testimony this day after three deputies who guarded the panel are reassigned amid charges of giving preferential treatment to white jurors.
May 1	Juror Tracy Hampton is dismissed because she can no longer take the stress of the trial and sequestration.
May 4	Goldman's father and sister file a wrongful death lawsuit against Simpson.
May 10	The testimony about DNA blood analysis begins; scientist Robin Cotton is the first witness to link Simpson to the murders through genetic tests.
May 26	Another juror is dismissed.
June 5	Two more jurors are dismissed. Juror makeup now is ten women and two men—nine African Americans, one Hispanic, and two Anglos.
June 12	On the anniversary of the killings, the estate of Nicole Brown Simpson files a lawsuit asserting that O. J. Simpson "brutally and with malice aforethought stalked, attacked, and repeatedly stabbed and beat" his ex–wife.
June 15	Simpson struggles to pull on the bloody gloves found at the slaying scene and at his estate. Prosecutors suggest that the gloves had shrunk.
July 6	The prosecution rests.
July 10	The defense calls its first witness—Simpson's grown daughter, Arnelle.
Aug. 15	Clark says she will ask Ito to remove himself from the trial because of an appearance of conflict of interest stemming from tapes Fuhrman made as part of a screenwriting project about the Los Angeles Police Department. In the tapes, Fuhrman made derogatory comments about Ito's police–captain wife and minorities.
Aug. 16	Clark backs down from her threat to seek Ito's recusal. Ito says he will rule on the admissibility of the Fuhrman tapes but allows another judge to determine whether his wife is a relevant witness.
Aug. 18	Superior Court judge John Reid rules that Ito's wife has nothing relevant to add to the trial.
Aug. 29	Excerpts of recorded interviews between Fuhrman and a screenwriter are played with the jury absent.

Aug. 31	Ito rules that the jurors will hear only two of the sixty-one excerpts the defense wants to present. Cochran calls Ito's ruling cruel and unfair. Lawyer Robert Tourtelot says he will no longer act as Fuhrman's spokesman and will no longer represent him.
Sept. 5	The jurors hear Fuhrman on the tape using racial epithets.
Sept. 6	Fuhrman returns to the witness stand, out of the jury's presence, and invokes the Fifth Amendment protection against self–incrimination. African American witness Roderic Hodge tells jurors that when Fuhrman arrested him in 1987, he used a racial slur.
Sept. 7	The defense ends months of speculation by saying that Simpson will not testify. Judge Ito agrees to the defense's request that jurors be told Fuhrman had become "unavailable," which they could consider in weighing his credibility. The prosecution appeals Ito's proposed instruction.
Sept. 8	An appeals court rejects Ito's jury instruction about Fuhrman.
Sept. 11	The defense refuses to rest its case pending an appeal on whether Fuhrman can be recalled for cross-examination about the racist issue; Judge Ito orders prosecutors to begin rebuttal.
Sept. 13	Cochran announces that he wants FBI agent Frederic Whitehurst to testify about problems in the FBI crime lab.
Sept. 14	The appeals court rejects the defense's request to recall Fuhrman for cross–examination about racist statements in taped interviews.
Sept. 18	The prosecution conditionally rests.
Sept. 19	Detective Philip Vannatter is grilled in court about statements he allegedly made to mob informants. Ito blacks out the trial for the first time in the case so informants can testify. Three FBI agents testify that Vannatter said he suspected "the husband" from the start.
Sept. 20	Ito bars Whitehurst's testimony about sloppy procedures in the FBI crime labs. Police commander Keith Bushey testifies that he gave orders for investigators to go to Simpson's estate and notify him of his ex–wife's slaying.
Sept. 21	Ito gives jurors the option of finding Simpson guilty of second–degree murder.

Sept. 22	The defense and the prosecution both rest. Simpson tells the judge, "I did not, could not, and would not have committed this crime." Ito reads the jury instructions.
Sept. 26	The prosecution begins closing arguments. Ito blacks out the trial when a court camera inadvertently pans to Simpson's hand as he is writing a note. The judge eventually allows the camera back on but fines the broadcast group $1,500.
Sept. 27	The prosecution finishes its closing arguments; the defense begins.
Sept. 28	During summation, Cochran upsets the Goldman family when he compares Fuhrman to Adolf Hitler. Goldman's father, Fred, tells a live TV audience that Cochran "is the worst kind of human being imaginable." Simpson's family counters this statement in a news conference saying, "It's wrong for someone to get up and personally attack our lawyers and say that they are liars."
Sept. 29	The prosecution presents rebuttal arguments. Final jury instructions are given by Judge Ito, and the case goes to the jury. A forewoman is selected in about three minutes.
Oct. 2	The jury deliberates less than four hours before reaching a verdict.
Oct. 3	The jury finds O. J. Simpson not guilty.
1996 Oct. 23	Opening statements in the civil trial begin. The jury is composed of nine whites, one black, one Hispanic, and one person of black and Asian ancestry.
Nov. 22	Simpson testifies before a jury for the first time when he is called adversely by the plaintiffs. He denies killing Brown Simpson and Goldman, but he cannot explain the physical evidence against him.
Dec. 9	Victim Ron Goldman's father, Fred Goldman, testifies. The plaintiffs rest.
Dec. 20	An Orange County judge awards Simpson custody of children, Sydney and Justin, in a separate custody hearing.
1997 Jan. 10	Simpson takes the stand again during the defense portion of the case and describes his ex–wife's increasingly erratic behavior.

Jan. 16	Both sides rest after hearing 101 witnesses in forty-one days of testimony.
Jan. 21	The plaintiffs make their closing arguments, and attorney Daniel Petrocelli points at Simpson and says, "There's a killer in this courtroom."
Jan. 22	The defense attorneys make their closing arguments, and attorney Robert Baker says, "It's law enforcement vs. O. J. Simpson."
Feb. 4	The jury unanimously finds Simpson liable in the slayings and awards $8.5 million in compensatory damages.
Feb. 12	Jurors return a verdict of $12.5 million in punitive damages for the death of Ron Goldman and $12.5 million for Nicole Brown Simpson's death. This portion of the verdict was not unanimous.

Appendix B: Juries from the Simpson Trials

Criminal Trial

The material below is adapted from Islandnet [Internet].
Available: http://www.islandnet.com/~walraven/the_jury.html.

Jurors Who Voted
Seat 1 (#230, Armanda Cooley): Cooley was the foreperson and an original juror. She was a fifty-one-year-old black female who was divorced. She had two years of college and was employed as a vendor. She lived in South Central L.A., and she is a co-author of *Madam Foreman: A Rush to Judgment?*, which she wrote with jurors Bess and Rubin-Jackson.

Seat 2 (#1492, Yolanda Crawford): Crawford was placed on the jury on June 6, replacing Farran Chavarria. Crawford was a twenty-five-year-old black female who was single. She had gone through one year of college and worked as a hospital employee. She lived in Gardena. She informed Judge Ito about a note written by Chavarria on a newspaper that was allegedly read by Florio-Bunten, causing their dismissals.

Seat 3 (#1290, Anise Aschenbach): She was placed on the jury March 17, replacing Tracy Kennedy. Aschenbach is a white female who was sixty-one and divorced. She had completed one year of college and is a retired gasoline company clerk. She lived in Norwalk and is one of two jurors who voted guilty in the first vote.

Seat 4 (#19, David Aldana): Aldana was an original juror. He was a thirty-three-year-old single Hispanic male. He is a high school graduate who was employed as a Pepsi delivery truck driver. Aldana lived in East L.A.

Seat 5 (#984, Marsha Rubin-Jackson): She was an original juror. Rubin-Jackson is a black female who was thirty-eight and married. She is a high school graduate and was a mail carrier for USPS. She lived in Bellflower and co-wrote *Madam Foreman: A Rush to Judgment?*

Seat 6 (#247, Lionel Cryer): Cryer was placed on the jury January 18. He was a forty-four-year-old black male. He is a high school graduate who worked as a phone company marketing representative. Florio-Bunten told Ito she thought that he might be writing a book. He gave Simpson a "power salute" after the verdict.

Seat 7 (#795, Brenda Moran): Moran was placed on the jury April 5, replacing Jeanette Harris. She was a forty-five-year-old black female who was single. She is a high school graduate and worked as a computer technician. She wrote a book with Gina Rosborough, titled *Inside the Simpson Jury: The Parallel Universe*.

Seat 8 (#1233, Sheila Woods): Woods was an original juror. She is a black female who was thirty-nine and single. She is a college graduate and was employed as an environmental health specialist. She lived in Inglewood. She told Ito she thought that Aschenbach, Florio-Bunten, and Chavarria disliked her because they suspected her of being behind the dismissal of Kathryn Murdoch.

Seat 9 (#98, Carrie Bess): Bess was an original juror. She was a fifty-three-year-old black female who was divorced. She is a high school graduate and worked as a postal clerk. She lived in South Central L.A. She is a co-author of *Madam Foreman: A Rush to Judgment?*

Seat 10 (#2179, Gina Rosborough): She was placed on the jury June 6, replacing Willie Craven. Rosborough was a twenty-year-old married black female. She is a high school graduate and worked as a postal employee. She wrote a book with Brenda Moran titled *Inside the Simpson Jury: The Parallel Universe*.

Seat 11 (#63, Annie Backman): Backman was an original juror. She was a twenty-three-year-old single white female. She is a college graduate who was working as an insurance claims adjuster and lived in Burbank. She is believed to be the other juror who initially voted "guilty" (Source: Aschenbach's interview on *Larry King Live*).

Seat 12 (#2457, Beatrice Wilson): Wilson was placed on the jury May 26. She replaced Francine Florio-Bunten, who replaced Michael Knox. Wilson was a seventy-two-year-old black female who was married. She has a tenth-grade education and is a retired cleaner who lived in L.A.'s West Adams.

Remaining Alternate Jurors

#165 (Watson Calhoun): Calhoun is a black male who was seventy-three and married. He is a retired security guard. According to the transcripts, he had several run-ins with the deputies and other jurors.

#1386 (Reyko Butler): Butler is a white female who was twenty-five and married. She worked as a fire department receptionist and lived in Altadena. She said she would have voted "guilty" in an interview with *American Journal*.

Dismissed Jurors

#228 (Roland Cooper): Cooper was dismissed January 18. He was a forty-nine-year-old black male who worked for the Hertz rental car company. He allegedly met Simpson at a Hertz function. (Motion was made by the prosecution; an objection was made by the defense.)

#320 (Name Unknown): Juror was dismissed January 18. She was a thirty-nine-year-old Hispanic female who worked as a letter carrier. Apparently, she was involved in an abusive relationship with her ex-boyfriend while serving on the jury. (Motion was made by the defense; an objection was made by the prosecution.)

#2017 (Kathryn Murdoch): Murdoch was dismissed February 7. She was a sixty-four-year-old white female who was a retired legal secretary. The court found out that she was a patient of the same doctor who had been treating Simpson for arthritis. The doctor was expected to be a defense witness. (Motion was made by the defense; an objection was made by the prosecution.)

#620 (Michael Knox): Knox was dismissed March 1. He was a forty-seven-year-old black male who worked as a courier. Before being empaneled, he reportedly offered to bet a week's wages that Simpson would be found innocent of double murder. At times, he wore a San Francisco 49ers cap while serving on the jury and allegedly spent too much time "admiring" Simpson's stuff during the jury's visit to Rockingham. After his dismissal, he co-wrote *The Private Diary of an O. J. Juror*. (Motion was made by the prosecution; an objection was made by the defense.)

#602 (Tracy Kennedy): Kennedy was dismissed March 17. He is an American Indian and white male. He was fifty-three and married at the time of the trial. He taught high school and interviewed prospective employees for Amtrak. He was first targeted by Robert Shapiro during a sidebar in mid-February for continually staring "out into space" and not paying attention in the jury box. Later, Kennedy was accused of writing a book. He was dismissed when he was apparently caught lying about having juror information on his notebook computer. He co-wrote *Mistrial of the Century* with his wife. (Motion was made by the defense; objection was made by the prosecution.)

#462 (Jeanette Harris): Harris was dismissed April 5. She was a thirty-nine-year-old married black female who worked as an employment interviewer. The court found out that she had past experience with domestic violence, which she failed to report in the juror questionnaire and during jury selection. (Motion was made by the prosecution; an objection was made by the defense.)

#452 (Tracy Hampton): Hampton was dismissed May 1. She is a black female who was twenty-six and single at the time of the trial. She was employed as a flight attendant. She told Ito she "couldn't take it anymore." After her dismissal, she posed for *Playboy*. (Motion was made by the court; no objection was made by either side.)

#353 (Francine Florio-Bunten): Florio-Bunten was dismissed May 26. She was a thirty-nine-year-old white female who was married. She worked as a technician at Pacific Bell. She told Ito she thought Cryer might be writing a book. An anonymous letter, claiming to be from a literary agent's receptionist, accused Florio-Bunten of contracting a book titled *Standing Alone—A Vote for Nicole*. However, according to Ito, she was "primarily" dismissed for lying about reading a note written on a newspaper by Chavarria. Now she says she likely would have voted "guilty." (Motion was made by the defense; an objection was made by the prosecution.)

#1489 (Willie Craven): Craven was dismissed June 5. He was a fifty-five-year-old black male who was married at the time of the trial. He was employed as a postal operations manager, and he was accused of being a "bully" and intimidating other jurors, especially Chavarria. (Motion was made by the prosecution; an objection was made by the defense.)

#1427 (Farran Chavarria): Chavarria was dismissed June 5. She is a Hispanic female who was twenty-nine and single. She was employed as a real estate appraiser. She accused Craven of harassing her and of wanting off the jury. She wrote a "clandestine" note on a newspaper and allegedly showed it to Florio-Bunten. (Motion was made by the defense; an objection was made by the prosecution.)

Civil Trial

The material below is adapted from the following sources:

Associated Press. (1997, January 28). *USA Today* [Internet]. Available:
http://www.usatoday.com/news/index/nns178.html
CNN Interactive [On-line] (1996, October 18). Available:
http://cnn.com/US/9610/18/oj.jurors/index.html
MSNBC [Internet]. (1997, August 3). Available:
http://www.islandnet.com/~walraven/c_jury.html

Seated Jurors
Seat 1 (#199): Seat 1 was a Jamaican-born male of mixed Asian and black descent in his twenties or early thirties. He had lived in the United States for ten years, and he has a bachelor's degree in math from California State, Fresno. He believed DNA is "like a genetic fingerprint." He said he was unsure of Simpson's guilt or innocence following the criminal trial, but he was surprised at the quick verdict in the criminal case. When asked if he believes physical force predisposes a person to more severe violence, he said, "Yes." He said he watched Simpson's criminal trial on television for "entertainment" only.

Seat 2 (#341): Seat 2 was a white female who appeared to be in her sixties. She worked as a security officer at a bank. On her juror questionnaire, she wrote that, in her opinion, the use of force in a relationship often predisposes a person to violence. She said there was not enough evidence at the criminal trial to convict Simpson, and she felt that he is probably not guilty. She also felt that interracial marriages can cause problems. She noted that Simpson seemed to have difficulty when he tried on the gloves, and she felt "that was kind of peculiar." She is a widowed mother of three; one son still lives with her. She did not understand the DNA evidence in the criminal case, saying, "That's over my head." When asked about Los Angeles police detective Mark Fuhrman, she said, "I was just amazed to hear they gave him probation when he lied on the witness stand."

Seat 3 (#186): Seat 3 was a white male in his twenties or thirties. He said he rarely followed the criminal case, and he found the attorneys in that case "annoying." He said he doesn't believe cops are all good or all bad, and he had no opinion on whether Simpson was responsible for the killings. He believed DNA is like "a fingerprint" and said most of his information on DNA came from watching the Discovery Channel and the movie *Jurassic Park*. He was worried about the verdict's effect, saying, "I'm afraid whatever the outcome, I will offend people." Although he said he didn't want people to dislike him, he said that he was willing to put that aside in reaching a decision.

Seat 4 (#294): Seat 4 was a white female in her twenties who worked in retail. She did not watch many news reports on the criminal trial. "The news depresses me. I try to avoid it." She had no opinion on whether Simpson was responsible for the killings. She felt some evidence could have been tampered with. Regarding Detective Mark Fuhrman, she said, "You can't base the trial on one man." She wrote that Simpson was "secure, athletic and wealthy" on her juror questionnaire, and she said that she grew up seeing Simpson as a hero because he endorsed "all the cool products." She replaced juror 78, a woman of mixed white and Hispanic descent in her thirties, who was dismissed for inappropriate behavior on November 25.

Seat 5 (#266): Seat 5 is a white female who was in her forties who grew up in the South. She worked as a stage manager for a nonprofit theater company. She believed that some witnesses during the criminal trial had an agenda. She thought Simpson was probably guilty of the killings but described her opinion as a "vague response" she could set aside. Evidence of domestic abuse is what made her lean toward guilt. Later, she heard police had mishandled evidence, which caused her to have doubts. She thought a police conspiracy was "unlikely, although anything is possible." She said she doesn't think the police were out to "get" Simpson, but added, "The criminal justice system is full of flaws, but it's standing up just like the Santa Monica Courthouse," a building full of cracks from an earthquake in 1994. She felt the media "speculated wildly" during the last case, and that troubled her because "this is very serious business."

Seat 6 (#257): Seat 6 was a Hispanic female in her twenties or thirties. She indicated on her juror questionnaire that she did not pay much attention to Simpson's criminal trial and had few opinions about the case. She said that at the beginning of the criminal trial, she thought Simpson was guilty, but "other things came up" that gave her doubts. She described Simpson's relationship with his ex-wife, Nicole Brown Simpson, as "dysfunctional," and she was saddened when she saw the pictures of Nicole's battered face. She said she thought the Bronco chase was silly and that she believed police were "sloppy" in handling evidence. But she also said she was confused because a professor told her that DNA was the best evidence, yet after seeing that evidence, the criminal jury found Simpson not guilty.

Seat 7 (#333): Seat 7 was a black female in her sixties. Her late husband was a parole officer for the California Youth Authority. Her brother-in-law was killed by a robber during a holdup at the liquor store he owned. She said she still trusts law enforcement but thinks evidence in the Simpson case could have been mishandled. She was worried that an unpopular verdict could have caused riots in her neighborhood. She is a grandmother and said many times that she feels sorry for Simpson's children—Sydney and Justin. She also told attorneys that she felt sympathy for Fred Goldman, the father of murder victim Ronald Goldman, because "[i]t's a parent's worst nightmare to have your child die before you do." She was not sure about Simpson's guilt or innocence, but she also said, "Celebrities are human beings, just as likely to kill as any other person." She said she did not watch a lot of the criminal trial because she was "in pain" for Denise Brown and the Goldmans, and she decided against watching all that pain.

Seat 8 (#290): Seat 8 was a white male in his forties, believed to be of Middle Eastern descent. He worked as a supervisor, specializing in arbitration. He described himself as a "good listener" and said he would "go in with an open mind." He said he decided not to watch the criminal trial. "The media had such a saturation campaign," he said, and he had "more important things" in his life. He thought the police treated Simpson differently during the low-speed chase. "Being of celebrity status, they extended some courtesy," he said. He didn't believe race was a big part of this case, saying, "It's about whether the defendant is responsible to the plaintiffs."

Seat 9 (#326): Seat 9 was a white male in his forties or fifties who was an unemployed cement finisher. He said police treated him fairly when he was once arrested for driving under the influence, but he also said that he has an open mind about police misconduct. He said it was "possible" that evidence in the case had been tampered with, and he was doubtful about blood found on a gate at Nicole Brown Simpson's home two months after the murders. He believes police are sometimes involved in coverups. "Of course they cover up for each other," he said. "It's been done before." He was not sure whether Simpson was responsible for the murders because of "tainted" evidence, but he also said that domestic abuse is never justified. He replaced Edgar Allan, a juror who was removed for an alcoholism problem.

Seat 10 (#400): Seat 10 was a white female in her fifties or sixties. She did invoices and paid bills for the legal department where she worked. She was married and had six children, three still living at home. She said because of her family and her ten- to eleven-hour workdays, she had little opportunity to follow Simpson's criminal trial. But she did remember Prosecutor Marcia Clark's hairdo. She said she was unsure of Simpson's guilt or innocence, but she thought the low-speed Bronco chance made Simpson appear guilty. She explained that her husband has some prejudice, but she doesn't share his opinions about race and other issues. "We disagree a lot," she said, and she indicated he would not influence her decision. She said her husband told her to just tell the court that Simpson was guilty so she could be done with jury duty. But instead, she said, "I could be fair." She also has strong religious beliefs but told attorneys that she is "not a fanatic." She said her daughter had been in a situation involving domestic violence with a boyfriend. She also heard that Simpson had "slapped around" Nicole, but that didn't necessarily mean he was the killer. She said that she thinks interracial couples should give careful thought to having children.

Seat 11 (#88): Seat 11 was a white married female in her thirties. She used to live near the crime scene and wrote on her questionnaire that Simpson was "probably guilty" of the murders. However, she thought a frame-up was a possibility. When asked if she would listen to arguments about evidence planting by police, she said, "I believe anything is possible." She said she disagrees with her husband, who strongly believes Simpson is innocent, and would not discuss the case with him. She said Mark Fuhrman would not make a trustworthy witness but added that the police tend to tell the truth. She said DNA could have a great impact on the case, comparing it to a fingerprint.

Seat 12 (#227): Seat 12 was a white male in his fifties or sixties. He first thought Simpson was innocent, but later concluded that Simpson was "probably guilty" because there did not seem to be another answer. "The prosecution failed to prove its case" during the criminal trial, he said. However, he hoped Simpson wasn't guilty because he admires him as an athlete. The juror said physical force cannot be justified, but he does not link domestic violence to murder. His father was a policeman, but he said that would not affect his decision in the case because police officers can make mistakes. He believes interracial marriages are "impractical" because they can pose problems.

Remaining Alternate Jurors

#369: Alternate juror #369 was an Asian male in his thirties who worked as a computer programmer. "I'm neutral," he said, but he believed planting of evidence is possible.

#206: He was a white male in his sixties who is a retired medical diagnostic lab worker. He said he knew little about the case because he was more concerned with problems in Yugoslavia.

#27: He was a white male. He has friends in the Los Angeles Police Department and has gone on police ride-alongs. He said he had ignored recent publicity and did not know about former detective Mark Fuhrman's no contest plea, saying "[T]here's two sides to every story."

#294: Alternate juror #294 moved to seat 4 on the jury after dismissal of juror 78.

#295: She is a black female who was in her forties and worked for a medical corporation. She said she would not be upset by gruesome photos in the case and added, "I would listen to the evidence and base my decision on the evidence."

Dismissed Alternate Jurors

#205: Alternate juror #205 was dismissed November 15. She is a white female who was in her twenties and a college student. She did not believe race was an issue in the Simpson case. She was dismissed for sleeping in court.

#330: He was dismissed December 17. He was a Hispanic male in his forties who said he was unbiased: "I call 'em as I see 'em."

#367: He was dismissed October 31. He is a white male who did desktop publishing in the marketing department of a law firm. He was a member of a previous jury that hung 10–2 for guilt. His dismissal was due to illness.

References

ABC world news tonight with Peter Jennings. (1997, February 10). R. N. Kaplan (Executive Producer). [Transcript #97121001-j04]. New York and Century City, CA: ABC Distribution Company.

Abramson, J. (1994). *We, the jury.* New York: Basic Books.

———, (Ed.). (1996). *Postmortem: The O. J. Simpson case. Justice confronts race, domestic violence, lawyers, money, and the media.* New York: Basic Books.

Adler, S. J. (1994). *The jury: Trial and error in the American courtroom.* New York: Random House.

Aldana, D. (1995, October 10). Hispanic Simpson juror says race not issue. *Houston Chronicle,* p. 3A.

Alexander, S. L. (1996, January/February). The impact of *California v. Simpson* on cameras in the courtroom. *Judicature, 79,* 169–72.

Alter, J. (1997, February 17). The O. J. legacy. *Newsweek, 129,* 126–29.

American Bar Association (ABA). (1997). Recommendation 7, p. 18 [Online]. Available: http://www.abanet.org/nedua/feb97/death.html.

Anastaplo, G. (1995). On crime, criminal lawyers, and O. J. Simpson: Plato's *Gorgias* revisited. *Loyola University Chicago Law Journal, 26,* 464–65.

Armstrong, B. (1979). *The electronic church.* Nashville, TN: Thomas Nelson Publishers.

Atkin, C., & M. Block. (1983). Effectiveness of celebrity endorsers. *Journal of Advertising Research, 23,* 57–62.

Auerbach, P. G. (1990). The effective opening statement. *Trial Diplomacy Journal, 13,* 27–39.

Barber, S. (1987). *News cameras in the courtroom.* Norwood, NJ: Albex.

Batson v. Kentucky, 476 U.S. 79 (1986).

Bennett, W. L., & M. S. Feldman. (1981). *Reconstructing reality in the courtroom: Justice and judgment in American culture.* New Brunswick, NJ: Rutgers University Press.

Benoit, W. L. (1995). *Accounts, excuses, and apologies: A theory of image restoration strategies.* Albany: State University of New York Press.

Benoit, W. L., & J. S. France. (1983). Review of research on opening statements and closing arguments. In R. J. Matlon & R. J. Crawford (Eds.), *Communication strategies in the practice of lawyering* (pp. 384–400). Annandale, VA: Speech Communication Association.

Bloom, J. (1996). The O. J. media circus. In J. Gorham (Ed.), *Mass media* (pp. 79–82). Connecticut: Dushkin Publishing Group.

Boorstin, D. (1978). *The republic of technology: Reflections on our future community.* New York: Harper & Row.

Bortner, M. A. (1984). Media images and public attitudes toward crime and justice. In R. Surette (Ed.), *Justice and the media* (pp. 15–30). Springfield, IL: Charles C. R. Thomas.

Boster, F. J., J. E. Hunter & J. L. Hale. (1991). An information-processing model of jury decision making. *Communication Research, 18,* 524–47.

Boyll, J. R. (1991). Psychological, cognitive, personality and interpersonal factors in jury verdicts. *Law and Psychology Review, 15,* 163–84.

Bridgeman, D. L. & D. Marlowe. (1979). Jury decision-making: An empirical study based on actual felony trials. *Journal of Applied Psychology, 64,* 91–98.

Brooks, P. (1996). The law as narrative and rhetoric. In P. Brooks & P. Gewirtz (Eds.), *Law's stories: Narrative and rhetoric in law* (pp. 14–22). New Haven, CN: Yale University Press.

Brooks, P., & P. Gewirtz (Eds.). (1996), *Law's stories: Narrative and rhetoric in law.* New Haven, CN: Yale University Press.

Brown, W. J., J. J. Duane & B. P. Fraser. (1997). Media coverage and public opinion of the O. J. Simpson trial: Implications for the criminal justice system. *Communication Law and Policy, 2,* 261–87.

Buchanan, R. W. (1983). Opening statements and closing arguments: A response from the communication perspective. In R. J. Matlon & R. J. Crawford (Eds.), *Communication strategies in the practice of lawyering* (pp. 449–60). Annandale, VA: Speech Communication Association.

Bugliosi, V. (1996). *Outrage: The five reasons why O. J. Simpson got away with murder.* New York: W. W. Norton & Company.

Burden of Proof (CNN). (1995, May 1–31). L. Ortarsh (Executive Producer). G. Van Susteran and R. Cossack. Washington, DC: Turner Program Services.

———. (1997, February 7). L. Ortarsh (Executive Producer). G. Van Susteran and R. Cossack. Washington, DC: Turner Program Services.

———. (1997, February 11). L. Ortarsh (Executive Producer). Laura Fast Khazaee [Interview]. Washington, DC: Turner Program Services.

Burnett Pettus, A. (1990). The verdict is in: A study of jury decision-making factors, moment of personal decision, and jury deliberations—from the jurors' point of view. *Communication Quarterly, 38,* 83–97.

Cal. Ann. Code, R. of Ct. 980(B) (West 1994).

Caplan, L. (1996). The failure (and promise) of legal journalism. In J. Abramson (Ed.), *Postmortem: The O. J. Simpson case: Justice confronts race, domestic violence, lawyers, money, and the media* (pp. 195–98). New York: Basic Books.

Cialdini, R. B., R. E. Petty & J. T. Cacioppo. (1981). Attitude and attitude change. *Annual Review of Psychology, 32*, 357–404.

Clark, M. (with T. Carpenter). (1997). *Without a doubt.* New York: Viking Penguin.

CNN. (1995, October 4a). D. Knapp, D. (Executive Producer). Atlanta, GA: Turner Program Services.

———. (1995, October 4b). B. Moran [Interview]. [Transcript #1321-4]. Atlanta, GA: Turner Program Services.

———. (1995, October 29). G. Rosborough [Interview]. [Transcript #1321-4]. Atlanta, GA: Turner Program Services.

CNN *live coverage of the O. J. Simpson trial.* (1995, September 26). Atlanta, GA: Turner Program Services.

Cochran, J. (with Jim Rutten). (1996). *Journey to justice.* New York: Ballantine Books.

Coke, T. E. (1994). Lady justice may be blind, but is she a soul sister? Race neutrality and the ideal of representative juries. *New York University Law Review, 66*, 354–55.

Commission to investigate allegations of police corruption and the anti-corruption practices of the police department. (1994, July 7). *Mollen Commission Report* [New York].

Comstock, G. (1980). *Television in America.* Newbury Park, CA: Sage Publications.

Conway, J. C., & A. Rubin. (1991). Psychological predictors of television viewing motivation. *Communication Research, 18* (4), 443–63.

Cooley, A., C. Bess & M. Rubin-Jackson. (1995). *Madam foreman: A rush to judgment?* Beverly Hills, CA: Dove Books.

Cornwell, T. (1997, February 7). O. J. waits for second damages bill. *The Independent,* p. 12.

Cottrol, R. J. (1996, Fall). Through a glass diversely: The O. J. Simpson trial as racial Rorschach test. *University of Colorado Law Review, 67*, 909–21.

Crawford, R. J. (1989). *The persuasion edge: Winning psychological strategies and tactics for lawyers.* Eau Claire, WI: Professional Education Systems.

———. (1990, Winter). Expanding the boundaries of the opening statement. *Trial Diplomacy Journal, 13*, 227–32.

Curriden, M. (1995, October). Blowing smoke. *ABA Journal, 81*, 56–60.

Darden, C. (with Walter, J.). (1996). *In contempt.* New York: Regan Books.

Darden, C. (1997, February 17). Justice is in the color of the beholder. *Time, 149,* 38–39.

Davis, J. H., N. L. Kerr, G. Stasser, D. Meek & R. Holt. (1977). Victim consequences, sentence severity, and decision processes in mock juries. *Organizational Behavior and Human Performance, 18,* 346–65.

Denniston, L. W. (1980). *The reporter and the law.* New York: Hastings House.

Dershowitz, A. M. (1996). *Reasonable doubts: The O. J. Simpson case and the criminal justice system.* New York: Simon & Schuster.

Deutsch, D. (1966). *The nerves of government.* New York: Free Press.

Djurkovic, D. (1997, February 11). Interview [On-line]. Available: http://www.usatoday.com.

Dominick, J. (1996). *The dynamics of mass communication* (5th ed.). New York: McGraw-Hill Companies.

Double justice: Race and the death penalty. (1997) *American Civil Liberties Union* [On-line]. Available: http://www.aclu.org/issues/death/death5.html.

Dunne, D. (1995, February). L.A. in the age of O. J. *Vanity Fair, 58,* 46–56.

———. (1997, April). Closing arguments. *Vanity Fair, 60,* 136–49.

Dyson, E. M. (1996a). Obsessed with O. J. In J. Abramson (Ed.), *Postmortem: The O. J. Simpson case: Justice confronts race, domestic violence, lawyers, money, and the media* (pp. 46–56). New York: Basic Books.

———. (1996b). *Race rules: Navigating the color line.* New York: Garamond Books.

Elias, T., & D. Schatzman. (1996). *The Simpson trial in black and white.* Los Angeles: General Publishing Group.

Eliot, M. (1995). *Kato Kaelin: The whole truth. The real story of O. J., Nicole, and Kato: From the actual tapes.* New York: Harper Paperbacks.

Fan, D. P., H. B. Brosius & H. M. Kepplinger. (1994). Predictions of the public agenda from television coverage. *Journal of Broadcasting & Electronic Media, 38* (2), 163–78.

Ferguson, R. A. (1996). Untold stories in the law. In P. Brooks & P. Gewirtz (Eds.), *Law's stories: Narrative and rhetoric in law* (pp. 84–98). New Haven, CN: Yale University Press.

Finkel, N. J. (1995). *Commonsense justice: Jurors' notions of the law.* Cambridge, MA: Harvard University Press.

Fisher, W. R. (1987). *Human communication as narration: Toward a philosophy of reason, value, and action.* Columbia: University of South Carolina Press.

Ford, A. (1995, October 9). The Simpson legacy. *Los Angeles Times,* p. S3.

Foss, R. D. (1976). Group decision processes in the simulated trial jury. *Sociometry, 39*, 305–16.

Foss, S. (1989). *Rhetorical criticism: Exploration & practice.* Prospect Heights, IL: Waveland Press.

Frankel, M. (1994, October 16). I am not a camera. *New York Times Magazine*, pp. 28–32.

Freedman, J. L., K. Krismer, J. E. MacDonald & J. A. Cunningham. (1994). Severity of penalty, seriousness of the charge, and mock jurors' verdicts. *Law and Human Behavior, 18*, 189–202.

Fuhrman, M. (1997). *Murder in Brentwood.* Washington, DC: Regnery Publishing.

Ganer, P. M., K. J. Congalton & C. D. Olson. (1991). Excuse making in argument: The reliance on ebmos. In F. H. VanEemeren, R. Grootendorst, J. A. Blair, & C. A. Willard (Eds.), *Proceedings of the second International Conference on Argumentation* (pp. 619–24). Amsterdam: SICSAT.

Garber, M., J. Matlock & R. L. Walkowitz. (1993). *Media spectacles.* New York: Routledge.

Gewirtz, P. (1996a). Narrative and rhetoric in law. In P. Brooks & P. Gewirtz (Eds.), *Law's stories: Narrative and rhetoric in law* (pp. 2–13). New Haven, CN: Yale University Press.

———. (1996b). Victims and voyeurs: Two narrative problems at the criminal trial. In P. Brooks & P. Gewirtz (Eds.), *Law's stories: Narrative and rhetoric in law* (pp. 135–61). New Haven, CN: Yale University Press.

Gibbs, J. T. (1996). *Race and justice: Rodney King and O. J. Simpson in a house divided.* San Francisco: Jossey-Bass.

Goffman, E. (1959). *The presentation of self in everyday life.* New York: Anchor.

———. (1971). *Relations in public.* New York: Harper Colophon Books.

Goldberg, H. M. (1996). *The prosecution responds: An O. J. Simpson trial prosecutor reveals what really happened.* Secaucus, NJ: Birch Lane Press.

Gottlieb, R. C. (1997, February 6). O. J. lost to new evidence, lawyers, judge. *Newsday*, p. A49.

Graber, D. (1979). Evaluating crime-fighting policies. In R. Baker & F. Meyer (Eds.), *Evaluating alternative law enforcement policies* (pp. 179–200). Lexington, MA: Lexington Books.

Graham, F. (1995, October 9). The Simpson legacy. *Los Angeles Times*, p. S3.

Hamilton, V. L. (1978). Who is responsible? Toward a social psychology of responsibility attribution. *Journal of Social Psychology, 47*, 316–28.

Harvey, J. H., A. L. Weber & T. L. Orbuch. (1990). *Interpersonal accounts: A social-psychological perspective.* Cambridge, MA: Basil Blackwell.

Haskins, W. A., & G. H. Gardner. (1990). Organizing opening and closing statements. *Trial Diplomacy Journal, 13,* 50–58.

Heider, F. (1958). *The psychology of interpersonal relations.* New York: Wiley & Sons.

Heuer, L., & S. Penrod. (1994). Juror note taking and question asking during trials. *Law and Human Behavior, 18,* 121–50.

Hewitt, J. P., & R. Stokes. (1975). Disclaimers. *American Sociological Review, 40,* 1–11.

Hodes, W. W. (1996, Fall). Lord Brougham, the dream team, and jury nullification of the third kind. *University of Colorado Law Review, 67,* 1075–1108.

Holden, B. A., L. P. Cohen & E. de Lisser. (1995, October 4). Color blinded? Race seems to play an increasing role in many jury verdicts; blacks express skepticism of the justice system; acquittals in the Bronx; the issue of nullification. *Wall Street Journal,* pp. A1, A5.

Holland, G. (1995, October 23). For Simpson, money picture not that dim. *USA Today,* p. 3A.

Holstein, J. A. (1985). Jurors' interpretations and jury decision making. *Law and Human Behavior, 9,* 83–100.

Howlett, D. (1995, October 5). Evidence alone was the key, jurors assert. *USA Today,* p. 5A.

Jamieson, K. H., & K. K. Campbell. (1990). The generic approach: Introduction to form and genre. In B. Brock & R. L. Scott (Eds.), *Methods of rhetorical criticism: A twentieth-century perspective* (pp. 331–42). Detroit: Wayne State University Press.

Jasinski, J. (1990). An explanation of form and force in rhetoric and argumentation. In D. C. Williams & M. D. Hazen (Eds.), *Argumentation theory and the rhetoric of assent* (pp. 53–68). Tuscaloosa: University of Alabama Press.

Johnson, L., & D. Roediger. (1997). "Hertz, don't it?" Becoming colorless and staying black in the cross-over of O. J. Simpson. In T. Morrison & C. B. Lacour (Eds.), *Birth of a nation'hood: Gaze, script, and spectacle in the O. J. Simpson case* (pp. 197–239). New York: Pantheon Books.

Jones, T. (1995, October 3). The silent persuader: Johnnie Cochran. *Washington Post,* p. B1.

Judge's order banning media coverage and gag order. (1996, August 23). Available: http://www.islandnet.com/~walraven/simpson/hf-gag.html.

Julien, A. S. (1982). *Opening statements.* Wilmette, IL: Gallaghan.

Jun, S. H., & C. Dayan. (1986). An interactive media event: South Korea's televised family reunion. *Journal of Communication, 3,* 73–82.

Jury socks O. J. with huge tab (1997, February 11). *Orlando Sentinel,* p. A1.

Kahle, L. R., & P. M. Homer. (1985). Physical attractiveness and the celebrity endorser: A social adaptation perspective. *Journal of Consumer Research, 11,* 954–61.

Kaplan, M. F. (1977). Discussion of polarization effects in a modified jury decision paradigm: Informational influences. *Sociometry, 40,* 262–71.

Kassin, S. M., & L. S. Wrightsman. (1979). On the requirements of proof: The timing of judicial instruction and mock juror verdicts. *Journal of Personality and Social Psychology, 37,* 1877–87.

Keeva, S. (1995, June). Storm warnings: After months of courtroom maneuvering in the O. J. Simpson case, the public is ready to indict the entire criminal justice system. *ABA Journal, 81,* 77–78.

Kennedy, R. (1994, November 14). Deliberating race: Should jurors in the O. J. Simpson trial use the nullification strategy? *California Lawyer, 11,* 61.

Kennedy, T., & J. Kennedy (with Abrahamson, A.). (1995). *Mistrial of the century: A private diary of the jury system on trial.* Beverly Hills, CA: Dove Books.

Key dates in the O. J. Simpson case. CNN [On-line]. Available: http://cnn.com/US/9702/05/oj.timeline/index.html.

Kittel, N. G. (1986). Police perjury: Criminal defense attorneys' perspective. *American Journal of Criminal Justice, 11,* 16–20.

Klonoff, R. H., & P. L. Colby. (1990). *Sponsorship strategy: Evidentiary tactics for winning jury trials.* Charlottesville, VA: The Michie Company.

KNBC news (Special report out of Los Angeles). (1997, February 10). N. Bauer-Gonzales (Executive Producer). Burbank, CA: NBC International, LTD.

Knox, M. (with M. Walker). (1995). *The private diary of an O. J. juror: Behind the scenes of the trial of the century.* Beverly Hills, CA: Dove Books.

Lafferty, E. (1997, February 17). The inside story of how O. J. lost. *Time, 149,* 29–36.

Lakoff, G., & M. Turner. (1989). *More than cool reason: A field guide to poetic metaphor.* Chicago: University of Chicago Press.

Landy, D., & E. Aronson. (1969). The influence of the character of the criminal and his victim on the decisions of the simulated jurors. *Journal of Experimental Social Psychology, 5,* 141–52.

Larry King live. (1995, July 18). M. Gregory (Executive Producer). Washington, DC: Turner Program Services.

―――. (1997, February 5). M. Gregory (Executive Producer). Washington, DC: Turner Program Services.

Lassiter, C. (1996, Spring). TV or not TV—That is the question. *Journal of Criminal Law and Criminology, 86*, 928–1018.

Leigh, L. J. (1984, Winter). A theory of jury trial advocacy. *Utah Law Review, 1984*, 763–806.

Levy, M. R. (1979). Watching TV news as parasocial interaction. *Journal of Broadcasting, 23*, 69–80.

Lichter, L., & S. Lichter. (1983). *Prime time crime*. Washington, DC: Media Institute.

Lind, E. A., & G. Y. Ke. (1985). Opening and closing statements. In S. M. Kassin & L. S. Wrightsman (Eds.), *The psychology of evidence and trial procedure* (pp. 229–52). Beverly Hills, CA: Sage Publications, Inc.

Loftus, E., & J. Palmer. (1974). Reconstruction of automobile destruction: An example of the interaction between language and memory. *Journal of Verbal Learning and Verbal Behavior, 13*, 585–89.

Loh, W. D. (1985). The evidence and trial procedure: The law, social policy, and psychological research. In S. M. Kassin & L. S. Wrightsman, *The psychology of evidence and trial procedure*. Beverly Hills, CA: Sage Publications.

Lotz, R. E. (1991). *Crime and the American press*. New York: Praeger Publishers.

Loury, G. C. (1997, February 17). Looking beyond O. J. *U.S. News and World Report, 122*, 29.

Lovitt, J. T., & R. Price. (1997, February 5). Plaintiffs' best witness was O. J. *USA Today*, pp. 1A, 2A.

Lubet, S. (1990). The trial as a persuasive story. *American Journal of Trial Advocacy, 14*, 77–95.

MacCoun, R. J. (1990). Experimental research on jury decision-making. *Jurimetrics Journal of Law, Science and Technology, 30*, 223–33.

MacNeil/Lehrer news hour (now called *The news hour with Jim Lehrer*). (1995, October 4). L. Crystal (Executive Producer). New York and Washington, DC: Public Broadcasting Service.

Manstead, A. S., & G. R. Semin. (1981). Social transgressions, social perspectives, and social emotionality. *Motivation and Emotion, 5*, 249–61.

Markus, R. M. (1981, December). A theory of trial advocacy. *Tulane Law Review, 56*, 95–131.

Matlon, R. J. (1991, October 10–13). *Opening statements and closing arguments: A research review*. Paper presented to the American Society of Trial Consultants Convention, San Francisco.

―――. (1993). *Opening statements/Closing arguments*. San Anselmo, CA: Stuart Allen Books.

McCombs, M. (1994). News influence on our pictures of the world. In J. Bryant & D. Zillman (Eds.), *Media effects: Advances in theory and research* (pp. 1–16). Hillsdale, NJ: Lawrence Erlbaum Associates.

McCracken, G. (1989). Who is the celebrity endorser? Cultural foundations of the endorsement process. *Journal of Consumer Research, 16*, 159–73.

McGuire, W. J. (1964). Inducing resistance to persuasion. In L. Berkowitz (Ed.), *Advances in experimental psychology* (pp. 192–231). New York: Academic Press.

McGuire, W. J., & D. Papageorgis. (1962). Effectiveness of forewarning in developing resistance to persuasion. *Public Opinion Quarterly, 26*, 24–34.

McQuail, D., & S. Windahl. (1993). *Communication models.* New York: Longman.

Meyrowitz, J. (1985). *No sense of place.* New York: Oxford University Press.

Miller, R. J., A. F. Chino, M. K. Harney, D. A. Haines & R. L. Saavedra. (1986). Assignment of punishment as a function of the severity and consequences of the crime and the status of the defendant. *Journal of Applied Social Psychology, 16*, 77–91.

Moldea, D. E. (as told by T. Lange & P. Vannatter). (1997). *Evidence dismissed: The inside story of the police investigation of O. J. Simpson.* New York: Pocket Books.

Moore, P. J., & B. B. Gump. (1995). Information integration in juror decision making. *Journal of Applied Social Psychology, 25*, 2158–79.

Morgan, B. (1996, Fall). The jury's view. *University of Colorado Law Review, 67*, 983–88.

Myers, M. A. (1979). Rule departures and making law: Juries and their verdicts. *Law and Society Review, 13*, 781–98.

National public radio (morning edition). (1997, February 14). M. Block (Reporter). Transcript #97021412-210.

Ng, S. H., & J. J. Bradac. (1993). *Power in language: Verbal communication and social influence.* Newbury Park, CA: Sage Publications, Inc.

Nielsen, A. C. (1994). *Reference supplement: Nielsen station index.* New York: Nielsen Media Research.

Nightline. (1994, March 14). T. Bettag (Executive Producer). Max Cordova [Interview]. New York and Century City, CA: ABC Distribution Co.

Ohanian, R. (1991). The impact of celebrity spokespersons' perceived image on consumers' intention to purchase. *Journal of Advertising Research, 31*, 46–54.

O'Keefe, D. J. (1990). *Persuasion: Theory and research.* Newbury Park, CA: Sage Publications.

Orfield, M. W., Jr. (1992). Deterrence, perjury, and the heater factor: An exclusionary rule in the Chicago criminal courts. *University of Colorado Law Review, 63,* 75–162.

Pennington, N., & R. Hastie. (1981a). A cognitive theory of jury decision making: The story model. *Cordoza Law Review, 13,* 519–58.

———. (1981b). Juror decision-making models: The generalization gap. *Psychological Bulletin, 89,* 246–87.

———. (1986). Evidence evaluation in complex decision making. *Journal of Personality and Social Psychology, 51,* 242–58.

———. (1990). Practical implications of psychological research on juror and jury decision making. *Personality and Social Psychology Bulletin, 16,* 90–105.

———. (1991). A cognitive theory of jury decision making: The story model. *Cordoza Law Review, 13,* 519–58.

———. (1992). Explaining the evidence: Tests of the story model for juror decision making. *Journal of Personality and Social Psychology, 62,* 189–206.

———. (1993). The story model for juror decision making. In R. Hastie (Ed.), *Inside the juror: The psychology of juror decision making* (pp. 192–218). New York: Cambridge University Press.

People v. O. J. Simpson [Computer software]. (1994–95). Boise, ID: Litigator Software.

Perlman, S. E. (1995, October 5). O. J. verdict. *Newsday,* p. A01.

———. (1996, November 24). Mixed review for O. J./Demeanor helped, his testimony hurt. *Newsday,* p. A03.

———. (1997, February 11). The jury. *Newsday,* p. A03.

Petrocelli, D. (1998). *Triumph of justice: Closing the book on Simpson.* New York: Crown Books.

Petty, R. E., & J. T. Cacioppo. (1977). Forewarning, cognitive responding, and resistance to persuasion. *Journal of Personality and Social Psychology, 35,* 645–55.

———. (1979). Effects of forewarning and persuasive intent and involvement on cognitive responses and persuasion. *Personality and Social Psychology Bulletin, 5,* 173–76.

Purdue, J. M., P. Perlman, M. S. Mandell, R. B. Conlin, L. S. Stewart & J. B. Zimmermann. (1996, March). Opening statements: Good beginnings. *Trial, 32,* 44–57.

Pyszczynski, T., & L. S. Wrightsman (1981). Effects of opening statements on mock jurors. *Journal of Applied Social Psychology, 11,* 301–13.

Rantala, M. L. (1996). *O. J. unmasked: The trial, the truth, and the media.* Chicago: Catfeet Press.

Reinard, J. (1991). *Foundations of argument.* Dubuque, IA: William C. Brown Publishers.

Reskin, B. F., & C. A. Visher. (1986). The impacts of evidence and extralegal factors in jurors' decisions. *Law and Society Review, 20,* 423–38.

Resnick, F. D. (with M. Walker). (1994). *Nicole Brown Simpson: The private diary of a life interrupted.* Beverly Hills, CA: Dove Books.

Rich, F. (1997, February 12). Take O. J. circus seriously, a sign of racial strife. *Albuquerque Journal,* p. A8.

Rieke, R. D., & M. O. Sillars. (1993). *Argumentation and critical decision making* (3rd ed.). New York: Harper Collins.

Rieke, R. D., & R. K. Stutman. (1990). *Communication and legal advocacy.* Columbia: University of South Carolina Press.

Roberts, P. (1995). *O. J.: 101 theories, conspiracies and alibis: Guilty or innocent? YOU be the judge.* Diamond Bar, CA: Goldtree Press.

Rogers, E. M., J. W. Dearing & D. Bregman. (1993). The anatomy of agenda-setting research. *Journal of Communication, 43,* 68–84.

Rosenberg, C. B. (1995, June). The law after O. J. *ABA Journal, 81,* 72–76.

Rosengren, K. E., & S. Windahl. (1972). Mass media consumption as a functional alternative. In D. McQuail (Ed.), *Sociology of mass communications* (pp. 166–94). New York: Oxford University Press.

Roshier, B. (1981). The selection of crime news in the press. In E. S. Cohen & J. Young (Eds.), *The manufacture of news* (pp. 40–51). Newbury Park, CA: Sage Publications.

Rubin, A. M., & E. M. Perse. (1987). Audience activity and soap opera involvement: A uses and effects investigation. *Human Communication Research, 14,* 246–68.

Rubin, A. M., E. M. Perse & R. A. Powell. (1985). Loneliness, parasocial interaction, and local television viewing. *Human Communication Research, 12,* 155–80.

Sandys, M., & R. C. Dillehay. (1995). First ballot votes, predeliberation dispositions, and final verdicts in jury trials. *Law and Human Behavior, 19,* 175–95.

Schiller, L., & J. Willwerth. (1996). *American tragedy: The uncensored story of the Simpson defense.* New York: Random House.

Schlenker, B. R. (1980). *Impression management: The self-concept, social identity, and interpersonal relations.* Monterey, CA: Brooks/Cole.

Schneider, E. M. (1996). What happened to public education about domestic violence? In J. Abramson (Ed.), *Postmortem: The O. J. Simpson case. Justice confronts race, domestic violence, lawyers, money, and the media* (pp. 75–82). New York: Basic Books.

Schonbach, P. (1980). A category system for account phases. *European Journal of Social Psychology, 10,* 195–200.

Schuetz, J. (1994). *The logic of women on trial: Case studies of popular American trials.* Carbondale: Southern Illinois University Press.

Schuetz, J., & K. Snedaker. (1988). *Communication and litigation: Case studies of famous trials.* Carbondale: Southern Illinois University Press.

Schultze, Q. J. (1991). *Televangelism and American culture.* Grand Rapids, MI: Baker Books.

Scott, M. H., & S. M. Lyman. (1968). Accounts. *American Sociological Review, 33,* 46–63.

Semin, G. R., & A. S. R. Munstead. (1983). *The accountability of conduct: A social-psychological analysis.* New York: Academic Press.

Shapiro, B. J. (1986). "To a moral certainty": Theories of knowledge and Anglo-American juries 1600–1850. *Hastings Law Journal, 38,* 153–93.

Shapiro, R. L. (with L. Warren). (1996). *The search for justice: A defense attorney's brief on the O. J. Simpson case.* New York: Warner Books.

Shaw, D. (1995, October 9). Obsession: Did the media overfeed a starving public? *Los Angeles Times* (Special Report), pp. S1–S12.

Sheppard v. Maxwell, 384 U.S. 33 (1996).

Shoop, J. G. (1995). Supporters of cameras in court see benefits of televising trials. *Trial, 31,* 70.

Simon, R. J. (1980). The rationality of jury deliberations and verdicts. In R. J. Simon (Ed.), *The jury: Its role in American society* (pp. 49–71). Lexington, MA: Lexington Books.

Simon, R. J., & L. Mahan. (1971). Quantifying burdens of proof: A view from the bench, the jury and the classroom. *Law and Society, 5,* 319–30.

Simon, S. (1996, September 18). Simpson trial resumes. *Los Angeles Times,* p. A10.

―――. (1996, December 9). Simpson team poised to launch counterattack. *Los Angeles Times,* pp. A1, A28.

―――. (1997, February 11). Simpson verdict: $25 million. *Los Angeles Times,* pp. A1, A19.

Simpson, O. J. (with L. Schiller). (1995). *I want to tell you: My response to your letters, your messages, your questions.* Boston: Little, Brown & Company.

The Simpson legacy. (1995, October 8–11). *Los Angeles Times,* Section S.

Simpson portrays Nicole as wild and wayward. (1997, January 10). *CNN Interactive* [On-line]. Available: http://cnn.com/US/9701/10/simpson.civil/index.html.

Simpson trial statistics [On-line]. (1997). Available: http://www.islandnet.com/~walraven/ojstats.html.

Skolnick, J. H. (1982, Summer/Fall). Deception by police. *Criminal Justice Ethics, 1,* 40–54.

Sleeper, J. (1996). Racial theater. In J. Abramson (Ed.), *Postmortem: The O. J. Simpson case: Justice confronts race, domestic violence, lawyers, money, and the media* (pp. 57–64). New York: Basic Books.

Sonaike, S. F. (1978). The influence of jury deliberation on juror perception of trial, credibility, and damage awards. *Brigham Young University Law Review, 1978,* 889–908.

Spence, G. (1993, June 15). Closing arguments. *U.S. v. Weaver* [transcripts], p. 88.

———. (1995, February). Let me tell you a story. *Trial, 31,* 72–79.

Squeezed: Where did O. J.'s money go? (1997, February 17). *Newsweek, 129,* 30.

Starr, V. H. (1983). From the communication profession: Communication strategies and research needs on opening statements and closing arguments. In R. J. Matlon & R. J. Crawford (Eds.), *Communication strategies in the practice of lawyering* (pp. 424–48). Annandale, VA: Speech Communication Association.

Stein, J. A. (1985). *Closing argument.* Wilmette, IL: Callaghan & Company.

Strauder v. West Virginia, 100 U.S. 303 (1880).

Sue, S., R. E. Smith & C. Caldwell. (1973). Effects of inadmissible evidence on the decisions of simulated jurors: A moral dilemma. *Journal of Applied Social Psychology, 3,* 344–53.

Surette, R. (1989). Media trials. *Journal of Criminal Justice, 17,* 293–308.

———. (1992). *Media: Crime and criminal justice.* Menlo Park, CA: Brooks/Cole Publishing.

Taff, M. L. (1996, July). The meaning of the O. J. Simpson verdict. *Journal of Forensic Sciences, 41,* 552.

Tanford, J. A. (1983). *The trial process.* Charlottesville, VA: The Michie Company.

Tanford, S., & S. Penrod. (1986). Jury deliberations: Content and influence processes in jury decision making. *Journal of Applied Social Psychology, 16,* 322–47.

Taylor, S., Jr. (1995, October). For the record. *American Lawyer,* p. 72.

Thomas, E. A., & A. Hogue. (1976). Apparent weight of evidence, decision criteria, and confidence ratings in juror decision making. *Psychological Review, 83,* 442–65.

Today show. (1995, October 9). J. Zucker (Executive Producer). Sheila Woods [Interview]. New York: NBC International 1, LTD.

Toobin, J. (1996). *The run of his life: The People v. O. J. Simpson.* New York: Random House.

———. (1996, September 9). The Marcia Clark verdict. *New Yorker, 71,* 58–71.

TRC refers to the trial record of *California v. Orenthal James Simpson.* TRL refers to the civil trial transcript in *Sharon Rufo, Plaintiff, v. Orenthal James Simpson, Defendant, and Fredric Goldman, Plaintiff,*

v. Orenthal James Simpson, Defendant, and Louis H. Brown, Plaintiff, v. Orenthal James Simpson. Authors have used the transcripts available on the Internet and have cited them by date. All of the transcripts are the unofficial records. Simpson trial records are available on the following Internet locations:
http://www.islandnet.com/~walraven/simpson/html
http://cnn.com/US/OJ/simpson.civil.trial/index.html
http://cnn.com/US/OJ/trial/index.html.

Trials have their own signatures. (1997, February 5). *USA Today*, p. 5A.

Turow, S. (1995, October 4). Simpson prosecutors pay for their blunders. *New York Times*, p. A21.

Uelman, G. F. (1996). *Lessons from the trial: O. J. Simpson.* Kansas City, KS: Andrews and McMeel.

Unreasonable doubt: The eclipse of civil reason. (1995, October 23). *New Republic, 213*, 7–8.

The verdict arrives. (1997, February 9). *USA Today*, p. 14A.

Ware, B. L., Jr., & W. Linkugel. (1973). They spoke in defense of themselves: On the generic criticism of apologia. *Quarterly Journal of Speech, 59*, 273–83.

Weinstein, H. (1997, February 11). Size of punitive damages is justified, legal experts say. *Los Angeles Times*, p. A21.

Weisberg, R. (1996). Proclaiming trials as narratives: Premises and pretenses. In P. Brooks & P. Gewirtz (Eds.), *Law's stories: Narrative and rhetoric in law* (pp. 61–83). New Haven, CN: Yale University Press.

Wesson, M. (1996, Fall). That's my story and I'm stickin' to it: The jury as fifth business in the trial of O. J. Simpson and other matters. *University of Colorado Law Review, 67*, 949–56.

West, C. (1991). *Race matters.* Boston: Beacon.

———. (1996). *Race and justice.* San Francisco: Jossey-Bass.

Williams, P. J. (1991). *The alchemy of race and rights.* Cambridge: Harvard University Press.

Woods, S. (1995, October 7). O. J. Simpson juror speaks on trial. UPI news release.

Zamichow, N., E. Malnic & M. Gold. (1997, February 11). Jurors were swayed beyond a doubt. *Los Angeles Times*, pp. A1, A20, A22.

Zeisel, H. (1988). A jury hoax: The superpower of the opening statement. *Litigation, 14* (4), 17–18.

Contributors

Ann Burnett is an associate professor of communication at North Dakota State University. She received her doctorate from the University of Utah in 1986, where her research focused on jury decision making. She has published numerous articles on juror behavior. Burnett completed her first year of law school at the University of Nebraska.

Diane Furno-Lamude is an associate professor in the Department of Communication and Journalism at the University of New Mexico, where she teaches and conducts research on audience behavior and the social consequences of mass media. She has published numerous articles on the use of mass media in the United States and the social effects of television. She received her doctorate from the University of Utah.

Patricia M. Ganer is a professor of speech communication at Cypress College. A former president of the American Forensic Association, she has published and presented papers to the Speech Communication Association, Western Speech Communication Association, and International Communication Association in areas of legal communication, political communication, and argumentation. She received her doctorate from the University of Utah.

Ann M. Gill is a professor and the chair of the Department of Speech Communication at Colorado State University. Gill holds a Ph.D. from the University of Denver and a J.D. from the University of Colorado. She has served as president of the national Cross-Examination Debate Association and is the author of two books and a number of articles and book chapters, many concerning freedom of speech and legal discourse.

Lin S. Lilley is the president of Southwest Trial Consulting, Inc., based in Austin, Texas, and has been a trial consultant for the past twenty years. During that time, Lilley has assisted attorneys in selecting over five hundred juries and has lectured extensively to legal groups about voir dire issues. She is a founding member of the American Society of Trial Consultants and a past president of the organization. Lilley received her doctorate in communication from the University of Iowa.

Janice Schuetz is a professor of communication at the University of New Mexico. She received her doctorate at the University of Colorado. Of the seven books she has written, two focus on legal communication—*Communication and Litigation: Case Studies of Famous Trials* (with Kathryn Holmes Snedaker) and *The Logic of Women on Trial: Case Studies of Popular American Trials*. Schuetz is the author of more than forty journal articles, many relating to communication and the law. She also has served as editor of a special edition of the *International Journal of Argumentation*, "American and Continental Perspectives on Law." Schuetz does communication training for lawyers, court clerks, and judges.

Index